PREMIER b

NO2

The Dunfermline Athletic squad at the start of their epoch-making season, 1986-87.
Back row, from left: Jim Bowie, Dave Young, John Waddell, Grant Reid, Ian Westwater, Hugh Whyte, Steve Morrison, Ian Campbell, Leslie Thomson and Rowan Hamilton. *Centre row:* Joe Nelson (coach), Gary Thompson, Ian McCall, Ian Heddle, Norrie McCathie, Grant Jenkins, Davie Moyes, Raymond Sharp, Stuart Grant, Graeme Davidson and Philip Yeates (physiotherapist). *Front row:* John Jobson (coach), Trevor Smith, John Watson, Eric Ferguson, Jim Leishman (manager), Bobby Robertson (captain), Bobby Forrest, Gordon Connolly and Gregor Abel (coach). (Dunfermline Press).

John Donald Publishers Ltd., 138 St Stephen Street, Edinburgh EH3 5AA.

ISBN 0 85976 203 3

Phototypeset by Nextext Composition Ltd., Glasgow.
Printed by Bell & Bain Ltd., Glasgow.

PREMIER BOUND

The Story of Dunfermline Athletic's
Return to the Big Time

JOHN HUNTER

JOHN DONALD PUBLISHERS LTD
EDINBURGH

About the Author

The author, John Hunter, was born in Whitburn, West Lothian, in June 1948. Educated at Bathgate Academy, he attended Edinburgh University where he graduated in 1970 with an honours degree in History. After completing a post-graduate diploma in Education, he began his teaching career at Dunfermline High School where he has been Head of History for the last 13 years.

His first book was a school textbook entitled *Mary Queen of Scots and John Knox.* In 1985, to commemorate the centenary of Dunfermline Athletic, he published an official history of the club which he spent several years researching and writing and which has been widely acclaimed. More recently, he was the co-producer of a 3-hour videotape on Dunfermline Athletic's marvellous years in the 1960s.

John and his wife, Irene, who also trained as a teacher, have three young daughters and live in their adopted town of Dunfermline, not far from East End Park. In his spare time he enjoys reading, walking, photography, squash, caravanning, cycling and travel.

Acknowledgements

I cannot pay too high a tribute to the *Dunfermline Press* whose reporters and photographers have compiled an excellent record of matches and events at the club; without their assistance and goodwill, this book could not have been published. I must also make special mention of the club's official photographer, Ian Malcolm, who has been exceedingly helpful in providing me with photographs and advice. Freelance photographer, Enzo Mincella, also very kindly supplied me with invaluable material. I am very much in debt to Mel Rennie and his colleagues on the Board and to Jim Leishman, Gregor Abel and all the playing and coaching staff for talking to me when they must have had weightier matters on their mind. I am also grateful to a number of individuals and agencies who have been of great help: Bill Fyfe, Mark Gribbin, George and Michael Simon, Joan Malcolm, Peter McAteer, the contributors to the *Pars News* and to the *Scottish League Review,* the staff of Dunfermline Public Library, the *Evening News* and the *Dundee Courier;* and to many others who have assisted in small, but important, ways. I will be eternally in debt to my excellent typists, Isobel Gillespie and Betty Duncan, who transcribed my handwriting in record time. Last, but by no means least, my thanks go to my wife Irene, for all her support and for relieving me, albeit temporarily, from my household chores.

Preface

On the morning of Saturday, April 25 1987, Jim Leishman woke up at 4.30 a.m. and could not get back to sleep. For several hours he paced the bedroom floor like a caged animal, his mind in turmoil. The most important day in his short career as manager of Dunfermline Athletic F.C. had dawned. His stomach heaved and his nerves tightened in the manner of a soldier about to engage the enemy in a decisive battle. His team, which had won the Second Division Championship a year earlier, were on the verge of writing a new chapter in the long and distinguished history of a once famous club which had recently sunk into near oblivion. A victory over visitors, Queen of the South, would guarantee the points that would kill off Dumbarton's stubborn challenge and make promotion certain.

As the morning progressed, the tension among the players began to mount as the adrenalin was pumped feverishly through their systems. Just as Moses had taken the children of Israel to view the Promised Land, Jim Leishman had taken his disciples to the threshold of a new era. Only Clydebank had ever gone before from the Second Division to the Premier League in successive seasons. For Dunfermline, the Premier Division had never been other than an elusive dream from its inception in 1975.

The large, expectant, demanding crowd began to drift in to occupy their familiar places; the players, with more than forty games behind them, nervously warmed up in the spring sunshine. Jim Leishman, normally the first to greet the fans with a hearty wave, remained in the background, not trusting his shaking legs.

The course of the match did little to allay his anxiety; an early goal from Dunfermline often looked like being cancelled by a Dumfries side desperate to avoid relegation. The ninety minutes of regulation time seemed like an eternity; there was no fast-forward switch in the arena to speed up the drama.

The final minutes ticked away as slowly as icicles melt off the north face of the Eiger. The sounding of the final whistle was hardly heard by the manager, his mind already anaesthetised by worry. As though a dam had burst, the delirious fans descended on him, burying him under a sea of scarves and outstretched hands. The celebrations began, the manager stood to receive the acclaim of the crowd and to welcome his ecstatic players. "It was," he later reflected, "the worst and best day of my life."

Dunfermline were back in the top drawer of Scottish football.

John Hunter

Greetings from . . .

The Chairman

Who would have thought when I was asked to take over at East End Park at the beginning of season 1986-87 that we would be sitting in the Premier League by the end of it? That must have been beyond anyone's dreams, especially since we had only arrived in the First Division at the end of season 1985-86. My thanks go to Jim Watters, my predecessor, for his leadership at that time.

We are here with an enormous task ahead. The close season is not going to be very relaxing for any of us if we hope to achieve success. The manager has already started on his programme for the future. Every one knows that East End Park is a super stadium but over the years time has caught up with us — especially as regards safety on the terracing. To make headway in this direction, each and every director has been allocated his own department for which he is responsible. Every one pulls his weight at the club.

On behalf of the Board of Directors of Dunfermline Athletic F.C., I would like to sincerely thank the many thousands of loyal fans who have turned up this season, both at East End Park and at away games, to support the team. It is this type of support, along with the team's performances, that has brought such positive media coverage to the club again this season.

Thanks must also go behind the scenes to the many people who, by working hard, make our position as Board members easier: the kitchen staff, groundsmen, gate-keepers, the programme editor, writers, photographers and programme sellers. In addition, the part-time and full-time coaching, administrative and commercial staff have all played a vital role in this season's success. We greatly appreciate all the businesses whose financial contributions through advertising and various other sponsorships have supported the club.

Last, but not least, to the Paragon Club, the Centenary Club and both the adult and junior supporters' clubs and committees, we give our sincere thanks for your contribution to the atmosphere at East End Park.

We look forward to your continued support in season 1987-88.

William M. Rennie
Chairman

The Manager

As a young boy of nine, I can recall standing on the terracing at East End Park watching Dunfermline play in that memorable Fairs' Cup match against Valencia. When I was a few years older, I used to leave school early and walk from my home in Lochgelly to spectate at Dunfermline's other European matches. These exciting days have always stuck in my mind. I was, understandably, thrilled to sign for the Pars as a teenager and for most of the last thirty years, Dunfermline Athletic has been an important part of my life. The events of the last two seasons have fulfilled my wildest dreams and I hope I have set the club on the right path towards re-creating those glorious days when the team's reputation was feared throughout the country.

When John presented me with a copy of his *Centenary History* last season, he inscribed on the inside cover: "To Jim, the man to take Dunfermline into the Premier League." In November 1985, few people in football would have put much money on that happening. Out of kindness, he did not state when it would occur.

When I took over at the club, I always knew in my heart that Dunfermline were too big a club for the Second Division and that I could give them promotion. It would be fair to say, however, that I did not expect us to get into the Premier League at the first attempt. It did begin to dawn on me and my directors around the turn of the year that the club might manage it after all.

As you read this book, you will be able to re-trace the steps which won us promotion in successive seasons. It will recall the chances that we took, the opportunities which we failed to grasp. That, alas, is life. It will bring back memories of successes, frustrations, despair and joy. It's amazing how, in the space of a couple of seasons, details can quickly be forgotten — that spectacular goal, that missed penalty, that night of torrential rain, that player who has now moved on. I'm sure you will enjoy re-living these two fantastic seasons which no-one connected with Dunfermline will ever forget.

I would like to thank everyone who has worked to make our triumphs on and off the field possible. I have had tremendous support from Mr. Rennie and the Board, from Gregor and all the backroom staff, from the players who have responded magnificently to the pressures and from many more hidden from public view. I must also pay tribute to my wife, Mary, without whose support and understanding, I could have achieved nothing.

We all look forward with anticipation to next season. Once again we are stepping up a grade and I would ask everyone to rally round the team, especially when events are going badly. Let's hope that we can consolidate our position in the Premier League and that the next book on Dunfermline Athletic will be celebrating its return to European Football.

Jim Leishman,
Manager

The Team Captain

Just over three years ago, on a reserve team coach to an evening fixture at Dumbarton, Jim Leishman and myself were sitting together. It was not a high point of either's career. Jim was reserve team coach striving, seemingly unnoticed, to establish himself back in football after his playing career was sadly ended by injury. I was struggling to combine my work as a junior hospital doctor with the commitment demanded by the club, and my football was suffering.

The Pars were lowly placed in the Second Division, the morale of the players was low, and the attendances had dropped below all previous records.

The town had lost its pride in Dunfermline Athletic F.C.

I can't remember a thing about that **vii**

match at Dumbarton, but with clarity, as if it was yesterday, I can recall how Jim and I talked long and passionately about the club we had both loved since boyhood. We talked about the glorious days of the sixties, we postulated many reasons for the decline in the seventies, and we despaired about the present, but with what seemed at the time totally inappropriate optimism, Jim talked about the future.

Six weeks later Jim Leishman was appointed manager of Dunfermline Athletic, and the future was his.

I am convinced that it was on that day that our club became 'big' again. The manager brought no new miraculous ideas or tactics; indeed, his inexperience was slightly alarming, and no money was forthcoming for a transfer-market spending spree. What did happen, however, was that immediately every player, whether first, reserve or youth team, was made aware that when you pull on a black and white jersey you are privileged to be part of a club with a tradition and history equal to any in the land. There would be hard work and hard times, but no talk of achievement until Dunfermline Athletic were firmly established back amongst the country's elite.

This book describes in detail the past three years. From the desperate disappointment of missing promotion in 1984-85 to the elation of the Second Division Championship the following season and promotion to the Premier League this year.

There have been wise coaching appointments in Gregor Abel, John Jobson and Ian Campbell, the signings of several quality players and the nurturing to fruition of talents already at the club.

The atmosphere in the dressing-room, training ground and field of play has been one of a unique camaraderie, enthusiasm and pride. In my life, inside or outside football, I have never experienced anything quite like it.

The coming seasons will determine whether the wildest dreams we dared discuss on that bleak coach trip three years ago can be achieved, but at least for now we can stick out our chests in that black and white jersey, because THE PARS ARE BACK.

Bobby Robertson, Club Captain

Contents

Karen Grega, the club's commercial consultant, at her desk at East End Park. She is certainly the best looking signing the Pars have made in recent years. She was born in Australia of a Scots mother and a Czech father. The dynamic 29-year-old was chosen out of 80 applicants for the commercial post vacated by Jim Leishman. Her energy, her drive and her enthusiasm will help Dunfermline to stay at the top of Scottish football. It is no coincidence that a photograph of herself with Jock Stein adorns her office. (Evening News)

Relaxing at home: Jim and his wife Mary with six-year old daughter, Kate, and the family pet, Fergus, a great dane. (Dunfermline Press).

New signing, Stuart Beedie, and backroom coach, Joe Nelson, pose with children of Centenary Club members during one of the holiday coaching courses at East End Park.

The catering students of the Lauder Technical College take the opportunity to celebrate the Pars successes during season 1986-87. Karen Grega, Jim Leishman and Eric Ferguson are the lucky diners. (Dunfermline Press)

DUNFERMLINE ATHLETIC
Formed: 1885
Division Two champions: 1926, 1986
Runners-up: 1913, 1934, 1955, 1958,
1973, 1979
Scottish Cup winners: 1961, 1968
Runners-up: 1965
Scottish League Cup runners-up:
1950
European Cup Winners Cup quarter-finalists
1962, semi-finalists 1969
European Fairs Cup quarter-finalists:
1966

An Illustrious Past

Dunfermline Athletic F.C. was formed in May 1885 as a result of a breakaway from the original Dunfermline club, an organisation whose main interest was in playing cricket in the summer while using football merely as a part-time pursuit in the winter to keep their players fit. The new club kicked off in their first match on June 13 against a team from Edinburgh University and beat them 2-1.

In the early days, the players enjoyed their football which was organised purely on an amateur basis. A committee was established to run the club, and by all accounts its work was never easy as it tried to organise fixtures, arrange training, raise funds and keep morale high. The increasing affluence of the working classes in late Victorian Britain, the development of the railways in Fife and the granting of a half-day on a Saturday certainly eased some of their problems. However, in footballing terms, Fife was a comparative backwater and when the Scottish League was set up in 1890, no teams from the Kingdom were to be included. The establishment of professionalism in 1893 increased the competitive element and brought about the creation of the Second Division, but Fife clubs were still noticeable by their absence.

At a local and district level, however, Dunfermline Athletic slowly began to prosper. In the early years of the twentieth century they moved their ground slightly east to occupy the present site at East End Park. The establishment of various district competitions such as the Northern, Midland and Central Leagues gave the club a great deal of experience.

It could be said that the club really came of age in season 1911-12 when it reached the final of the prestigious Qualifying Cup and went on to beat Dumbarton, the Second Division champions, 1-0. The first national trophy had been secured at East End Park. This gave them entry to the Scottish Cup itself where they drew the mighty Celtic in Glasgow, the first of many famous clashes between the clubs. The team put up a very creditable performance and lost only 1-0 to a very questionable goal. Despite this setback, Dunfermline went on to complete their most successful season ever — winners of the Central League (for the second successive year), the Loftus Cup, the Fife Cup and the Penman Cup.

Their successes and endeavour were rewarded nationally when the Scottish League took note and gave them entry to the Second Division for season 1912-13. Dunfermline had arrived at last! They were kitted out in the colours which have remained with them over the years: black and white striped jerseys with black shorts. At this time the local newspapers began calling them 'the Pars' because of the parallel lines on their jerseys and because they were now on a par with, or equal to, the best in the land.

For newcomers, Dunfermline performed exceptionally well in the Second Division, coming second in the league, one point behind Ayr. Nowadays, this would have meant **1**

The side that won the Scottish Qualifying Cup in 1911. *Back row:* T.A. Robertson (vice-president), A. Liddell, W. Crichton, R. Philp (secretary). *Third row:* E. Millar (treasurer), J. Philp (trainer), D.Donaldson, D. Izatt, J. Brown (captain), A. Wilkie, J. Thomson, T. Ballantyne, J. Bewick (secretary). *Second row:* G. Anderson (vice-president), J. Murray, M. Slavin, F.Gibson. G. Newlands-Robertson, J. Farrell (president). *First row:* J. McLaughlan (trainer), C. Duncan. The Loftus Cup and the Calder Shield are also displayed. (Dunfermline Press)

automatic promotion, but in those days the management of the League selected whom they wanted and they preferred the West of Scotland clubs, Ayr and sixth-placed Dumbarton. Dunfermline undoubtedly had a good team and it can only be a matter of speculation how far they might have advanced if their just reward had been accorded to them.

In any event, the First World War broke out in 1914 and football, like so many other activities, took a very low priority. When the hostilities ended in 1918, there was a great resurgence of football. At Dunfermline in 1919 a limited liability company was floated with £3,000 of capital raised through £1

shares, a sign that the sport was indeed entering a new age which could not be entrusted to a handful of volunteers.

Rather than suffer the indignity of having to be invited to join the top division, Dunfermline and the other clubs, who had pressed for automatic promotion and relegation, broke away from the Scottish League and formed themselves into the Central League. Since they were outwith the jurisdiction of the Scottish League they could entice star players to their grounds, pay them high wages but not have to pay any transfer fee. It was under this arrangement that the club secured the services of one of the all-time greats of

The team which took Dunfermline into the First Division as champions for the first time in 1926. *Back row:* T. Burns, R. Wyllie, E. Miller, G. Turner. *Middle:* E. Dowie, Bain, Mitchell, Herd, Gibb, Wilson, Clark, Masterton. *Front:* Paterson (manager), Ritchie, Sutton, Skinner, Dickson, Stein, J. Fraser, and J. Farrell (linesman). (Dundee Courier)

Scottish football, Andy Wilson. This high-scoring and entertaining goal-scorer (more than 100 goals in two seasons) brought in crowds of over 10,000 and his exploits were to earn him six Scottish Caps while he was at East End Park.

The overwhelming success of the rebel league finally persuaded the authorities to grant promotion on merit, and from 1921 Dunfermline reverted to playing in the old Second Division. They stayed there until season 1925-26 when they finally won the Championship, scoring 109 goals in the process, and were admitted for the first time to the First Division. Their success was due in

no small part to another hero in the East End Hall of Fame, Bobby Skinner, whose 53 goals in 38 games is still a club record and unlikely to be broken. The manager then was Sandy Paterson, recently brought in from Cowdenbeath F.C.

As is often the case, it is difficult for a promoted club to do well amongst the giants of the game and Dunfermline struggled for the next two seasons before being relegated at the end of season 1927-28. Their pointage had come to a mere 12, with 126 goals conceded for only 41 scored.

The Great Depression which affected the country generally did nothing to

The team that took Dunfermline back into Division One in 1934 as runners-up to Albion Rovers. *Back row:* J. Low, E. Dowie. *Middle:* Laidlaw, R. Drever, Currie, Rarity, Steele, Rodgers, R. Wylie, J. Anderson, W. Knight. *Front:* Reid, Dobson, Paterson, McKendrick, Watson, Weir, Garland. (Dundee Courier)

boost the club's fortunes and several lean years followed, although there was the club's record league win to record: an 11-2 victory against Stenhousemuir on September 27, 1930. To increase its flagging finances, the club allowed a company to set up greyhound racing on the track and this soon proved to be very popular.

After narrowly missing out on promotion in season 1932-33, Dunfermline were guided back into the First Division the following season by manager Willie Knight. This time new players were bought but they could only give the club three years in the top

drawer before relegation once again befell them in 1937.

Another World War ensured there would be no quick return to the First Division for the team. The national leagues were suspended although football did continue and the Dunfermline public was entertained by several guest players, Billy Liddell in particular.

The return to normality after the war saw Dunfermline continue to struggle. Long-serving manager, Sandy Archibald, died in 1946 and was replaced by Willie McAndrew who saw his new charges slump almost immediately to their

Going for promotion, February 1958. Standing: Duthie, Sweeney, Beaton, Mailer. Seated: Peebles, McWilliam, Dickson, Watson, Napier. (Dundee Courier)

heaviest league defeat: 10-0 at Dens Park on March 22, 1947. He did not last long and his successor, former referee Bobby Calder, lasted even less – six months. With the Board then managing the team during season 1948-49, Dunfermline were desperately unlucky not to win promotion on the last day of the season. They travelled to Kirkcaldy, needing to take at least a point from fellow contenders, Raith Rovers. Early in the game the Pars lost the services of goalkeeper Michie and, with no substitutes allowed, went on to lose 4-0.

Raith were promoted and Dunfermline languished in the Second Division.

It was left to the newly-appointed manager, Webber Lees, to put Dunfermline back on the footballing map. In the autumn of 1949 he took the club to the final of the League Cup, a new competition which had only begun formally after the war. Dunfermline beat a much fancied Hibs side containing six internationalists in the semi-final at Tynecastle. In the final at Hampden Park on October 29 they met an East Fife side, managed by Scot Symon, which **5**

of
by
igh
April
gain
to go
Andy
afloat
ook an
the last
to seal

Thomson,
out the future.
s erected and
ht to strengthen
n, Bain, Watson,
d Alec Smith. In April
on promotion again,
s runners-up to Stirling
ough a pool of full-time
as established and plans drawn
install floodlighting, Dunfermline
continued to struggle and their fate hinged once again on the results of the final day of the league programme. In a match which has now become a legend at East End Park, the Pars thrashed Partick Thistle 10-1 to dispel any doubts about their First Division status that season. Recent signing Harry Melrose grabbed six goals that famous afternoon. As a reward, the players were taken on holiday to Switzerland, their first European visit though certainly not their last. It was at this time that George Miller, John 'Cammy' Fraser and David Thomson joined the club.

The following spring saw the club once again face near certain relegation and manager Dickson resigned. His successor did not cause much stir at the time — a relatively unknown and inexperienced John Stein, a former miner, who had enjoyed only limited success as a player with Albion Rovers, Llanelly Town and Celtic. Very soon, however, his name was to be well known, at least in local circles, as he instilled enough confidence into his dispirited charges to let them win their next six matches on the trot, a sequence which is a record for the club in the old First Division.

Dunfermline were thus saved from relegation and for the next decade were to enjoy a period of amazing success, witnessed neither before nor since. They were, indeed, the years of "Black and White Magic" so vividly recalled by authors Jim Paterson and Douglas Scott. Stein brought discipline, stability, belief and good working practices to a club which seemed destined to oscillate like a pendulum between the two divisions.

His first success was to take the team to the final of the Scottish Cup for the first time in 1961, by way of Berwick, Stranraer, Aberdeen and Edinburgh, before beating the mighty Celtic 2-0 in a replay at Hampden. Stein then took Dunfermline into Europe where they acquitted themselves with distinction in the European Cup-Winners' Cup and the old Inter-Cities Fairs Cup, claiming the scalps of Everton, the Bank of England team, in the process.

Stein knew how to pick up good players — and at low cost. Willie Cunningham, Tommy McDonald, Jackie

Sinclair, Dan McLindon, Willie and Tommy Callaghan, Alec Edwards, John Lunn, Jim Thomson, Bert Paton, Jim McLean, Jim Fraser and others were all brought by Stein to East End Park. Prudent budgeting, wise selling and increased gates allowed the Board to build the present stadium, still the envy of many visiting teams.

By the time Stein left to seek a more challenging position at Easter Road in 1964, he had established Dunfermline as a team which expected to do well regularly in domestic and European football. His successor, his former captain and coach, Willie Cunningham, carried on in the same expert manner. Under him, the Pars narrowly lost the 1965 Cup Final to Celtic and missed the First Division Championship in the same season by one crucial point. European participation continued in each of Cunningham's seasons with the club, and more fine players arrived at East End: Alex Ferguson, Hugh Robertson, Alex Totten, Bent Martin and Roy Barry.

A disenchanted Willie Cunningham shocked the footballing world in 1967 by announcing his resignation and George Farm, the former international goalkeeper, was appointed in his place. The success continued, almost as surely as night followed day. Another visit to Hampden in 1968 saw Hearts easily disposed of and the Scottish Cup returned to the Boardroom at East End Park. European sorties saw West Bromwich swept aside, making Dunfermline the only Scottish side to eliminate two English clubs from Europe. In the same season only a single goal prevented Dunfermline from reaching the final of the Cup-winners'

Jock Stein (1922-85). The first manager to bring the Scottish Cup to East End Park, in April 1961. He also brought fame to Dunfermline in Europe.

Cup. Olympia of Greece, Bordeaux of France and Gwardia of Poland were other clubs which Dunfermline consumed with ease. It took the invocation of the 'away goals' rule for Anderlecht to finally knock Dunfermline out of Europe in January 1970. During Farm's period of office, the fans savoured the skills of more exciting players: Pat Gardner, George McLean, Doug Baillie and Barry Mitchell.

The bubble burst in the autumn of 1970 when a series of poor league results plus the absence of the club from European competition persuaded the Board to dismiss George Farm. His successor, Alec Wright, did not have a happy stay at East End Park, his tenure overshadowed by a severe financial crisis which almost made the club

The successful team display their trophies of 1960-61 — the Fife Cup, the Scottish Cup and the Penman Cup. *Back Row:* Fraser, Mailer, Connachan, Herriot, Miller, Sweeney, Cunningham. *Middle:* McLindon, Peebles, Smith, Thomson, Dickson, Melrose, McDonald, Williamson. *Front:* Stevenson, Jack, Torrie, Thomson, Watson, McConville, Stein. (Dunfermline Press)

bankrupt. Economies were made, players were transferred, older and experienced ones were not replaced, youth teams were disbanded and younger players were blooded before they were fully ready.

Former captain, George Miller, was appointed manager in February 1972, but was too late to save the club from relegation at the end of the season, a fate which all connected with the club thought had been cast aside for ever. The enthusiastic and untiring Miller did succeed in bringing the club back into Division One at the first attempt, though it was a hard struggle and Dunfermline

could only manage the runners-up spot to Clyde. Although Miller tried hard to keep a struggling ship afloat, the club was but a pale shadow of its former self.

In its wisdom, the Scottish League decided to re-organise the league structure after 1975 to the current set-up of three leagues. For Dunfermline, this momentous change came just too late. Although it seemed possible at one stage that the team might secure an exclusive place in the Premier League, a dramatic loss of form saw the Pars, in effect, relegated to the new First Division.

Miller resigned and another former

Cup-winning side, 1968. Standing: J. Stevenson, P. Gardner, T. Callaghan, J. McGarty, B. Martin, B. Paton, R. Barry, J. Thomson, J. Lunn, G. Farm. Seated: J. Yellowley, R. Torrie, I. Lister, W. Callaghan, A. Watson, H. Robertson, A. Edwards, L. Jack, J. McConville.

favourite, Harry Melrose, took over in the driving seat, only to see Dunfermline drop even further into the new Second Division in 1976, which forced the club to revert to part-time football once again. Dunfermline found it a great struggle to escape from the nether reaches of the league, coming third top in 1977 and 1978. With little money at his disposal, Melrose put together a team which finally secured promotion in May 1979 although, as observers will remember, it was a close run affair. The struggle went to the last game when visitors Falkirk required to beat Dunfermline to achieve promotion themselves. In a nail-biting game, it took a dramatic penalty equaliser by player-coach Andy Rolland

to salvage the point which put Dunfermline up. The crowd on that memorable night, almost 6,000, is still a record for the new Second Division.

By now, Dunfermline were certainly the poor relations of Scottish Football and admission to the First Division ensured no let-up in the struggle. Disappointing results brought about Melrose's resignation in December 1980 and the Board turned again to Central Park to find their new manager, Pat Stanton. If skill and achievement on the football field had any bearing on success in football management, then the darling of the crowds at Easter Road, and latterly Parkhead, would have been assured of a high place on the pedestal. **9**

Dunfermline's record crowd (27,816) at the match against Celtic on Tuesday, 30th April, 1968, when the Cup holders played the League Champions.

Sadly, though he brought several promising players to the club in McCathie, Jenkins, Forrest and Morrison, he was unable to revive Dunfermline's fortunes and he resigned in September 1982.

He was succeeded by the 'iron man' of Scottish football, Tom Forsyth, his career at Rangers cut short by a knee injury. The newcomer made changes but still failed to come up with the successful formula. With the club's most expensive signing, Doug Considine, walking out on the club in mid season,

the team slithered towards the foot of the league and were relegated once again to the backwater of Scottish football. It was no surprise when Forsyth left the club in October 1983.

Dunfermline's fortunes seemed at an all-time low point. Gates had fallen alarmingly low, sometimes below the thousand mark, the players were dispirited, an air of doom hung over the dressing-room and promotion seemed far away. Clubs like Aberdeen and Dundee United, whom Dunfermline had once taken on and beaten with relative ease, were the ones now making the headlines in Scotland and in Europe. They had found their Jock Stein in Alex Ferguson and Jim McLean. For Dunfermline, the prospect of Europe, or even the Premier League, seemed light years away. That is, until a certain Jim Leishman, whom some supporters had a vague recollection of as a player whose career had been cut short in the mid-seventies through injury, was appointed in October 1983. Almost immediately the transformation imperceptibly began. For the first time since the war, the job was held in a part-time capacity.

The untried manager, a mere 29 years old, hardly knew where to begin. Although there was little money available, Leishman acquired a player who soon proved to be an excellent marksman, the red-haired John Watson, signed for very little from Hong Kong Rangers. Leishman was appointed too late to alter the club's poor record in the league and in finishing ninth in the Second Division, the Pars put in their poorest performance for 30 years. There was, however, a glimmer of hope when Dunfermline came within nine minutes in January of knocking Rangers out of the Scottish Cup at Ibrox. Leishman also found a coach of proven ability whose services were to prove invaluable – Gregor Abel, formerly manager of Falkirk.

Off the field, an enthusiastic manager – now doubling up as commercial manager also – relentlessly carried out public engagements which would have left members of the Royal Family gasping. The local community certainly knew that the renaissance at East End Park had begun.

Leishman acquired more new players – Rowan Hamilton, Davie Young, Davie Moyes and Ian Westwater — and came within a whisker of promotion in 1985, the club's centenary year. No Pars' fan needs to be reminded of Saturday May 11 when Dunfermline beat Berwick, thanks to two coolly converted penalties from young Trevor Smith, and thought they had pipped Alloa for promotion. Alas, earlier radio reports that Alloa had failed to win the necessary victory over Arbroath proved to be unfounded and as delight turned to despair, the crowd at East End Park could only hope for better fortune another day. That day, all the richer when it finally dawned, was not now to be far away.

Just Champion
Season 1985-86

During the summer of 1985, one of the wettest on record, the citizens of the Auld Grey Toun had double cause for celebration. While the trustees of Andrew Carnegie were marking the 150th anniversary of the birth of the world's greatest philanthropist, the management at East End Park were making the final preparations to note another great anniversary – the centenary of Dunfermline Athletic Football Club, founded in an age when air travel, the radio, the telephone, the television, penicillin, family allowances, unemployment benefit and old age pensions were but dreams of the future.

From June until August the local museum mounted an extremely popular exhibition entitled 'Black and White' which brought together an amazing

The 1985-86 squad. *Back row:* Strachan, Forrest, Jenkins, Bowie, Campbell, McGinlay, Houston, Foggo, Lobban. *Middle:* Nelson, Gordon, Smith, Whyte, Westwater, McGregor, Grant, Young, Jobson. *Front:* McCathie, Hamilton, Pryde, Leishman, Irvine, Heddle, Watson. (Absent: Abel [coach], Forsyth, Morrison, Moyes and Robertson.)

amount of Pars memorabilia — old programmes, souvenirs from various campaigns, photographs, badges, scarves, jerseys, medals, indeed almost anything connected with the famous club over the last century. It is estimated that more than 4,500 visitors turned out, making it easily the museum's most popular exhibition and giving proof, if proof were needed, of the high standing of the club in the community. The crowds were no doubt boosted by the appearance on August 10th of former manager Jock Stein and several of the cup-winning team of 1961 at the museum — complete with that most elusive of trophies, the Scottish Cup.

The summer of 1985 was indeed a time for nostalgia but the Board of Directors rightly realised that the future of the club was more important and in an effort to put the club on a more secure financial footing a new venture was launched on July 31st, the Centenary Club. While actor Russell Hunter was meticulously rehearsing his brilliant one-man characterisation of the life of Andrew Carnegie in that famous hall named after him, only a few hundred yards away the premises of the local night spot, 'Night Magic', were packed by supporters of the club to hear of the launch of this latest bold initiative.

One of the guest speakers, the legendary Nat Lofthouse, one of England's greatest forwards, outlined how a similar venture had resurrected the financial fortunes of his old club, Bolton Wanderers. The idea was essentially fund raising — members would contribute £2 weekly and in return could not only stand a chance of winning the weekly £500 draw or the

The Ground Staff — John Mackie, Sam and Danny Hutchison. Their work keeps the ground in tip-top condition.

quarterly prize of £2,500, but they would be able also to participate in a series of social functions to draw members closer together. The evening was a great success and the Centenary Club has gone from strength to strength, providing the club with vital revenue for expansion.

Another celebration, a special Centenary Dinner at Dunblane Hydro, the venue for many training sessions in the glorious 'sixties, allowed over 300 guests under the guidance of Master of Ceremonies, Bob Crampsey, another opportunity to wander down memory lane with such speakers as Doug Baillie while at the same time boosting the club's funds. The first draw for the Centenary Club was made and a delighted Neil Moffat found himself richer to the tune of £500.

The highlight, however, of the centenary celebrations in the summer was undoubtedly the challenge match on August 7th against Premier League champions, Aberdeen, managed by none other than former Dunfermline **13**

Players spanning almost every decade in the 100-year history of Dunfermline Athletic gathered at East End Park for the challenge game against Aberdeen on August 7.

Before the match and afterwards, at a buffet, the former players, coaches, physiotherapists and managers recalled just a handful of the events which go together to form the history of the Pars.

There was a particularly good response from players who represented the club in the 1950s and, among those who attended, were Gerry Mays and Jimmy Cannon, of the side beaten in the final of the League Cup in 1949. (Dunfermline Press).

striker, Alex Ferguson, at that time assistant to Jock Stein at international level. The match, played on a beautiful summer's evening, was a splendid occasion. Before the kick-off, scores of former players were introduced to the crowd, with a warm welcome being reserved for former winger, Jimmy Tonner, who had played for the Pars in 1912! A special programme was produced for this unique occasion and at half-time an exhibition six-a-side, comprising fit and not-so-fit players of the past, entertained an appreciative crowd of just under 6,000 spectators.

The game itself, sponsored by financial consultant John Goldie, was thrilling and gave the home crowd, starved of top sides for so long, the opportunity to savour the skills of internationalists such as Jim Leighton and Alex McLeish and of emerging stars like Joe Miller. When young Ian Heddle of Dunfermline struck home what proved to be the only goal of the game in the 29th minute, the disappointments and despair experienced at the last league game of last season were all but forgotten. Dunfermline was on the way back! Fergie was full of praise for his

Special guests at the "Black and White" Exhibition in the local museum on August 10, 1985. Councillor Cameron, former managers Willie Cunningham and Harry Melrose, Scotland team boss Jock Stein, and former players Alex Smith, Alex Edwards and Jim Thomson. An appreciative group of young fans display momentoes from the exhibition which proved to be very popular in the town. (Dunfermline Press).

opponents, claiming the victory should have been greater, and once again, an air of expectancy hung around the stadium that night as the fans trooped home. Was this victory a propitious omen? Were the gods going to smile on Dunfermline this season?

Once the parties and celebrations had ended, it was down once again to the more mundane, but important, world of league business. On the playing side,

manager Jim Leishman made few changes to his squad which had so narrowly failed the previous season. David Houston, a first-team regular with newly relegated Alloa, was signed on a free transfer. It was hoped that this skilful player would lend strength and guile to that most important department, midfield. Striker Willie McGinley was signed up from Preston Athletic and Roddy Grant, young Willie Callaghan (a family name which needs no **15**

John Watson scores the winning goal against Cowdenbeath, August 31, 1985. (Dunfermline Press)

introduction at East End Park) and Peter Pryde were called up from the lower grades. The most significant news, however, was that Norrie McCathie, one of the Pars' most reliable and skilful players, had re-signed on a long-term contract.

The Pars' opening match of the season on Saturday, August 10th against Arbroath at Gayfield should have been a fairly easy encounter, considering that the home side had ended the previous season at the foot of the Second Division. However, Dunfermline were under no delusions and realised that their opponents had been revitalised

under the experienced hand of a new manager, the evergreen Jimmy Bone.

With skipper Bobby Robertson unavailable because of hospital duty and others out through injury, Leishman had to re-arrange his side, dropping Moyes to full back. Veteran Ian Campbell, brought back from Brechin earlier this year, scored after five minutes but shortly afterwards Ian Heddle, the hero of the Aberdeen match, headed under pressure through his own goal. Encouraged by this, Arbroath pressed forward and shocked the visitors by going into a 2-1 lead before the interval. It was left to prolific scorer John Watson,

Red-haired striker John Watson levels the score at 2-2 against Raith Rovers, September 14, 1985 at East End Park. (Dunfermline Press)

who had earlier delighted his fans by signing a new two-year contract, to twice beat Arbroath's off-side tactics and put his side once again ahead. However, with only seven minutes left, McCathie handled in the box and Arbroath equalised from the spot to level the match at 3-3.

Behind the scenes, Leishman made several backroom changes. Reserve coach Andy Young, who had brought on so many young players in the past, including the manager himself, left the club through pressure of work. The services of Willie Mackie, the scout in the Falkirk area for the past seven years, were dispensed with.

The first home league game brought initial disappointment to the sun-drenched crowd of 2,000 when the visitors, Berwick, went into the lead after only five minutes. Dunfermline struggled in the first half against a solid defence, well organised by former Scottish internationalist, John Brownlie. The vital breakthrough for Dunfermline came just before half-time when the advancing McCathie, rumoured to be the target of bids from several clubs, drilled home the equaliser through a crowded penalty area. The second half presented a happier picture with substitute Bowie causing the Borderers' defence all sorts of problems. Three quick goals from **17**

Bill Rolland and Jessie Arnott of the Centenary Club in front of the Trophy Cabinet in the Boardroom.

Campbell, Heddle and Watson put the home side into the driving seat and though Berwick pulled one back, Dunfermline were never again in danger and should have added to their lead.

The following Monday, August 19th, brought Stenhousemuir as visitors in the first round of the Skol Cup, the old League Cup. This tie should have been played the previous Wednesday but torrential rain that day had obliged the referee to postpone the match, leaving local fans to wonder if their opening home fixture of the season had ever been postponed before because of inclement weather. A crowd of around 2,500, including a few Premier League managers, watched the home side run out worthy winners by 4-0, despite the spoiling off-side tactics of the visitors.

Ian Campbell grabbed three goals and was nominated Man of the Match by the sponsors. Jenkins scored Dunfermline's fourth.

Only two days later the team, backed by a strong travelling support, had to journey to Greenock to fulfil their second round Skol Cup-tie against Morton who had played the previous season in the Premier League and who had seasoned campaigners in O'Hara, Richardson and McNamara on their books. Dunfermline belied their inferior league position and it was no surprise when Watson turned a Smith corner into the net. In 37 minutes Morton equalised and in the second half slack defensive work allowed Anderson to head home a Lex Richardson free kick. However, inside two minutes Watson again outjumped the home defence to head in the equaliser. The game went to extra time and the red-haired striker was unfortunate not to clinch the winner. To their credit, Dunfermline seemed the stronger side at the end but misfortune in the penalty shoot-out allowed Morton to convert four kicks to the visitors' three, the normally reliable McCathie and Watson missing from the spot. It was small consolation for the latter to be nominated Man of the Match.

The sequence of four games in eight days caught up with Dunfermline when they visited Glasgow on August 24th. Queen's Park, smarting from a 4-0 defeat at Stenhousemuir, started brightly and had a lot of early pressure. It was no surprise when their nippy forward, a certain Ian McCall, ignored claims that he was off-side and chipped the ball over the advancing Westwater. In 27 minutes Queen's Park went two up when

Watson heads home a Forrest cross against Raith Rovers, September 14, 1985. (Dunfermline Press)

a powerful cross from McLaughlin, assisted by the famous Hampden swirl, deceived Westwater and found the net. Almost immediately Watson pulled one back, heading home a Moyes cross but with only ten minutes left, McCall clinched it for the home side with a breakaway goal, sending the visitors to their first league defeat.

Against Cowdenbeath the following week at East End Park, Dunfermline seemed to be on the verge of losing further league points when goals from ex-Par McGlashan and from Doig put the visitors into the lead. Stevie Morrison pulled one back in 31 minutes with a

beautifully struck 30-yard volley and just before half-time, a well rehearsed free kick saw a terrific shot from Heddle, 25 yards out, crash into the net. Twenty minutes from time, Jenkins split the visitors' defence to allow Watson to score the winner in a match which had everything expected of a derby match: excitement, tension, entertainment, great goals, near misses, defensive clearances and competitive challenges which kept the fans on tenterhooks for 90 minutes.

A goalless draw at Palmerston Park a week later was regarded by manager Jim Leishman as a point gained. Queen of the South, joint second top of the **19**

Stevie Morrison, the Rivelino of East End Park, scores a memorable goal against Meadowbank, October 12, 1985. (Dunfermline Press)

league, had a well drilled defence which had conceded only one goal, and an own goal at that. The hero of the match was undoubtedly goalkeeper Ian Westwater who pulled off many fine saves. His counterpart, Alan Davidson, however, was not inactive either, saving well from Watson, Morrison and Young.

During the following week everyone in Scottish football, not least in Dunfermline, was stunned by the death of Scotland team manager, Jock Stein, after collapsing at the end of the crucial World Cup Qualifying Match against Wales at Cardiff on September 10th. It hardly needs repeating that it was Dunfermline Athletic which gave the former Albion Rovers and Celtic player his first opening into football management; it is also part of football legend how he miraculously saved a struggling Dunfermline team from certain relegation and took them to their first Scottish Cup Final in 1961, which was duly won in a replay against Celtic. Thereafter, Stein put Dunfermline onto a firm footing and brought them not inconsiderable European glory.

Only as recently as the previous May, as part of the Andrew Carnegie

A penalty from Grant Jenkins puts the Pars two goals up against Albion Rovers at East End Park on October 26, 1985. (Dunfermline Press)

celebrations, he and football broadcaster and author, Bob Crampsey, had shared the stage of the Carnegie Hall where they reminisced over an illustrious career and looked forward to the next World Cup. It was a fascinating evening for those privileged to attend and showed Stein to be the very warm, humane yet private man that he was. He also came over as a man who did not suffer fools gladly, reserving particular condemnation for armchair critics and, worse, the inebriated in public houses who made inane contributions to radio phone-in programmes. Even at the end of a long and tiring evening, he still found the time to sign every autograph book thrust at him. Throughout the summer Jock Stein paid another two visits to the town which had been his home for four happy years.

Before Dunfermline's home match against Raith Rovers on September 14th the crowd stood for one minute's silence, a tribute reverently repeated in all grounds, in memory of the colossus who dominated Scottish football for over a quarter of a century. The old maestro would have enjoyed the exciting, action-packed game that followed between the Fife rivals. Since league reconstruction in 1975, Dunfermline had beaten their

21

Jenkins scores the goal of the season against Queen of the South, November 9, 1985. (Dunfermline Press)

neighbours only once at East End Park and that statistic was not to change.

Early in the game Heddle fouled a Raith player in the box and Paul Smith scored from the spot. Three minutes later Watson rose majestically to head home a Forrest cross but only minutes later the home defence gifted a second goal. Undaunted, Dunfermline pressed on and were rewarded when Jenkins equalised. Dunfermline winger Jim Bowie was again in dazzling form. His curling crosses, his accomplished passing and his intricate dribbling confirmed him as one of the division's most talented players. Early in the second half Dunfermline went into the lead for the first time when the aerial brilliance of Watson again showed why he was the division's top scorer. Raith refused to surrender and fifteen minutes from time they equalised to grab a share of the points.

Dunfermline's weakness in gifting goals was again in evidence in a

midweek benefit match against Hearts in aid of funds for the long-serving Hugh Whyte, Bobby Robertson, Jim Bowie and the recently departed Paul Donnelly. As the game progressed, the Pars tired against a strong Hearts side and lost 2-0.

One week later, in a fixture postponed from the previous Saturday because of rain, Dunfermline travelled to Muirton Park to face a St. Johnstone side which only two seasons earlier had been playing in the Premier League. Relegation in successive seasons for this once successful club had brought about the resignation of manager Alex Rennie, and the appointment of Ian Gibson, now the youngest manager in Scotland.

After a goalless first half the Perth men shocked the large travelling support by going ahead in the 70th minute. Dunfermline knuckled down to their task and equalised through a free kick from Morrison after which Jenkins netted the winner. Disturbingly for the visiting support, both the goal scorers

Ian Heddle scores in the second minute in the Cup against Raith, December 7, 1985.
(Dunfermline Press)

had refused to sign long-term contracts. More worrying was that while the Dunfermline attack were finding the back of the net with relative ease, only Albion Rovers' defence had conceded more goals than Dunfermline's in the Second Division.

Both of these characteristics were to be in evidence on the last Saturday of September when visitors Stenhouse-muir, who had lost five goals in midweek to Meadowbank, kept the 2300 home crowd on edge right until the end. In the first half all Dunfermline had to show for incessant pressure was a single goal scored after 30 minutes by a fine header

from Jenkins. Almost immediately after the break Dunfermline paid the penalty for their ineffective finishing. Goalkeeper Westwater uncharacteristically missed the ball in the goalmouth and it fell nicely for that old East End favourite, Sandy McNaughton, to notch up the equaliser. Six minutes later that prolific scorer was again on hand to round Westwater and put his side into a shock 2-1 lead. Another former Pars' player, 33-year-old Jim Meakin, disadvantaged his side by being sent off in 68 minutes for persistent fouling. In a masterful stroke which swung the game, Leishman sent on substitutes Campbell

Keeper Ross of Queen's Park cannot hold McCathie's shot. January 11, 1986. (Dunfermline Press)

and Smith to harass a visiting defence whose main tactic was to repeatedly spring off-side traps to the great annoyance of a frustrated home crowd. A goalkeeping error from the normally reliable Lindsay Hamilton gave Heddle the easiest of chances to grab the equaliser with 15 minutes left. In the dying minutes McCathie, playing a true captain's part, headed home a deserved winner from Bowie's corner.

Ever mindful of the pressing need to recruit the best of the available youngsters in the neighbouring areas, Leishman appointed new scouts: Sandy Brown, one of the best-known figures in youth football in Edinburgh and the founder of that fertile producer of talent, Melbourne Thistle; and Jim Fraser, from Inverkeithing, who would concentrate his attentions on Fife. An under-18 and an under-18 side were soon to be set up.

At the beginning of October, five bus loads of Dunfermline supporters made the long journey to Stair Park; even at that, Dunfermline played to their lowest crowd of the season: 510. Though the local programme noted that Stranraer had only won two of their 19 league encounters with Dunfermline, the visitors were taking nothing for granted, especially with top-scoring forward John Watson unable to play.

The game started with plenty of excitement. In the first minute, Hamilton scored a simple goal from close range but three minutes later the home side, in their first venture up field, equalised. After that the game died for a long period with little to enthuse the small crowd. Before the break an own goal put Dunfermline 2-1 up which was increased five minutes before time when substitute Trevor Smith scored a great goal to wrap up the points and put his side into second top position.

Encouraged by the re-signing of Morrison and Jenkins (till the end of the current season at least) and by the return of skipper Robertson after an absence of five games, Dunfermline prepared to face Meadowbank, recently relegated from Division One and lying three places below the Pars. A magnificent goal in seven minutes from a well struck free kick by the powerful Morrison, the Rivelino of East End Park, put Dunfermline into the lead. While the Dunfermline defence kept the eager Edinburgh forward line at bay, the home forwards were unable to capitalise on their early lead and allowed their guests back into the game in the second half. Watson, restored to the team, was unlucky not to score before he was replaced by Bowie who brought more depth and scope to the home attack. With only four minutes left, Dunfermline's early pressure was nullified when Meadowbank equalised through Jackson to snatch a share of the points.

Dunfermline's fears at visiting Firs Park on October 19th proved to be totally groundless. The team which had knocked the Pars out of the Cup the previous season found themselves on the receiving end of a 4-0 thrashing. Watson put the visitors ahead after six minutes and his side never looked back even though Trevor Smith missed a penalty on the half-hour mark. Before and after half-time Jenkins scored two goals, the second from the spot, and five minutes from time Morrison boosted his side's goal difference by adding his name to the score sheet.

The Dunfermline goal-scoring machine was now in top gear as visitors Albion Rovers, with only one victory to their credit in the league, found out to

Memories of bygone days — a special football train from Dunfermline station for a Scottish Cup-tie.

their cost. On a mudbath of a field which the *Press* reporter likened to a First World War battlefield, Dunfermline rattled in six goals with the Coatbridge side unable to reply. After only four minutes that all-action centreback, Norrie McCathie, headed home to open the flood gates. Eight minutes later Jenkins made it number two when he converted a penalty after Watson was floored. With only 14 minutes gone big centre half Davie Young killed the game as a contest with a brilliant header. After the break, Watson scored his side's fourth goal and in 64 minutes, not to be outdone, defender Bobby Forrest added a fifth. McCathie finished off a fine day's work with a looping header from 18

25

Ian Campbell, opens the scoring against Queen's Park on January 11, 1986. (Dunfermline Press)

yards out to complete the rout.

Off the field the centenary festivities continued. At a dinner held at Keavil House Hotel on Thursday October 31st representatives from virtually all the country's senior sides, officials of the S.F.A. and Scottish League, local dignitaries and invited guests were welcomed by Chairman Jimmy Watters. He paid generous tributes to his predecessors and thanked all the people, many of them hidden from public view, who had worked so hard over the years to keep the club functioning. One of the finest speeches was given by Harry Melrose who gave a unique and humorous insight into the club as a player, manager and supporter over a 27-year period. A special presentation was made to secretary Jimmy McConville to mark 33 years of unbroken service to the club.

Three days later Dunfermline made the relatively short trip to Annfield to take on Stirling Albion, determined to keep up their challenge for honours in their centenary season. Though the home side had most of the early play and created several chances, they were unable to beat the splendid Westwater in goal. It was John Watson, again, who came to his side's rescue when he blasted home the only goal of the game from the edge of the penalty box early in

McCathie dives to head home Ian Heddle's cross for goal no. 1 against E. Stirling. January 18, 1986. (Dunfermline Press)

the second half. Though the visitors diced with death several times, they held out to clinch the two valuable points which kept them in second top position, just one point behind their next opponents, Queen of the South.

The top of the table clash attracted more than four and a half thousand spectators, a figure which was the envy of sides from the First Division, not to mention a few from the Premier League. Dunfermline put up a well disciplined performance. The *Press* hailed the 'magnificently aggressive attack of Watson, the bubbling artistry of Bowie and the calculated restraint of McCathie'.

Despite torrential rain and a sodden pitch, the home side adapted well to the swampy playing surface, using the long ball and the early cross to good effect.

Although it took Dunfermline 30 minutes to score the opening goal, it was well worth waiting for and would have been an outstanding candidate for 'Goal of the Season'. Winger Bowie flighted over a first-time cross from the right for Jenkins to nod it in at the near post. In 58 minutes, Watson picked up a loose ball to bury it behind the advancing Davidson. Queen's battled away and were rewarded with a goal three minutes from time. Dunfermline, **27**

New Directors, Blair Morgan and Roy Woodrow, co-opted in January, 1986, on to the Board.

however, held out to record a famous victory. With foul and unfair play seemingly never far from the sporting headlines, it is pleasing to recall an incident which reminds fans of the truly caring side of the game. Midway through the second half, Dumfries player Tony Gervaise collapsed in a fit, suffering, it was later diagnosed, from hypothermia. Jim Bowie had no hesitation in almost dragging the referee over to stop play for what was clearly not an act. In inflicting on the Dumfries side their first league defeat, the Pars were now proudly sitting at the top of the table with just over a third of the season gone.

Not surprisingly, Dunfermline took another large support to Kirkcaldy to boost the gate there to over 3,300. To say that Bobby Wilson's team was unpredictable would be something of an understatement. Two weeks earlier they had inflicted a humiliating 9-2 thrashing

on Stenhousemuir, only to lose the next match 6-0 at Meadowbank. Although Raith lay eighth in the league, Leishman did not underestimate the challenge ahead. On a heavy, spongy pitch the Pars were more than a match for their rivals, with their drive, pace and stamina triumphing in the end.

Dunfermline went ahead in 21 minutes when Jenkins converted the penalty awarded for a foul on John Watson. Only minutes later Jenkins might have made it two if his header had been slightly lower. A relieved home side were encouraged by this escape and Marshall soon equalised for them. In the second half the large travelling support thought Watson had won both points for them but his strike was disallowed. However, justice was done a few minutes from time when Jenkins, accepting a pass from Watson, blasted the ball into the net, demonstrating yet again what a fine partnership they had struck up.

It was a confident Dunfermline, therefore, unchanged for the fifth successive game, which took on third placed St. Johnstone on November 23rd in front of another excellent gate of over 4,000. While the Pars displayed speed, guile and expert finishing, the Perth men relied on fierce tackling which saw five of their players booked and one ordered off. Westwater had little to do, giving him plenty of time to admire a series of fine crosses from Bowie which tormented the visitors' defence. Jenkins, whom Leishman had earlier contemplated selling to Muirton Park, opened the scoring in 25 minutes when he finished off a beautifully executed move on the right. Jenkins added another one after a surging, solo run after the interval and

The Pars are top of the pops! The Pars hit the high notes as the Dunfermline football squad line up with a few friends from the pop world to cut a pop disc in an Edinburgh Studio. Manager, Jim Leishman led the lads in song with some help from Director, Blair Morgan. The minstrels later made two appearances on T.V.: "Reporting Scotland" and "Pebble Mill at One". (Evening News)

then the other half of the deadly duo, Watson, took over, grabbing a brace for himself as well. With 42 goals scored Dunfermline had the best shooting record in British league football.

The following weekend should have kept the spotlight on Dunfermline as most of the Premier League action was postponed to accommodate Scotland's International team on World Cup duty in Australia but frosty weather caused the away game at Stenhousemuir to be postponed. The launch, however, that

morning of the author's *Centenary History of Dunfermline Athletic* in the newly opened Kingsgate Centre, with members of past and present teams available to sign autographs, drew a crowd which many clubs would have been proud to see on their terracings.

An official reception hosted by Provost Mill for the players at the Town Chambers two days later ended what had been a marvellous year of celebrations for the club in their centenary; it was equally pleasing to see **29**

I AM THE BOSS'S FAVOURITE PLAYER

The club's top scorer, John Watson, probably merits this accolade from Jim Leishman. (Evening News)

the club perched proudly at the top of the league, encouraging fans to think of a brighter future.

By coincidence, two friendlies took place during the cold snap to allow the Dunfermline management to gauge how their team was shaping up against superior opposition. On the bitterly cold night of Tuesday November 26th a Rangers X1, depleted by the absence of most of the first team in Majorca, brought out a crowd of over 2,000 to see a first-half hat-trick from John MacDonald swing the game to the visitors.

One week later a stronger Pars team took the field at Easter Road to play for the Tom Hart Memorial Trophy. Though it took a Jenkins second-half penalty and very late goals from Watson

to make the defeat respectable (3-5), Dunfermline took a lot of credit and encouragement from the tussle, realising that a part-time team lacks the pace and fitness that full-time training brings.

To strengthen his squad, Leishman signed the former Newtongrange defender, Gordon Wilson (22), recently released by Meadowbank. Allan Forsyth, one of his first signings, and Andy Irvine, formerly with Derby County, both left the club.

The first Saturday in December was Scottish Cup day with Raith Rovers being drawn to come to East End Park. Over the last century, these deadly rivals had clashed on five occasions with Raith coming off marginally better. Interestingly, on the last occasion in 1972 Raith had surprisingly won 2-0, forcing an irate manager, Alex Wright, to blood new youngsters: a certain Ken Mackie and a young Jim Leishman were the beneficiaries of that ill wind.

Torrential rain had left the ground heavy and had kept many spectators away, though 5,558 did pay £5,540 to see their teams do battle. The home side got off to a dream start in the first minute when a defensive lapse by More allowed the eager Heddle to drive a Watson cross low past McLafferty. Wright came close on two occasions for the visitors while at the other end the ever alert Watson almost capitalised on a short pass-back by Philip. On the stroke of half-time another dreadful error by Philip was punished by Watson to effectively kill the game. Full backs Forrest and Robertson kept the visitors' lively forwards at bay. Jenkins was unfortunate not to have his name on the

The 1961 Cup-winning side meet up 25 years later: *(Back)* D. Thomson, A. Smith, C. Dickson, G. Miller. *(Centre)* G. Peebles, J. Sweeney, W. Cunningham. *(Front)* Chairman J. Watters, R. Mailer, H. Melrose. (Dunfermline Press)

score sheet when his 'goal' was adjudged off-side.

With the return to league action, the home fans expected lowly Stranraer, whose earlier 6-1 humiliation by Arbroath had brought about the resignation of manager Dave Sneddon, to fall easy victims to the Dunfermline goal machine. What they had failed to take into account was an heroic performance from 'keeper Brian Noonan who, when he was not stopping certain goals with his hands or feet, could call upon other parts of his anatomy to do the needful. The visitors' stuffy 4-4-2 formation totally frustrated the home side and it took until midway through the second half before Bowie broke the deadlock when he neatly volleyed the ball over an inspired 'keeper for his first goal of the season. Sadly, he fell victim to a fierce tackle and had to be carried from the field. With Stranraer having so little of the play, it would have been a travesty if McGuire had scored near the end instead of fluffing his shot.

The last game of a momentous year took the league leaders to England to play a dispirited home side which lay second bottom in the league with only two home victories to their credit. The suspension of Heddle allowed the creative Houston the chance to claim a regular berth in the visitors' side which was showing its first change in eight games. The fans who made the trek to Shielfield Park saw an amazing game, due in no small part to a gale force wind which caused panic in both goal areas. Romaines unsettled the visitors by scoring after 12 minutes though this was cancelled in 28 minutes when a Morrison corner hung in the wind and dropped behind the 'keeper for the ubiquitous Watson to crack the ball home. Berwick, however, rising to the challenge, forged ahead through Sokoluk and Conroy before the interval. The latter's shot would normally have gone high and wide but was caught by the wind and, much to the embarrassment of Westwater, went in at the top corner.

The 'keeper's misery was compounded at the start of the second half when a harmless cross eluded him and went in off the post. Most teams would have crumbled at 4-1 down but to their credit Dunfermline staged a near miraculous recovery. Jenkins finished off an impressive build-up with a goal, only to find himself dismissed with Davidson for a goalmouth fracas. On the hour mark, Forrest pulled another one back and 20 minutes later substitute Campbell expertly slid home a penalty kick after Smith was brought down in full flight in the box. With a bit more luck the visitors might even have won the contest to give them the victory they required to equal the club's record run of eight consecutive victories, established in 1957-58. Leishman, while grateful for the point, could only wonder how his team, which had conceded only four goals in 10 games, could suddenly lose as many in 35 minutes!

The end of the year brought the club's A.G.M. which reported a healthy situation. Though takings from the lotteries were down from £41,000 to £14,000, the success of the team on the field had increased the gate money from £71,000 to £99,000. Moreover, the Centenary Club, now up to 500 members, was bringing in the sum (before payments) of £1,000 per week. The transfer of Paul Donnelly and Rab Stewart had brought in £17,000 to reduce the overdraft to the not inconsiderable sum of £58,000. Clearly, Jim Leishman, whose 'sterling work' on and off the field was singled out, would not have a blank cheque book at his disposal when he went out to strengthen

Office Secretary, Sheila Peters, and Peter McAteer of the Junior Supporters' Club.

his team. While players might be sold if an exceptional offer came along, chairman Jimmy Watters stressed that 'there are no bargain buys for any club at East End Park. We've already had a few offers for one or two, but they were far below what we would want'.

The first Saturday of the New Year traditionally means Cup football and more than a thousand Pars' fans made the long and potentially hazardous trip to Meadow Park, Castle Douglas, home of the unknown Threave Rovers. Formed only in 1953, this country club was making only its third appearance in the Scottish Cup, and that by virtue of reaching the semi-final of the Qualifying Cup (South). With Hamilton and Jenkins both out through suspension, Dunfermline brought in Heddle and Moyes for a match that any senior club could not anticipate with relish, especially when the Arctic weather had made the frozen pitch a great leveller. Experienced full back Forrest only made the line-up with difficulty, after missing the team bus and having to resort to a £70 taxi ride to arrive in time.

The day the fans had dreamed of for so long — promotion to Division One. An ecstatic crowd acclaims its heroes. (Dunfermline Press)

Dunfermline were almost caught cold in the opening minutes by an energetic, enthusiastic, bustling forward line which looked upon this second-round tie as their cup final. After an exasperating first half, aggravated by falling sleet, Watson finally secured the goal the team was looking for when, in 42 minutes, after excellent work from Robertson on the right, he prodded the ball home with his left foot.

After a roasting from the manager at the interval and with the wind in their favour, Dunfermline set about demolishing their opponents in the second half. Two quick goals from

Heddle and Watson, both engineered by Trevor Smith, made the rest of the game academic. Soon afterwards, Watson completed his hat-trick and went on to score a fourth when he converted a penalty kick after Campbell had been up-ended to bring his tally to 21 goals. It was a good-natured contest with no bookings and, judging by the later exchange of friendly letters in the local papers, evidence that football can still bring communities together in friendship.

The New Year saw the Board inject young blood into their midst when they co-opted two new directors: 38-year old

Further scenes of jubilation on the day that promotion was gained against East Stirling on April 19, 1986. (Dunfermline Press)

solicitor, Blair Morgan, and 44-year old Roy Woodrow, the owner of a soft drinks company. It was hoped that some of the skills, ambition, drive and business acumen which had made these two men successful in their own particular fields would assist the club in their determined drive to return Dunfermline Athletic to the top of Scottish football.

By this time, it must be remembered, a new, intriguing factor had been added to the Scottish football scene which threatened the very basis upon which the sport had been organised for almost a century. The problem had begun at the start of the season when the Old

Firm asserted their right to ban the screening of live matches, a stance which the League Management Committee could not countenance. The dispute quickly developed to include related items such as sponsorship, the division of Pools' revenue and the very organisation of the leagues.

As the season progressed, there seemed the distinct possibility that the top, full-time, ambitious clubs might break away from the Scottish League and set up their own independent structure, inviting other like-minded clubs to join them. It was widely speculated that Dunfermline, with its

Celebrations in the dressing room after promotion had been secured to the First Division. (Dunfermline Press)

traditions, its fine stadium, its drawing power and its recent resurrection, would be asked to join Scotland's élite. Dunfermline were certainly putting their house in order, on and off the park, to deal with any eventuality.

It was, however, back to the more important job of amassing league points that faced Dunfermline, demoted to second top position after Queen of the South's victory over East Stirling the previous week, when third-placed Queen's Park, their only conquerors so far, visted East End Park on Saturday

January 11th for a crucial encounter. On a muddy pitch and facing a strong, gale-force wind, Dunfermline, without captain Robertson, had to battle hard against the talented amateurs. They were given the perfect start when, after misses by Campbell and Heddle, Campbell opened the scoring in eight minutes when 'keeper Ross failed to hold a Jenkins shot. To the crowd's great delight, the ever-alert McCathie made it 2-0 six minutes later by driving home a Morrison corner from the edge of the box. Five minutes from half-time the

35

visitors' pressure paid off when a wind-assisted drive from Cairns from all of 30 yards out left Westwater stranded and after the break Caven stunned the home support by heading low into the net.

In a masterful stroke, Leishman sent on his two substitutes, Bowie and Smith, who swung the game in Dunfermline's favour. In fact, it was from Smith that Dunfermline's 50th league goal came — he dribbled the ball into the box and crossed to Watson who touched the ball home with his left foot to gain his side another two valuable points and check the challenge of the Hampden side. This gritty, fighting display took the Pars to their 16th league game without defeat, thus equalling the record set in season 1978-79.

The record was duly smashed the following week when lowly East Stirling made their way into the lion's den at East End Park though Dunfermline's performance was anything but inspiring. Although the home side were boosted by the return of Robertson, the team lacked rhythm and creativity and it was left, not for the first or last time, for defender McCathie to score two fine headers in each half to show his blushing forwards how it should be done. As is often the case at East End Park against lesser-quality opposition, Dunfermline failed to convert their superiority into goals and could only blame themselves when Maskrey pulled one back near the end for 'Shire to make their performance appear slightly more respectable.

A welcome break from league business came with the third round of the Scottish Cup which took the Pars back to Easter Road to face a Hibs side under John Blackley. This was, unbelievably, the fourth time the two sides had met in the Cup in the last decade. In 1976, Hibs won 3-2 and though the ties in 1979 and 1981 went to replays, the Edinburgh side triumphed on each occasion. Dunfermline fans had to go back to 1965, the year their team lost to Celtic in the final, to remember their last victory, 2-0 at Tynecastle in the semi-final.

Although Hibs lay third bottom in the Premier League, they had fine, established players in international goalkeeper, Rough, and in twin strikers Cowan and Durie who had already netted 30 goals; in May, Collins and Kane they had promising youngsters. As the full-time side Hibs were clearly favourites but that did not deter a Fife support in excess of 5,000 making the short journey on Sunday January 26th to give Hibs their biggest crowd of the season: 15,491 which brought in healthy receipts totalling £32,624.

The part-timers did well to frustrate the home side in the first half and goalkeeper Westwater was seldom in real danger. Indeed, the best chance of the half fell to Jenkins, put through in the clear by Watson, but the bearded striker shot over from the edge of the box. The turning point in the game came 11 minutes into the second half when gritty midfielder Davie Moyes received his second caution from referee Delaney and was duly sent off.

With Watson obliged to drop into midfield, the Pars' attack was blunted and though substitute Morrison bolstered the midfield, Hibs scented victory and pressed home their advantage. In the 63rd minute May

A unique photo by Ian Malcolm has captured the scene on the night that Dunfermline won the championship at Stenhousemuir on April 29, 1986.

found it an easy task to head home the opening goal and at that point the tie slipped from Dunfermline's grasp. Ten minutes from time Cowan made it safe for Hibs by slotting home his side's second goal. Despite valiant efforts from Young and McCathie, the visitors were denied the consolation goal which their stout-hearted challenge had merited. Though outclassed by a side which played every week in the cauldron of the Premier League, Dunfermline could take a lot of encouragement from a brave performance which gave no cause for dejection.

It was back to league business on February 1st when Stirling, who had failed to beat the Pars in their last six meetings, visited East End Park. Though Dunfermline played well in the first half and were unlucky not to be in the lead, they found the visitors to be a well organised team, with forwards Irvine and Ormond in particularly fine form. Finding themselves a goal down at the interval, Irvine scoring in 42 minutes, Dunfermline attacked in the second half and could have scored through Jenkins (twice), Forrest and Morrison. In 71 minutes Stirling punished these misses by going further ahead when a short pass-back from Forrest was seized on by Thompson who rounded Westwater and scored.

In a last throw, Leishman sent on substitutes Houston and Smith and **37** pushed McCathie forward. The gamble seemed to have paid off when Smith's corner was rammed home by Young and then in injury time Smith equalised with the aid of a deflection from close-in. The home fans' joy at this remarkable escape was, alas, to turn to despair within seconds when Stirling centred the ball, ran up the field and netted a shock winner as the referee prepared to blow for full-time. Thus, Dunfermline's record breaking run of 17 games without defeat came to an end. Fortunately, Dunfermline's rivals had also dropped points and during the week, Queen's Park did them a favour by beating Queen of the South 1-0.

Though continuing bad weather caused the postponement of Dunfermline's game against Albion Rovers, the team were far from inactive off the field. When the social history of the late 20th century is written there will doubtless be a place in it for the extremely popular B.B.C. soap opera, 'East Enders'. Throughout the season the Pars fans had adopted the catchy theme music as their unofficial anthem and the signature tune became a popular request with 'Radio Pars'.

In an inspired moment, director Blair Morgan and his 16-year old son, Steven, wrote lyrics to go with the music, with the 'East End' of Dunfermline in mind rather than the more popular district featured in the series. Using his contacts in the music publishing world, Blair organised a recording session in Edinburgh with the players and, following an appearance on 'Reporting Scotland', a record was duly cut. Coach Gregor Abel obliged by penning and singing the 'B' side, the plaintive but melodic 'Pars Song'. The B.B.C. magazine programme, 'Pebble Mill at One', heard of this enterprising venture and invited the squad to give a live performance on the show in Birmingham on Thursday February 13th. Thus a national audience of several million was reminded that Dunfermline Athletic were back on song once again.

It was, therefore, a rather tired squad, reminiscent of the return of the conquering heroes of the 1960s from a European campaign, which went to Kirkcaldy to take on a home side which, with no manager, was certainly on the slide with crowds dropping below the thousand mark. On a bone-hard surface it seemed that Dunfermline were going to add to the home side's misery. In the opening minutes a cross from the enterprising Bobby Forrest was nodded down by Watson for Campbell to score. A few minutes later, Campbell returned the compliment and set up an easy goal for the red-haired striker. Shortly afterwards the rejuvenated Campbell was unlucky not to kill the game off with goal number three. The home side's relentless endeavour, however, paid off when Herd shot through a ruck of players after 21 minutes to give his side a glimmer of hope.

In the second half Raith quickly equalised through Wright to put the outcome of the game in the balance. This was the first time in more than three months that Raith had scored more than two goals in a game. The introduction of Houston and new signing, Ian Pryde, as substitutes seemed to do the trick when Watson blasted a 25-yarder into McLafferty's net

East Enders – The Words

1. We're the boys from East End Park
    We've been on the go for One Hundred years, and
    We're the team in black and white
    Football is our game we're getting it right, and

    What's our Name
    Our Claim to Fame
    We are the Pars, Dunfermline Athletic.

2. Come along to East End Park,
    Come and watch us win, there's no better reason
    We're the team they call the Pars
    Promotion is our Aim and this is our Season

    What's our Name
    Our Claim to Fame
    We are the Pars, Dunfermline Athletic

3. Come along to East End Park
    Come and watch us win, there's no better reason
    We're the team they call the Pars
    Promotion is our Aim and this is our Season

SPEAK OVER:

In 1885 Dunfermline Athletic Football Club were formed. In 1903 Dunfermline Athletic moved to East End Park. In 1912 Dunfermline Athletic played in black and white for the first time and the local newspapers referred to them as The Pars. In 1926 Dunfermline Athletic entered the Scottish First Division. In 1961 and 1968 Dunfermline Athletic won the Scottish Cup.

4. We're the boys from East End Park
    We've been on the go for One Hundred years, and
    We're the team in black and white
    Football is our game we're getting it right, and

5. Come along to East End Park
    Come and watch us win, there's no better reason
    We're the team they call the Pars
    Promotion is our Aim and this is our Season

    La La La La La ....

Lyrics by Blair and Steven Morgan. Music by arrangement with the B.B.C. At one stage it was planned to tape the voices of the crowd during the home match against St. Johnstone on February 22 to provide the chorus for the record. Unfortunately, adverse weather conditions caused the fixture to be postponed and the idea was abandoned. However, the record was an outstanding success and though it never reached the Top Ten, there have been many impromptu renditions of it in recent months.

in the 76th minute. Lack of concentration again let Raith back in the game when Herd squeezed home a Sweeney corner, leaving the visitors to ponder how they had contrived to drop a point which might prove invaluable at the end of the season.

With winter refusing to relax its icy grip, it was Wednesday March 5th before Dunfermline could set about catching up on Queen of the South who were now four points ahead but with two more games played. The Pars now faced eight games in the space of one month.

An occasion to savour — Captain Bobby Robertson receiving the Second Division Championship Cup from Eric Mitchell of the Scottish League. Jimmy Watters and Jim Harrison look on.

Dunfermline made the short trip to Cowdenbeath, under new manager Joe Craig, to play the fixture which had been postponed from Ne'erday. Dunfermline were at full strength against a dispirited side which had not played at Central Park since November 30th.

The first-footers were in determined mood on a bitterly cold night, made more uncomfortable by a strong westerly wind and heavy showers which made good football virtually impossible. Dunfermline put in a workmanlike performance and were on top both halves. Goalkeeper Westwater had little to do, protected as he was by a strong defence which the home side could not break down. Trevor Smith put in a notable performance, probably his best of the season, the highlight of which was his scoring of the only goal of the night.

The second half is best remembered for the torrential rain against which a partially burned out stand offered little protection.

The visit of Queen's Park to East End Park three days later was eagerly awaited. While Dunfermline and Queen of the South were shaping up to be promotion contenders, the Glasgow men were fast creeping up on the front runners, though they had played more games. Once again the Dunfermline defence found they had a game on their hands as they faced a tricky forward line which, thanks to undersoil heating at Hampden, was fully match-fit. The muddy park made for a dour, midfield struggle with Queen's Park getting the better of the early exchanges, causing Westwater to make fine saves from Caven, Smith and Crooks.

Ian Heddle (left) and Rowan Hamilton (right) coaching keen youngsters at the Dunfermline Centre. There is never a shortage of applicants for these very popular courses.

Even the introduction of fresh men for Dunfermline — Houston and Jenkins — could not swing the game for the home side who were missing the services of winger Bowie. Leishman was not unhappy with the point which kept the Pars four points clear of Queen's Park with the bonus of four games in hand.

A chance to go further ahead in a re-arranged midweek fixture against lowly Stenhousemuir was squandered. The Ochilview bogey continued, with Dunfermline's dismal record of not having won there for eight years continuing. More than 1,500 fans from Dunfermline journeyed through but were disheartened after only four minutes when the home side went ahead.

Dunfermline missed several good chances to equalise, with Watson being repeatedly held up for off-side. Young Gordon Connelly, making his league debut, found it a difficult match when so many of his colleagues were off-form. A certain element of luck is required to win championships and fortune certainly favoured Dunfermline in the second half when a Houston mis-kick conveniently ricocheted off a defender's back into the path of Watson who brought a huge sigh of relief to the visiting support by neatly scoring the equaliser. Try as they might, Dunfermline could not grab the winner and could not even capitalise on the dismissal of McIntosh which reduced the home side to 10 men.

A quick return to Central Park against an injury-hit home side brought Dunfermline another two valuable points, completing a hat trick of wins over their neighbours and stretching their unbeaten away run to 11 games. Dunfermline went ahead through Hamilton who shrugged off protests of

41

Programme Editor, Ken Richards (standing) and public address announcer, Bob Johnston.

off-side to coolly stroke the ball past 'keeper Allan. Despite playing into a strong wind, Dunfermline spurned further good chances to go ahead, largely due to the excellence of Allan. Robertson and Forrest were allowed to burst forward at will while the solid pillars of McCathie and Young gave Westwater an easy afternoon. It took until the 79th minute when Rutherford failed to control the ball to let in Campbell to finally seal Cowden's fate.

It was just as well Dunfermline were doing well on the field; in the smoke-filled headquarters of the Scottish League it was announced during the week that the threatened breakaway by the 'rebel' nine clubs had been averted. For Dunfermline, as they had always imagined anyway, it meant there would be no short cut back to the top; hard graft, not divine favour, would be the arbiter.

Though Meadowbank's promotion hopes had been dented in recent weeks,

there was little chance of them lying down to Dunfermline when they visited the Capital for a re-arranged fixture on Tuesday evening, March 18th, and so it proved to be. Twice Dunfermline took the lead and twice a jittery defence let Meadowbank back into the game. After 20 minutes the Pars thought they had gone ahead when a Campbell strike seemed to have crossed the line but, to howls of protest, World Cup referee Brian McGinlay waved play on and booked the protesting McCathie for dissent. However, in 34 minutes, Campbell did get his name on the scoresheet when a well worked set-piece from Hamilton found the veteran striker who crashed the ball in from close range.

Five minutes later, Dunfermline conceded a poor equaliser when a Moyes mis-kick was watched by an immobile defence to let Lawrence in with a chip over the advancing Westwater. Watson restored the visitors' pride just after the interval when he headed home a great overhead kick from Jenkins. When centre half Davie Young limped off with 20 minutes to go, a re-arranged rearguard of Robertson in the centre and Hamilton at full back bolstered by substitute Morrison in midfield was subjected to a barrage of shots from a home side confident of equalising. The goal duly came, though it was a poor shot from Lawrence, wickedly deflected, that finally beat Westwater to complete an unsatisfactory evening. Hamilton was ordered off in the dying minutes following a goalmouth clash.

Whether it was due to the busy session the players had on the Saturday

On the very last day of the season, East Fife applaud Dunfermline as champions onto the field for the forthcoming Fife Cup-tie. (Ian Malcolm)

morning signing autographs in local record shops during the hectic, but successful, launch of 'East Enders' or whether it was due to a tough midweek game, the team struggled to their second successive goalless draw at home. A young Arbroath side with seven players under 19 years did more than hold their own against a home side who had Ian Westwater to thank, yet again, for coming to their rescue on numerous occasions. The Pars had their chances but goal-line clearances or poor finishing saw only one point gained, when two had been confidently expected. On leaving East End, Jimmy

Bone pleased the home fans when he proclaimed that 'the race is now on for third place'. Although Dunfermline and Queen of the South still battled it out for top spot, it seemed that nearest rivals, Queen's Park, would require something of a miracle to make up the four-point gap, considering they had played three games more.

With almost a whole league separating Stranraer from their hosts, it was hardly surprising that the Pars ran out worthy winners though, on closer inspection, it was disturbing to see how Dunfermline could drift out of a game. Torrential rain again left the pitch in a

43

Jim Leishman conducting one of the very popular coaching sessions at East End Park for the children of Centenary Club members.

sodden state and the visitors, with little incentive, were happy to punt speculative balls upfield; the chances which did come their way were generously squandered.

Jenkins should have opened the scoring in the 10th minute but his penalty kick was saved. Four minutes later Hamilton, restored to the side after suspension, made amends by driving the ball home from 12 yards. Minutes later Dunfermline suffered a setback when Forrest was taken off injured and his cover, Gordon, almost gifted Stranraer an equaliser with a poor pass back which brought out a point-blank save from Westwater. Just before half-time Bowie provided another of his excellent crosses which Watson cleverly dummied to allow Jenkins to score from

18 yards. In the second half, although Stranraer pulled a goal back through a penalty, Watson and Morrison added a goal apiece to boost Dunfermline's goal difference column.

Such was the drawing power of Dunfermline that when their re-scheduled match against Albion Rovers was fixed for Monday, March 31st, Airdrie's ground at Broomfield was booked to accommodate a larger than usual crowd. Although under new manager, Lisbon Lion Tommy Gemmell, the Coatbridge side had enjoyed something of a mini-revival, going seven games without defeat, Dunfermline were hungry for both points to take them nearer promotion. The visitors opened well, with early chances falling to Heddle, McCathie, Watson and

Bowie, and they were rewarded with a goal in 14 minutes, thanks to 'keeper McKeown who, suspiciously weak on high cross balls, palmed a harmless header from Campbell into his own net. Two minutes before half-time, in one of the best moves of the game, Hamilton worked a neat one-two with Houston to chip the ball past the advancing 'keeper. Near the end of a miserable, wet night Campbell linked well with substitute Pryde to finish off a good evening's work which saw Dunfermline restored to the top of the league.

To strengthen his squad in the run-in to the end of the season, Leishman paid £5,000 to secure the services of 29-year old Gary Thomson from Alloa. The aggressive midfield dynamo, who had helped frustrate Dunfermline's promotion bid in the penultimate game of last season, would first have to serve out a four-match suspension before joining the team. Leishman made another shrewd acquisition in persuading former Raith manager, Bobby Wilson (44), to join the backroom set-up at East End. His duties were to oversee the scouting system and to draw up files on Dunfermline's opponents.

The only major hiccup to affect Dunfermline's promotion bid came in early April. For the club's crucial visit to Dumfries, the manager found himself without the services of three key players. Talented midfielder Stevie Morrison announced he wished to play in Australia during the summer and when he indicated that he wanted to go early, an infuriated Leishman promptly left him out of his squad altogether. Forrest's recent injury had not fully cleared and Gordon was drafted into the defence.

Head gate-checker, Alex Bowman, who has served the club for 35 years.

The severest blow, without doubt, was the suspension of Norrie McCathie for two games. If ever proof were needed that Dunfermline without McCathie was like *Hamlet* without the Prince, then spectators need look no further than the Pars' performances without him.

The 2,500 fans who made the visit south saw their team labour against a side which, after several disappointing results, needed the two points to put them back on top of the league. Captain Robertson seemed less than fit, Young missed the cover of McCathie and too much was expected of young Gordon Wilson on his league debut. After only six minutes Dunfermline were unlucky not to take the lead when a shot from Watson was blocked by the 'keeper's foot. Encouraged by this escape, Queen's pressed the visitors' goalmouth and were rewarded with a goal following a corner after 15 minutes. Shortly afterwards, Hamilton seemed to have an equaliser teed up, only to shoot wildly over the bar. On the half hour, the home side struck again when a dreadfully short pass back by Gordon let Cochrane increase the lead.

A second-half revival, orchestrated by Bowie and Watson, was firmly squashed when a long ball out of the Queen's defence gave Cochrane plenty of space to add a third goal. Although Bowie later pulled one back for the Pars, the visit was one that would be quickly forgotten. The match ended Dunfermline's marvellous run of 13 away games without defeat.

For the first and only time that season, the Pars followed one miserable defeat with one that was even more inglorious. In a re-arranged game on Tuesday, April 8th at Meadowbank the *Press* headline summed it all up: 'Pars played off the Park'. The first shock of the evening was the appearance of 38-year-old Hamish McAlpine in goal for Dunfermline. Earlier in the day Ian Westwater had gone down with a virus and with reserve 'keeper Whyte on holiday, Leishman had a day of panic before finally fixing up the loan of the veteran Tannadice player.

Unfortunately for the guest, the Pars' defence struck rock bottom that night, driving some of the visiting support to bay, quite unfairly, for the manager's blood. Aided by a swirling wind in the first half, Meadowbank seemed much faster than their opponents and picked up every loose ball, forcing Dunfermline to clear the ball off the line several times. Midway through the first half, goals from Jackson and Scott put the home side at ease while for the visitors only Watson and Thompson, who made a promising debut, came near to scoring. Eight minutes into the second half, McGachie volleyed home a corner to put the issue beyond doubt.

Despite the introduction of the substitutes and a policy of all-out attack, Dunfermline failed to score and indeed allowed McGachie at the other end to complete the rout with a simple header. Had it not been for the woodwork and a point-blank save from McAlpine, the damage could have been much greater. In inflicting on the Pars their worst defeat of the season, the home side also had the satisfaction of recording their first ever victory over their longer-established rivals.

After two dismal performances, the need for a good home result against Albion Rovers was never greater and the Pars duly obliged with a sparkling 4-0 victory to complete a hat-trick of wins over the club, scoring 13 goals and conceding none in the process. Tommy Gemmell, 'Manager of the Month' for March, had no answer to a Dunfermline inspired by the return of McCathie. Top scorer Watson was back on form, creating two goals out of nothing in the first half and giving him his 50th goal for the club. Newcomer Gary Thompson controlled the midfield well and deservedly got his name on the score sheet for the first time with a well-struck shot from a Bowie corner. It was Thompson too who supplied Campbell with the ball for him to poke it through the keeper's legs for goal number four.

With only six games left for Dunfermline, the countdown now began. Though they were three points behind leaders Queen of the South, they had a precious game in hand. More importantly, although they led third-placed Queen's Park by only two points, they had three games in hand over the

The Squad which won the Second Division championship. *Front row:* Gregor Abel (coach), Trevor Smith, Ian Westwater, Dave Houston, Jim Leishman (manager). *Middle row:* Philip Yeates (physiotherapist), Ian Heddle, John Watson, Bobby Robertson (captain), Grant Jenkins, Norrie McCathie, John Jobson (backroom), Joe Nelson (backroom). *Back row:* Ian Gordon, Rowan Hamilton, Bobby Forrest, Ian Campbell, Dave Moyes, Gary Thompson.

Glasgow side. Victory against St. Johnstone in a re-arranged match at home on Wednesday April 16th was essential and again the Pars came up trump, soundly beating the slipshod Perth side 4-0.

Campbell opened the scoring after 11 minutes, thanks to a 30-yard pass from Thompson. A goal from the uncompromising Moyes, his first for the club, settled the team. The highlight of the evening was undoubtedly the third goal by Watson whose left-foot shot from just inside the box in the 53rd minute made him the first striker in Scotland to reach 30 goals. His reward, apart from immense personal satisfaction, was a crate of champagne and 'The Golden Shot' Trophy from the *Daily Record.* Thomson rounded off the scoring by forcing Adam to put through his own net to send Dunfermline one stage nearer the First Division.

The scene was set for an intriguing game when East Stirling provided the opposition at home on Saturday April 19th. If Cowdenbeath could take a point at Hampden and if Dunfermline could win, then promotion would be secured although many thought the idea to be premature.

For the first half hour Dunfermline, not for the first time, did not look too impressive against a team far below them until Gary Thompson, the inspiration of the day, drove a fine goal past Bowie to calm a few nerves. Before the interval Hamilton netted his fifth goal of the season to put the Pars into a more confident mood, especially when it was learned that Cowdenbeath were ahead. The same player missed an excellent chance to make it number three after the interval and Davie Young, supreme in the air, was desperately unlucky with a header. However, a goal from Campbell in 73 minutes following good play from Watson and Bowie, and a brave header from substitute Jenkins 10 minutes later completed Dunfermline's hat-trick of victories.

The real drama of the afternoon was still to unfold. Pandemonium and jubilation broke out amongst the 3,300 fans when Bob Johnston announced over the public address system that Queen's Park had lost, indicating that promotion was now secure. Unlike last season, this was no cruel rumour — the Pars had fought their way back into the First Division for the first time since that Andy Rolland penalty sunk Falkirk in 1979. For twenty minutes the delighted fans stayed on the field to salute their heroes and to savour that special moment that only promotion can bring.

Inside the stadium the revelry and celebrations continued unabated as officials and players drank each other's health. 'I'm delighted', 'Magic',

'Tremendous' were the reactions of players who could not believe that the gruelling season, the hard training and dedicated application had finally paid off — and with four games to spare! Although Jim Leishman had been part of the successful promotion squad of 1972-73, this occasion was certainly more exciting for him in his new role as manager. Looking ahead, but without the aid of a crystal ball, Jim was confident about next season. 'I'm not saying we're going to win the First Division title, but I think we'll do very well.'

One player sadly missing was Stevie Morrison who, at that very moment, was flying to Australia to join Perth Azzurri on a temporary contract.

For the club chairman Jimmy Watters, who had seen the club's fortunes fluctuate considerably since he became a director in 1970, the occasion was a particularly proud one, especially after the heartbreak of last season. 'Obviously we are delighted: for the manager who worked hard, for the players who got promotion in style with three 4-0 wins, and for the fans who have supported us all year. The last few weeks seem to have taken forever, but the job is still not finished. We are still looking to go up as champions.

It was with that elusive championship in mind that Dunfermline took on Arbroath on Tuesday April 22nd on another rainy night — when did it not rain that season at East End? The Red Lichties operated a well-drilled off-side trap, much to the annoyance of the home crowd, which, coupled with hard, physical endeavour, kept them on level terms at half-time. It took an error in the

46th minute from right back Mitchell when he turned a header into his own net to give Dunfermline the vital breakthrough. A second goal followed when a volley from the enterprising McCathie was saved by Jackson, but the slippery ball slithered out of his hands into the path of the eager Young to record only his third goal of the season.

One of the most exciting moments of the night came after the final whistle when it was announced that Stirling had beaten championship contenders, Queen of the South, 3-1, a result which put Dunfermline back on top of the league by one point and with the cushion of a superior goal difference. Indeed, Dunfermline's goal-machine had now smashed Berwick's goal record (82) for the new Second Division in Season 1978-79.

With only three games to go, anticipation was high in the Dunfermline camp that the championship could come to East End for the first time since 1925-26 when Skinner, Sutton and Stein had written their names into the history books. For once, Dunfermline had a relatively easy game at Shielfield Park against a Border side which was simply playing out the season. Full backs Forrest and Hamilton, with little to trouble them, advanced at will and still left Westwater with an easy afternoon. Just one minute before half-time, 'keeper Watson failed to cut out a Bowie cross and his deadly namesake made no mistake.

Bolstered by the news that Queen of the South were losing 2-0 at home to Stranraer and driven on by a lecture by their manager, Dunfermline stepped up a gear in the second half and took over

the game. Another cross from Bowie set up the second goal for Campbell. Thus the scorer of the first goal of the season was also the scorer of the 100th strike of that remarkable season. It was the same player, written off earlier by his critics, who engineered his side's third goal when he cut a delightful ball back to give David Moyes an easy goal against his old team. The left winger was again in the thick of the action when he scored goal number four to send home the large travelling support in good cheer, heartened by the news that the Palmerston side had suffered yet another defeat.

In this season of anniversaries, it did not go unnoticed amidst all the excitement by the faithful in the Paragon Social Club that April 1986 marked the 25th anniversary of Dunfermline winning the Scottish Cup for the first time. Accordingly, the winning team was invited back to a dinner and, amazingly, nine of the 11 made the pilgrimage. Goalkeeper Eddie Connachan and full back Cammy Fraser both worked and lived abroad and could not be present. The others, looking perhaps slightly greyer and longer in the tooth but still possessing that sparkle, loyalty and camaraderie which distinguished their group, were greeted as heroes. Old stories were re-told, news of families was exchanged and everyone's health was drunk.

The memories of past glories and the prospect of new triumphs were thus in the minds of the 3,000 fans who made the important journey to Ochilview on Tuesday April 29th for the Pars' eighth game in a month. As has already been noted, the Larbert ground was anything **49** but a happy hunting ground for the visitors and that night was to be no exception.

As many expected, it was a dour game with a stuffy home side playing before their largest gate of the league programme. But for two fine saves from Westwater, Stenhousemuir could have been two up inside five minutes as the Warriors went on the warpath. Despite the discouraging news from Central Park that Queen of the South were leading 3-1, a revitalised Pars side showed more enterprise in the second half and were unlucky not to score from good efforts from Campbell, Hamilton, Moyes and Robertson. Westwater had the satisfaction of recording his sixth successive shut-out as his team played out a goalless draw.

Once again, the real drama took place after the final whistle as the players shook hands and the disgruntled faithful moved towards the exits. When a rather hesitant announcer, perhaps not fully realising the significance of his news, informed his expectant listeners that Cowdenbeath had pulled back to draw 3-3, the balloon, as they say, went up. Dunfermline Athletic, for only the second time in their long and distinguished history, had won the Second Division Championship. Once again, fans, players and officials greeted one another in almost disbelief as the significance of the night's proceedings sank in. To the tune of 'We are the Champions', the long convoy of cars and buses made its contented way back to Dunfermline where, in the hostelries across the burgh, the festivities carried on into the early morning.

In an extremely friendly gesture, too often absent from the modern game, the defeated Palmerston party, content to be runners-up to a side with which they had battled all season, joined in on the celebrations at the Paragon Club on their long way home.

The last day of an arduous but successful league programme dawned on Saturday May 3rd. Before the players could get to grips with the scalp hunters at Annfield, they generously gave of their time, as they had so often, to launch the club's new 'Candy' strip, designed with broader stripes more in the fashion of that worn in earlier years. For over three hours in the Co-op Sports Shop, Jim Leishman and his heroes presided over the sale of more than 1,500 outfits, obliging the manageress to order more.

The game against Stirling was a big disappointment to the large travelling support, eager to acclaim the new League Champions. Stirling, the only side to win at East End, set out to spoil the party, and succeeded though it looked different at half-time when the Pars went in 1-0 up to a Campbell goal that had more than a suspicion of offside about it. In the second half the visitors, suffering perhaps from the after effects of too much champagne during the week and missing the aerial skills of the suspended Watson, went off the boil and allowed a fast moving, skilful home side to rip them apart.

The *Press* reporter noted that a certain Willie Irvine, reportedly interesting Hibs, was 'the tormentor-in-chief. He was proving as difficult to hold on to as a bar of soap in the bath'. He went on to score two fine goals with McTeague adding another with a cracking header, and though McCathie

During the season, the gym at East End Park was used as a practice area for local pop groups. The result of Jim's audition was not disclosed. (Dundee Courier)

pulled a late goal back, Dunfermline were made to suffer their first defeat in seven games. As Gregor Abel admitted, 'the edge has gone off us a wee bit'. The problem of how to deal with a team with imagination and pace would be one that could be expected oftener in the season ahead.

The following day brought the last game of the season, the semi-final of the Fife Cup at East End against East Fife who had been narrowly pipped for promotion to the Premier League. An ordinary Sunday afternoon was turned into a unique occasion by the presentation by Cowdenbeath Chairman, Eric Mitchell, a member of the League Management Commitee, of the Championship Cup to captain Bobby Robertson, celebrating 10 years with the club. Centenary Club organiser Jim Harrison announced each member of the squad on to the field to collect the medal that would become a family heirloom.

After a great ovation and a lap of honour, it was down to the football which, alas, had an end of season staleness about it. An opening goal by Trevor Smith after 18 minutes did rouse the crowd as he caught on to an incisive pass from Watson which he slotted home from 10 yards. A defensive error before half-time allowed Stead to equalise which, with no further scoring, took the game to a penalty shoot-out. Everybody scored, bar the unfortunate Smith, and East Fife marched into the final. A sleepy Sabbath afternoon was perhaps not the ideal occasion to measure Dunfermline's chances against First Division opposition.

Thus the curtain came down on a season which will be talked about in Dunfermline for a long time. With relatively few changes to the side which just failed in 1984-85, Jim Leishman, in only his second full season as manager, had taken the Pars halfway towards their rightful place at the top of Scottish football. While a newly appointed Graeme Souness was splashing out money as though it was going out of fashion, a thrifty, cautious Board achieved their goal by dipping into their resources only once – a modest cheque for £5,000 for Gary Thompson, a sum which was quickly repaid.

Statistics revealed by the Scottish League disclosed that, outwith the Premier League, Dunfermline had the best support in Scottish football, 57,158 paying customers passing through the turnstiles in 20 games. This figure was not only 20,000 more than the next best supported club, Queen of the South (36,227), but it was nearly 10,000 more than the best supported club in the First Division. Champions Hamilton could only muster 47,221 and second top Falkirk, of similar size to Dunfermline, attracted a similar number, 47,171.

It looked likely that visiting Pars fans would easily outnumber the home fans in the First Division when their gates are revealed:
Brechin (12,639), Montrose (13,882), East Fife (17,416), Clyde (18,044), Dumbarton (22,236), Morton (23,118), Airdrie (26,666) and Killie (38,981).

It was a season which Dunfermline controlled from early on and increasingly a two-horse race with Queen of the South looked likely. Apart from a slight falter in early April at Palmerston and at Meadowbank, it could be fairly said that Dunfermline won at a canter. It was a season which John Watson will remember for his goal-scoring exploits which began to have the old faithful comparing him to Charlie Dickson and Alex Ferguson. Ian Westwater, Leishman's best buy, achieved no less than 21 shut-outs and missed only one league game as did the dependable Davie Young. McCathie missed only two games – and it showed! The team as a whole scored 91 League goals, the highest in Britain; they failed to score on only five occasions. When it is considered that four of the squad played in only five games, the first team pool in effect comprised only 17 players.

The club's list of 19 retained players confirmed none of the rumours which had been sweeping the town. Dave Houston, who made only eight full appearances, was freed as were I. Pryde, G. Wilson and W. McGinley; Willie Callaghan was not to keep the family name going and was soon transferred to a junior club. P. Pryde and R. McGregor would not be called up. For Leishman the headaches were just beginning as he tried to persuade current players to re-sign and as he searched for new blood. He was less than pleased by press speculation that he had over £150,000 to spend, noting that such talk made selling clubs greedy. Nonetheless, he set off for a well deserved holiday in Tenerife with his wife and daughter, away from the rigours of a job which claims a casualty almost every week.

Season 1985-86
All the results

August 10 1985

ARBROATH (2) 3   DUNFERMLINE (1) 3
Heddle (o.g. 25)   Campbell (5)
Curran (34, pen. 83)   Watson (49, 65)

ARBROATH: Jackson, Lynch (Kirkcaldy), Hill, Young, Glover, Taylor, Curran, Mackie, McWalter, Brannigan, Paterson (Kennedy)

Bookings: Hill, Glover, Taylor

DUNFERMLINE: Westwater, Moyes, Forrest, McCathie, Young, Heddle, Smith (Bowie), Hamilton (Jenkins), Watson, Morrison, Campbell

Bookings: Young, Heddle, Moyes

Referee: I.R. Cathcart, Bridge of Allan
Attendance: 1,100

Berwick	0	Albion Rovers	0
Cowdenbeath	3	Meadowbank	1
Queen of South	2	Stenhousemuir	0
Queen's Park	2	Stranraer	1
Raith	0	St Johnstone	2
Stirling	0	East Stirling	1

	P	W	D	L	F	A	Pts
Cowdenbeath	1	1	0	0	3	1	2
Queen of South	1	1	0	0	2	0	2
St Johnstone	1	1	0	0	2	0	2
Queen's Park	1	1	0	0	2	1	2
East Stirling	1	1	0	0	1	0	2
Arbroath	1	0	1	0	3	3	1
DUNFERMLINE	1	0	1	0	3	3	1

August 17 1985

DUNFERMLINE (1) 4   BERWICK (1) 2
McCathie (43)   Sokoluk (5, 76)
Campbell (69)
Heddle (71), Watson
(73)

DUNFERMLINE: Westwater, Robertson, Forrest, McCathie, Young, Heddle, Smith (Bowie), Moyes, Watson, Morrison, Campbell (Jenkins)

BERWICK: Glynn, Smith, Conroy, McGovern, Douglas, Brownlie, Davison, Romaines, Parker, Sokoluk, Hamilton (Cavanagh)

Bookings: Conroy, Romaines

Jim Leishman participating in one of his many fund-raising campaigns for charity.

Referee: L.B. Thow, Ayr
Attendance: 1,971
Mascot: Mark Devlin, 5 Keir Hardie Terrace

Albion	1	Stirling	3
Arbroath	3	Meadowbank	0
East Stirling	0	Queen of South	0
St Johnstone	0	Cowdenbeath	0
Stranraer	3	Raith	2
Stenhousemuir	4	Queen's Park	0

	P	W	D	L	F	A	Pts
Arbroath	2	1	1	0	6	3	3
DUNFERMLINE	2	1	1	0	7	5	3
Cowdenbeath	2	1	1	0	3	1	3
Queen of South	2	1	1	0	2	0	3
St Johnstone	2	1	1	0	2	0	3
East Stirling	2	1	1	0	6	3	3
Queen's Park	2	1	0	1	2	5	2

Monday August 19 1985
Skol Cup, First Round

DUNFERMLINE (3) 4   STENHOUSEMUIR (0) 0
Campbell (18, 20, 44)
Jenkins (86)

DUNFERMLINE: Westwater, Robertson, Forrest, McCathie, Young, Heddle, Bowie (Smith), Moyes, Watson, Morrison (Jenkins), Campbell

STENHOUSEMUIR: Hamilton, Cairney, Hamill, Erwin, Oliver, McComb, Butler, Bateman, Sinnet, Gillen (Grant), Wilson (Hyslop)

Booking: Hamill

Referee: J.F. McGilvray, Edinburgh
Attendance: 2,581
Mascot: Barry Haddow, 13 Clentry Cres, Kelty

Wednesday August 21 1985
Skol Cup, Second Round

MORTON (1) 2   DUNFERMLINE (1) 2
Robertson (37)   a.e.t.
Anderson (55)   Watson (18, 57)

Morton won 4-3 on penalties
McNeil, Gillespie   Morrison, Forrest
Doak, Holmes   Jenkins

MORTON: McDermott, O'Hara, Holmes, †McNamara, Anderson, Doak, Richardson, Robertson, Gillespie, McNeil, McCafferty
Subs: Docherty, Turner

Bookings: Anderson, Gillespie

DUNFERMLINE: Westwater, Robertson, Forrest, McCathie, Young, Heddle, Smith (Jenkins), Moyes, Watson, Morrison, Campbell (Bowie)

Bookings: Morrison, McCathie

Referee: W. McLeish, Stonehouse
Attendance: 1,386

August 24 1985

QUEEN'S PARK (2) 3   DUNFERMLINE (1) 1
McCall (20, 80)   Watson (29)
McLaughlin (27)

QUEEN'S PARK: Ross, Wilson, McLaughlin, McNamee, Brannigan, Walker (Fraser), McLean, Crooks, Nicholson, McCall, Shearer
Sub: Cairns

DUNFERMLINE: Westwater, Robertson, Heddle, McCathie, Young, Houston (Bowie), Smith, Moyes, Watson, Morrison, Campbell (Jenkins)

Bookings: Robertson, Morrison

Referee: T. Muirhead, Stenhousemuir
Attendance: 1,010

Berwick	0	Arbroath	2
Cowdenbeath	1	Raith	4
St Johnstone	0	Queen of South	3
Stenhousemuir	4	Albion	2
Stirling	1	Meadowbank	2
Stranraer	0	East Stirling	1

	P	W	D	L	F	A	Pts
Arbroath	3	2	1	0	8	3	5
Queen of South	3	2	1	0	5	0	5
East Stirling	3	2	1	0	7	3	5
Stenhousemuir	3	2	0	1	8	4	4
Queen's Park	3	2	0	1	5	6	4
DUNFERMLINE	3	1	1	1	8	8	3

August 31 1985

DUNFERMLINE (2) 3   COWDENBEATH (2) 2
Morrison (31), Heddle   McGlashan (15), Doig
(40), Watson (70)   (25)

DUNFERMLINE: Westwater, Robertson (Bowie), Forrest, McCathie, Young, Heddle, Smith, Moyes, Watson, Morrison, Campbell (Jenkins)

COWDENBEATH: Allan, Williamson, Shields, Rutherford, Wilcox, Cochrane, Quinn (Armour), McCulloch (Hackett), McGlashan, Doig, Duncan

Bookings: Cochrane, McGlashan, Williamson

Referee: G.A. Evans, Bishopbriggs
Attendance: 2,953
Mascot: Calum Bruce, 65 Camden Cres, Rosyth

Albion	0	Queen's Park	2
Arbroath	1	St Johnstone	0
East Stirling	0	Stenhousemuir	2
Meadowbank	0	Berwick	3
Queen of South	1	Stranraer	1
Raith	1	Stirling	1

	P	W	D	L	F	A	Pts
Arbroath	4	3	1	0	9	3	7
Stenhousemuir	4	3	0	1	10	4	6
Queen of South	4	2	2	0	6	1	6
Queen's Park	4	3	0	1	7	6	6
DUNFERMLINE	4	2	1	1	11	10	5
East Stirling	4	2	1	1	2	2	5
Raith	4	1	1	2	7	7	3
Stirling	4	1	1	2	5	5	3
Berwick	4	1	1	2	7	6	3
Stranraer	4	1	1	2	5	6	3
Cowdenbeath	4	1	1	2	6	8	3

September 7 1985

QUEEN OF SOUTH   DUNFERMLINE (0) 0
(0) 0

QUEEN OF SOUTH: Davidson, G. Robertson,✠ Gervaise, Parker, Hetherington, Cloy, Reid, Cochrane, Bryce, McBride, J. Robertson
Subs: Dick, Young

DUNFERMLINE: Westwater, Hamilton, Forrest, McCathie, Young, Heddle, Smith (Bowie), Moyes, Watson, Morrison, Campbell (Jenkins)

Bookings: Young, Smith

Referee: A.W. Waddell, Edinburgh
Attendance: 1,102

Cowdenbeath	3	Albion	0
East Stirling	2	Queen's Park	1
Raith	1	Meadowbank	1
St Johnstone	2	Stirling	0
Stenhousemuir	1	Arbroath	1
Stranraer	2	Berwick	0

	P	W	D	L	F	A	Pts
Arbroath	5	3	2	0	10	4	8
Stenhousemuir	5	3	1	1	11	5	7
Queen of South	5	2	3	0	6	1	7
East Stirling	5	3	1	1	4	3	7
DUNFERMLINE	5	2	2	1	11	10	6

September 14 1985

DUNFERMLINE (2) 3   RAITH ROVERS (2) 3
Watson (27, 48)   Smith (pen. 24)
Jenkins (33)   Gavine (31, 75)

DUNFERMLINE: Westwater, Hamilton, Forrest, McCathie, Young, Heddle, Bowie, Moyes, Watson, Morrison (Smith), Jenkins (Campbell)

Bookings: McCathie, Heddle, Young

RAITH ROVERS: McLafferty, Candlish, Sweeney, Marshall, Voy (Herd), Gavine, Smith, Elvin, Leitch, Robertson, Wright (McNeil)

Bookings: Leitch, Candlish, Elvin, Gavine

Referee: D.T. McVicar, Carluke
Attendance: 3,119
Mascot: Stuart Hannah, 51 Forrest Place, Townhill

Albion	1	East Stirling	2
Arbroath	0	Cowdenbeath	5
Berwick	1	Stenhousemuir	1
Meadowbank	1	Stranraer	1
Queen's Park	1	St Johnstone	1
Stirling	2	Queen of South	2

	P	W	D	L	F	A	Pts
East Stirling	6	4	1	1	6	4	9
Stenhousemuir	6	3	2	1	12	6	8
Queen of South	6	2	4	0	8	3	8
Arbroath	6	3	2	1	10	9	8
Cowdenbeath	6	3	1	2	14	8	7
DUNFERMLINE	6	2	3	1	14	13	7

September 21 1985

Cowdenbeath	P	Berwick	P
East Stirling	1	Arbroath	2
Queen of South	5	Albion	2
Raith	P	Queen's Park	P
Stenhousemuir	P	Meadowbank	P
Stranraer	P	Stirling	P
St Johnstone	P	Dunfermline	P

Tuesday September 24 1985

ST JOHNSTONE (0) 1   DUNFERMLINE (0) 2
Mitchell (70)   Morrison (74)
                   Jenkins (80)

ST JOHNSTONE: Balavage, McGurn, McGonigle, Barron, Winter, Morton, Gibson, Johnston, Ward, Reid, Mitchell
Subs: Williamson, Paterson

Booking: McGurn

DUNFERMLINE: Westwater, Hamilton, Forrest, McCathie, Young (Smith), Heddle, Bowie, Moyes, Watson (Campbell), Morrison, Jenkins

Booking: Heddle

Referee: R.B. Valentine, Dundee
Attendance: 1,562

Cowdenbeath	4	Berwick	2
Raith	3	Queen's Park	1
Stenhousemuir	1	Meadowbank	5
Stranraer	3	Stirling	2

	P	W	D	L	F	A	Pts
Queen of South	7	3	4	0	13	5	10
Arbroath	7	4	2	1	12	10	10
Cowdenbeath	7	4	1	2	18	10	9
DUNFERMLINE	7	3	3	1	16	14	9
East Stirling	7	4	1	2	7	6	9

September 28 1985

DUNFERMLINE (1) 3   STENHOUSEMUIR (0) 2
Jenkins (30), Heddle   McNaughton (46, 52)
(75), McCathie (87)

DUNFERMLINE: Westwater, Hamilton, Forrest, McCathie, Young, Heddle, Bowie, Moyes (Smith), Watson (Campbell), Morrison, Jenkins

55

Booking: Watson

STENHOUSEMUIR: Hamilton, Cairney, Hamill, Meakin, Erwin, Buchanan, McComb, Christie, Sinnet, McNaughton (Strange), Gillen
Sub: Smith

Bookings: Buchanan, Cairney; Meakin sent off

Referee: J. Duncan, Gorebridge
Attendance: 2,298
Mascot: D. Birnie, 16A Couston Street

Albion	2	Raith	0
Arbroath	1	Stranraer	0
Berwick	1	East Stirling	1
Meadowbank	4	St Johnstone	1
Queen's Park	1	Queen of South	2
Stirling	0	Cowdenbeath	0

	P	W	D	L	F	A	Pts
Queen of South	8	4	4	0	15	6	12
Arbroath	8	5	2	1	13	10	12
DUNFERMLINE	8	4	3	1	19	16	11
Cowdenbeath	8	4	2	2	18	10	10

October 5 1985

STRANRAER (1) 1   DUNFERMLINE (2) 3
McGuire (4)   Hamilton (1), Filson
                         (o.g. 33), Smith (85)

STRANRAER: Strachan, O'Donnell, Cousar, Quinn, McDougall, Filson, Logan, McCaig, Mauchlen, McCabe, McGuire
Subs: Brown, Lindsay

Booking: Cousar

DUNFERMLINE: Westwater, Hamilton, Forrest, McCathie, Young, Heddle (Smith), Robertson, Moyes, Campbell, Morrison, Jenkins
Sub: Bowie

Bookings: Forrest, Hamilton

Referee: D.T. McVicar, Carluke
Attendance: 510

Cowdenbeath	2	Queen's Park	2
East Stirling	1	Meadowbank	3
Queen of South	2	Berwick	0
Raith	2	Arbroath	1
St Johnstone	7	Albion	1
Stenhousemuir	2	Stirling	5

	P	W	D	L	F	A	Pts
Queen of South	9	5	4	0	17	6	14
DUNFERMLINE	9	5	3	1	22	17	13
Arbroath	9	5	2	2	14	12	12
Cowdenbeath	9	4	3	1	20	12	11

October 12 1985

DUNFERMLINE (1) 1   MEADOWBANK (0) 1
Morrison (7)   Jackson (86)

DUNFERMLINE: Westwater, Robertson, Forrest, McCathie, Young, Heddle, Smith (Campbell), Hamilton, Watson (Bowie), Morrison, Jenkins

Booking: Smith

MEADOWBANK: McQueen, Hendrie, Boyd, Wilson, Stewart, Armstrong, Lawrence, Lawson, Jackson, Nisbet, Sprott
Subs: Korotkitch, Robertson

Bookings: Boyd, Lawson

Referee: M. Delaney, Cleland
Attendance: 2,612
Mascot: Barry Deeman, 5 Watson Place

Albion	0	Arbroath	0
Berwick	4	Raith	3
Queen of South	6	Cowdenbeath	1
St Johnstone	3	East Stirling	0
Stenhousemuir	1	Stranraer	2
Stirling	0	Queen's Park	0

	P	W	D	L	F	A	Pts
Queen of South	10	6	4	0	23	7	16
DUNFERMLINE	10	5	4	1	23	18	14
Arbroath	10	5	3	2	14	12	13
Cowdenbeath	10	4	3	3	21	18	11

October 19 1985

EAST STIRLING (0) 0   DUNFERMLINE (2) 4
                        Watson (6), Jenkins
                        (37, pen 70), Morrison
                        (85)

DUNFERMLINE: Westwater, Robertson, Forrest, McCathie, Young, Heddle, Smith (Houston), Hamilton, Watson (Campbell), Morrison, Jenkins

Bookings: Forrest, Smith, Heddle

EAST STIRLING: Tulloch, Laird (Tollan), Mason, Innes, Rennie, Gilchrist, Doig, Hamilton, McGonigal, Harvey (Leetion), Maskrey

Bookings: Harvey, Rennie, Maskrey

Referee: D. Downie, Edinburgh
Attendance: 1,100

Arbroath	1	Stirling	0
Cowdenbeath	2	Stenhousemuir	0
Meadowbank	1	Albion	1
Queen's Park	2	Berwick	0
Raith	0	Queen of South	1
Stranraer	0	St Johnstone	2

	P	W	D	L	F	A	Pts
Queen of South	11	7	4	0	24	7	18
DUNFERMLINE	11	6	4	1	27	18	16
Arbroath	11	6	3	2	15	12	15
Cowdenbeath	11	5	3	3	23	18	13
St Johnstone	11	5	2	4	19	12	12
Meadowbank	11	4	4	3	19	17	12
Queen's Park	11	4	3	4	15	16	11

October 26 1985

DUNFERMLINE (3) 6   ALBION ROVERS (0) 0
  McCathie (4, 88)
  Jenkins (pen 12)
  Young (14), Watson
  (46), Forrest (64)

DUNFERMLINE: Westwater, Robertson, Forrest, McCathie, Young, Heddle, Bowie (Smith), Hamilton, Watson, Morrison (Houston), Jenkins

ALBION ROVERS: Thompson, Rodgers, Deakin, Edgar (Conn), Gallagher, Greene, Kasule, Clelland, McKay, Paisley (Nolan), McAteer

Booking: McAteer

Referee: J. Duncan, Gorebridge
Attendance: 2,386
Mascot: Guy Moffat

Arbroath	1	Queen's Park	0
Berwick	1	Stirling	0
East Stirling	0	Raith	2
Meadowbank	0	Queen of South	0
Stenhousemuir	3	St Johnstone	2
Stranraer	1	Cowdenbeath	2

	P	W	D	L	F	A	Pts
Queen of South	12	7	5	0	24	7	19
DUNFERMLINE	12	7	4	1	33	18	18
Arbroath	12	7	3	2	16	12	17
Cowdenbeath	12	6	3	3	25	19	15

November 2 1985

STIRLING (0) 0   DUNFERMLINE (0) 1
                  Watson (52)

STIRLING: Graham, Dawson, Spence, Anderson, McTeague, Maxwell, Thomson, Walker, Irvine, Grant, Hoggan
  Subs: Ormond, Aitchison

Booking: Spence

DUNFERMLINE: Westwater, Robertson, Forrest (Smith), McCathie, Young, Heddle, Bowie (Houston), Hamilton, Watson, Morrison, Jenkins

Booking: Forrest

Referee: I. Cathcart, Bridge of Allan
Attendance: 1,738

Albion	2	Stranraer	3
Cowdenbeath	1	East Stirling	1
Queen of South	2	Arbroath	0
Queen's Park	2	Meadowbank	1
Raith	9	Stenhousemuir	2
St Johnstone	3	Berwick	2

	P	W	D	L	F	A	Pts
Queen of South	13	8	5	0	26	7	21
DUNFERMLINE	13	8	4	1	34	18	20
Arbroath	13	7	3	3	16	14	17
Cowdenbeath	13	6	4	3	26	20	16
St Johnstone	13	6	2	5	24	17	14
Raith	13	5	3	5	39	22	13
Meadowbank	13	4	5	4	20	19	13
Queen's Park	13	5	3	5	17	18	13

November 9 1985

DUNFERMLINE (1) 2   QUEEN OF SOUTH
  Jenkins (30), Watson   (0) 1
  (58)   Cochrane (87)

DUNFERMLINE: Westwater, Robertson, Forrest, McCathie, Young, Heddle, Bowie, Hamilton (Houston), Watson, Morrison, Jenkins
  Sub: Campbell

Booking: Heddle

QUEEN OF SOUTH: Davidson, Robertson, Gervaise, Parker, Hetherington, Cloy, Reid, Cochrane, Bryce, McBride, J. Robertson
  Subs: Dick, Young

Booking: Gervaise

Referee: D.D. Hope, Erskine
Attendance: 4,577
Mascot: Stephen Ravenscroft, Morar Rd, Crossford

Albion	2	Cowdenbeath	1
Arbroath	1	Stenhousemuir	4
Berwick	2	Stranraer	2
Meadowbank	6	Raith	0
Queen's Park	1	East Stirling	0
Stirling	0	St Johnstone	2

	P	W	D	L	F	A	Pts
DUNFERMLINE	14	9	4	1	36	19	22
Queen of South	14	8	5	1	27	9	21
Arbroath	14	7	3	4	17	18	17
St Johnstone	14	7	2	5	26	17	16
Cowdenbeath	14	6	4	4	27	22	16

November 16 1985

RAITH ROVERS (1) 1   DUNFERMLINE (1) 2
Marshall (26)   Jenkins (pen. 21, 81)

RAITH ROVERS: McLafferty, Candlish (Herd), Sweeney, Philip, More, Reid, Smith, Elvin (McNeil), Marshall, Robertson, Wright

Booking: Reid

DUNFERMLINE: Westwater, Robertson, Forrest, McCathie, Young, Heddle, Bowie, Hamilton, Watson, Morrison (Houston), Jenkins
Sub: Campbell

Booking: Watson

Referee: W.N. Crombie, Edinburgh
Attendance: 3,331

Cowdenbeath	1	Arbroath	0
East Stirling	5	Albion	1
Queen of South	3	Stirling	1
St Johnstone	1	Queen's Park	0
Stenhousemuir	3	Berwick	1
Stranraer	0	Meadowbank	1

	P	W	D	L	F	A	Pts
DUNFERMLINE	15	10	4	1	38	20	24
Queen of South	15	9	5	1	30	10	23
St Johnstone	15	8	2	5	27	17	18
Cowdenbeath	15	7	4	4	28	22	18
Meadowbank	15	6	5	4	27	19	17
Arbroath	15	7	3	5	17	19	17

November 23 1985

DUNFERMLINE (1) 4   ST JOHNSTONE (0) 0
Jenkins (25, 53)
Watson (55, 87)

DUNFERMLINE: Westwater, Robertson, Forrest, McCathie, Young, Heddle, Bowie, Hamilton, Watson, Morrison, Jenkins
Subs: Campbell, Houston

ST JOHNSTONE: Balavage, Millen, McGonigle, Barron, Winter, Morton, Gibson, Brown, Evans, Addison, Adam
Subs: McGurn, Johnston

Bookings: Millen, Brown, Evans, Gibson
Adam sent off

Referee: G.D. Cumming, Carluke
Attendance: 4,245
Mascot: Neal Ravenscroft, Morar Rd, Crossford

Albion	1	Queen of South	5
Arbroath	2	East Stirling	1
Berwick	1	Cowdenbeath	1

Meadowbank	3	Stenhousemuir	1
Queen's Park	0	Raith	0
Stirling	3	Stranraer	0

	P	W	D	L	F	A	Pts
DUNFERMLINE	16	11	4	1	42	20	26
Queen of South	16	10	5	1	35	11	25
Meadowbank	16	7	5	4	30	20	19
Cowdenbeath	16	7	5	4	29	23	19
Arbroath	16	8	3	5	19	20	19

November 30 1985

Cowdenbeath	1	Stirling	2
East Stirling	P	Berwick	P
Queen of South	P	Queen's Park	P
Raith	P	Albion	P
St Johnstone	P	Meadowbank	P
Stenhousemuir	P	Dunfermline	P
Stranraer	P	Arbroath	P

December 7 1985
Scottish Cup, First Round

DUNFERMLINE (2) 2   RAITH ROVERS (0) 0
Heddle (2),
Watson (45)

DUNFERMLINE: Westwater, Robertson, Forrest, McCathie, Young, Heddle, Bowie, Hamilton, Watson, Morrison, Jenkins
Subs: Houston, Campbell

Bookings: Heddle, Hamilton

RAITH ROVERS: McLafferty, Herd, Sweeney (McNeil), Gavine, More, Philip, Smith, Elvin (Leitch), Marshall, Robertson, Wright

Booking: Marshall

Referee: W.N. Crombie, Edinburgh
Attendance: 5,558
Mascot: Symon Dick, 13 Thorn Grove

Division Two
Stranraer   1   Arbroath   6

	P	W	D	L	F	A	Pts
DUNFERMLINE	16	11	4	1	42	20	26
Queen of South	16	10	5	1	35	11	25
Arbroath	17	9	3	5	25	21	21
Meadowbank	16	7	5	4	30	20	19
Cowdenbeath	17	7	5	5	30	25	19
St Johnstone	16	8	2	6	27	21	18
Queen's Park	16	6	4	6	18	19	16

December 14 1985

DUNFERMLINE (0) 1   STRANRAER (0) 0
Bowie (64)

DUNFERMLINE: Westwater, Robertson, Forrest, McCathie, Young, Heddle, Bowie (Campbell), Hamilton, Watson, Morrison, Jenkins
Sub: Houston

STRANRAER: Noonan, O'Donnell, Cousar, Quinn (Brown), McDougall, McDonald, Logan, McCabe, Mauchlen, Newman (Sweeney), McGuire

Booking: Cousar

Referee: R.B. Valentine, Dundee
Attendance: 2,835
Mascot: Derek Cowan, 8 Brucefield Feus

Albion	2	St Johnstone	4
Arbroath	2	Raith	2
Berwick	0	Queen of South	1
Meadowbank	2	East Stirling	1
Queen's Park	2	Cowdenbeath	0
Stirling	1	Stenhousemuir	0

	P	W	D	L	F	A	Pts
DUNFERMLINE	17	12	4	1	43	20	28
Queen of South	17	11	5	1	36	11	27
Arbroath	18	9	4	5	27	23	22
Meadowbank	17	8	5	4	32	21	21
St Johnstone	17	9	2	6	31	23	20

December 21 1985

BERWICK (3) 4	DUNFERMLINE (1) 4
Romaines (12)	Watson (28, 60)
Sokoluk (36), Conroy	Jenkins (51)
(43), Cavanagh (47)	Campbell (pen. 80)

BERWICK: Watson, Fraser, McCann, McGovern, Marshall, Muir, Davidson, Romaines, Conroy, Sokoluk, Cavanagh
Subs: Douglas, Tait

Bookings: Fraser, Conroy, Marshall, Romaines
Davidson sent off

DUNFERMLINE: Westwater, Robertson, Forrest, McCathie, Young, Houston, Smith, Hamilton, Watson, Morrison (Campbell), Jenkins
Sub: Moyes

Bookings: Morrison, Hamilton
Jenkins sent off

Referee: D.D. Hope, Erskine
Attendance: 950

Arbroath	2	Meadowbank	2
Cowdenbeath	P	St Johnstone	P
Queen of South	P	East Stirling	P
Queen's Park	3	Stenhousemuir	2
Raith	P	Sranraer	P
Stirling	2	Albion	0

	P	W	D	L	F	A	Pts
DUNFERMLINE	18	12	5	1	47	24	29
Queen of South	17	11	5	1	36	11	27
Arbroath	19	9	5	5	29	25	23
Meadowbank	18	8	6	4	34	23	22

December 28 1985

Albion	P	Berwick	P
Dunfermline	P	Arbroath	P
East Stirling	0	Stirling	2
Meadowbank	1	Cowdenbeath	1
St Johnstone	4	Raith	1
Stenhousemuir	P	Queen of South	P
Stranraer	P	Queen's Park	P
Queen's Park	2	Stranraer	1

Wednesday January 1 1986

Berwick	0	Meadowbank	0
Cowdenbeath	P	Dunfermline	P
Queen's Park	2	Albion	0
St Johnstone	P	Arbroath	P
Stenhousemuir	P	East Stirling	P
Stirling	P	Raith	P
Stranraer	0	Queen of South	2

January 4 1986

THREAVE ROVERS (0) 0	DUNFERMLINE (1) 5
	Heddle (46)
	Watson (42, 49, 59, pen. 81)

THREAVE ROVERS: Shanks, Connelly, Gallagher (Austin), McVittie, D. Thomson, I. Bendall, S. Bendall, Houston (Thomson), Rudd, Maxwell, Semple

DUNFERMLINE: Westwater, Robertson, Forrest, McCathie, Young, Heddle (Gordon), Smith, Moyes (Morrison), Watson, Campbell, Houston

Referee: L.B. Thow, Ayr
Attendance: 1,600
Receipts: £2,200

Division Two

Queen of South	2	East Stirling	1
St Johnstone	1	Arbroath	0

	P	W	D	L	F	A	Pts
Queen of South	19	13	5	1	40	12	31
DUNFERMLINE	18	12	5	1	47	24	29
St Johnstone	19	11	2	6	36	24	24
Meadowbank	20	8	8	4	35	24	24
Queen's Park	20	10	4	6	27	22	24
Arbroath	20	9	5	6	29	26	23
Cowdenbeath	19	7	6	6	31	28	20

January 11 1986

DUNFERMLINE (2) 3   QUEEN'S PARK (1) 2
  Campbell (8)   Cairns (40), Caven
  McCathie (14)   (65)
  Watson (74)

DUNFERMLINE: Westwater, Hamilton, Forrest, McCathie, Young, Heddle, Campbell (Bowie), Morrison (Smith), Watson, Moyes, Jenkins

QUEEN'S PARK: Ross, Boyle, Wilson, McNamee, Brannigan, Walker, Cairns, Fraser, Smith, Caven, Crooks
  Subs: Ward, McKay

Referee: W.N. Crombie, Edinburgh
Attendance: 2,772
Mascot: Rebecca Haddow, 13 Clintry Cres., Kelty

Albion	P	Stenhousemuir	P
Arbroath	P	Berwick	P
East Stirling	3	Stranraer	1
Meadowbank	P	Stirling	P
Queen of South	P	St Johnstone	P
Raith	0	Cowdenbeath	1
Albion	0	Berwick	0

	P	W	D	L	F	A	Pts
Queen of South	19	13	5	1	40	12	31
DUNFERMLINE	19	13	5	1	50	26	31
St Johnstone	19	11	2	6	36	24	24
Meadowbank	20	8	8	4	35	24	24
Queen's Park	21	10	4	7	29	25	24
Arbroath	20	9	5	6	29	26	23
Cowdenbeath	20	8	6	6	32	28	22

January 18 1986

DUNFERMLINE (1) 2   EAST STILRING (0) 1
  McCathie (21, 69)   Maskrey (80)

DUNFERMLINE: Westwater, Robertson, Forrest, McCathie, Young, Heddle, Bowie, Hamilton (Morrison), Watson, Moyes, Jenkins
  Sub: Campbell

Booking: Robertson

EAST STIRLING: Bowie, Laird, Leetion, Harvey (McDonald), Rennie, Gilchrist, Doig, Wylde, Gaffney, Maskrey, McGonigal
  Sub: Tasker

Booking: Wylde

Referee: K.F. O'Donnel, Airdrie
Attendance: 2,663
Mascot: Mark Bett, 28 Watson Place

Albion	3	Meadowbank	2
Berwick	0	Queen's Park	5

Queen of South	2	Raith	0
St Johnstone	4	Stranraer	0
Stenhousemuir	1	Cowdenbeath	0
Stirling	1	Arbroath	0

	P	W	D	L	F	A	Pts
Queen of South	20	14	5	1	42	12	33
DUNFERMLINE	20	14	5	1	52	27	33
St Johnstone	20	12	2	6	40	24	26
Queen's Park	22	11	4	7	34	25	26
Meadowbank	21	8	8	5	37	27	24
Arbroath	21	9	5	7	29	27	23
Cowdenbeath	21	8	6	7	32	29	22

Sunday January 26 1986
Scottish Cup, Third Round

HIBS (0) 2   DUNFERMLINE (0) 0
  May (63), Cowan (80)

HIBS: Rough, Sneddon, Munro, Chisholm, Fulton, Hunter, May, Kane, Cowan, Durie, Collins
  Subs: Rae, Tortolano

DUNFERMLINE: Westwater, Robertson, Forrest, McCathie, Young, Heddle, Bowie (Morrison), Hamilton, Watson (Campbell), Moyes, Jenkins

Booking: Robertson
Moyes sent off

Referee: M. Delaney, Cleland
Attendance: 15,491

February 1 1986

DUNFERMLINE (0) 2   STIRLING (1) 3
  Young (84),   Irvine (42),
  Smith (88)   Thompson (71),
                       Walker (89)

DUNFERMLINE: Westwater, Robertson, Forrest, McCathie, Young, Heddle (Houston), Campbell (Smith), Hamilton, Watson, Morrison, Jenkins

Booking: Watson

STIRLING: Graham, Dawson, Spence, Walker, McTeague, Maxwell, Thompson, Hoggan (Cousin), Irvine, Grant, Ormond
  Sub: McCulley

Bookings: Irvine, McTeague

Referee: A.W. Waddell, Edinburgh
Attendance: 2,541
Mascot: Peter Lawrie

Arbroath	2	Queen of South	2
Berwick	3	St Johnstone	1
East Stirling	2	Cowdenbeath	1
Meadowbank	2	Queen's Park	1
Stenhousemuir	2	Raith	0
Stranraer	0	Albion	2

	P	W	D	L	F	A	Pts
Queen of South	21	14	6	1	44	14	34
DUNFERMLINE	21	14	5	2	54	30	33
St Johnstone	21	12	2	7	41	27	26
Meadowbank	22	9	8	5	39	28	26
Queen's Park	23	11	4	8	35	27	26
Arbroath	22	9	6	7	31	29	24
Stirling	22	9	4	9	29	25	22
Cowdenbeath	22	8	6	8	33	31	22
Stenhousemuir	20	8	2	10	36	43	18
East Stirling	22	7	3	12	24	34	17
Berwick	22	4	8	10	27	41	16
Raith	21	5	5	11	34	41	15
Stranraer	23	5	3	15	23	46	13
Albion Rovers	22	4	4	14	23	57	12

Midweek

Queen of South	0	Queen's Park	1
Stranraer	2	Stenhousemuir	0
Raith	1	Albion	0

February 8 1986

Division Two

Albion	P	Dunfermline	P
Cowdenbeath	P	Stranraer	P
Queen of South	1	Meadowbank	0
Queen's Park	1	Arbroath	2
Raith	P	East Stirling	P
St Johnstone	P	Stenhousemuir	P
Stirling	P	Berwick	P

February 15 1986

RAITH ROVERS (1) 3   DUNFERMLINE (2) 3
   Herd (21, 84)   Campbell (3)
   Wright (53)   Watson (14, 76)

RAITH ROVERS: McLafferty, Philip, Sweeney, Herd, Voy, More, Marshall, Anderson, Smith, Wright, Leitch (McNeil)
Sub: Gavine

Bookings: Smith, Marshall

DUNFERMLINE: Westwater, Robertson, Forrest, McCathie, Young, Gordon, Campbell (I. Pryde), Hamilton, Watson, Morrison (Houston), Jenkins

Booking: McCathie

Referee: G.B. Smith, Edinburgh
Attendance: 3,200

Cowdenbeath	P	Albion	P
East Stirling	P	Berwick	P
Queen of South	P	Queen's Park	P
St Johnstone	P	Stirling	P
Stenhousemuir	P	Arbroath	P
Stranraer	1	Meadowbank	2

	P	W	D	L	F	A	Pts
Queen of South	23	15	6	2	45	15	36
DUNFERMLINE	22	14	6	2	57	33	34
Meadowbank	24	10	8	6	41	30	28
Queen's Park	25	12	4	9	37	29	28
St Johnstone	21	12	2	7	41	27	26

Midweek

Queen of South	2	St Johnstone	1
Meadowbank	1	Stirling	1
Raith	3	Berwick	1

February 22 1986

Albion	P	Queen of South	P
Arbroath	0	Cowdenbeath	1
Berwick	P	Stranraer	P
Dunfermline	P	St Johnstone	P
Meadowbank	P	Raith	P
Queen's Park	4	East Stirling	2
Stirling	P	Stenhousemuir	P

March 1 1986

Albion	P	East Stirling	P
Cowdenbeath	P	Berwick	P
Meadowbank	P	Arbroath	P
Queen's Park	2	St Johnstone	0
Raith	P	Stranraer	P
Stenhousemuir	P	Dunfermline	P
Stirling	P	Queen of South	P
Arbroath	5	Berwick	1

	P	W	D	L	F	A	Pts
Queen of South	24	16	6	2	47	16	38
DUNFERMLINE	22	14	6	2	57	33	34
Queen's Park	27	14	4	9	43	31	32
Meadowbank	25	10	9	6	42	31	29

Wednesday March 5 1986

COWDENBEATH (0) 0 DUNFERMLINE (1) 1
                Smith (36)

COWDENBEATH: Allan, Wilson, Wilcox, Shaw, McCulloch, Rutherford, Baillie, Williamson, Grant, McGlashan (McKenzie), Shields

Bookings: Williamson, Baillie

DUNFERMLINE: Westwater, Robertson, Forrest, McCathie, Young, Gordon, Smith, Moyes, Watson (Jenkins), Morrison, Campbell
Sub: Houston

Booking: Moyes

Referee: A. Huett, Edinburgh
Attendance: 1,781

61

Arbroath	1	Albion	1
Berwick	4	Stranraer	0
Stirling	4	Stenhousemuir	0
Meadowbank	0	Raith	3
East Stirling	1	St Johnstone	3

	P	W	D	L	F	A	Pts
Queen of South	24	16	6	2	47	16	38
DUNFERMLINE	23	15	6	2	58	33	36
Queen's Park	27	14	4	9	43	31	32
Meadowbank	26	10	9	7	42	34	29
Arbroath	26	11	7	8	39	33	29
St Johnstone	24	13	2	9	45	32	28
Cowdenbeath	24	9	6	9	34	32	24

March 8 1986

DUNFERMLINE (0) 0   QUEEN'S PARK (0) 0

DUNFERMLINE: Westwater, Robertson, Forrest, McCathie, Young, Gordon, Smith, Moyes, Watson, Morrison (Houston), Campbell (Jenkins)

Bookings: Gordon, Morrison, Robertson

QUEEN'S PARK: Ross, Boyle, McLaughlin, McNamee, Brannigan, Walker, Cairns, Fraser, Smith, Caven, Crooks
Subs: McCall, McKay

Bookings: Smith, McLaughlin

Referee: M. Delaney, Cleland
Attendance: 3,112
Mascot: Paul Graham, 7 Loughborough Rd, Kirkcaldy

Berwick	1	Albion	2
East Stirling	2	Stenhousemuir	0
Meadowbank	4	Stirling	1
Queen of South	3	Cowdenbeath	0
St Johnstone	1	Raith	3
Stranraer	1	Arbroath	5

	P	W	D	L	F	A	Pts
Queen of South	25	17	6	2	50	16	40
DUNFERMLINE	24	15	7	2	58	33	37
Queen's Park	28	14	5	9	43	31	33
Meadowbank	27	11	9	7	46	35	31
Arbroath	27	12	7	8	44	34	31
St Johnstone	25	13	2	10	46	35	28
Stirling	25	10	5	10	35	30	25
Raith	26	9	6	11	47	46	24
Cowdenbeath	25	9	6	10	34	35	24
East Stirling	25	8	3	14	29	41	19
Stenhousemuir	23	8	2	13	36	51	18
Berwick	26	5	8	13	34	51	18
Stranraer	27	6	3	18	27	57	15
Albion	25	5	5	15	26	60	15

Wednesday March 12 1986

STENHOUSEMUIR (1) 1 DUNFERMLINE (0) 1
Erwin (4)   Watson (55)

STENHOUSEMUIR: Hamilton, Cairney, Hamill, Buchanan, Beaton, Erwin, McIntosh, Bateman (McComb), Sinnet, McNaughton (Butler), Gillen

Bookings: Cairney, Hamill
McIntosh sent off

DUNFERMLINE: Westwater, Robertson, Forrest, McCathie, Young, Gordon (Morrison), Connelly (Campbell), Moyes, Watson, Houston, Jenkins

Bookings: Moyes, Westwater, Watson

Referee: J. McGilvray, Edinburgh
Attendance: 1,900

Queen of South	0	Queen's Park	3
Cowdenbeath	1	St Johnstone	3
Raith	1	Stranraer	0

	P	W	D	L	F	A	Pts
Queen of South	26	17	6	3	50	19	40
DUNFERMLINE	25	15	8	2	59	34	38
Queen's Park	29	15	5	9	46	31	35
Meadowbank	27	11	9	7	46	35	31
Arbroath	27	12	7	8	44	34	31
St Johnstone	26	14	2	10	49	36	30

March 15 1986

COWDENBEATH (0) 0   DUNFERMLINE (1) 2
                          Hamilton (25)
                          Campbell (79)

COWDENBEATH: Allan, Williamson, Wilcox, Oliver, McCulloch, Rutherford, Brown, Armour, McKenzie, Wilson (Baillie), Grant (Doig)

Booking: Rutherford

DUNFERMLINE: Westwater, Robertson, Forrest, McCathie, Young, Gordon, Campbell, Moyes, Watson, Hamilton, Jenkins
Subs: Morrison, Houston

Booking: McCathie

Referee: D.D. Hope, Erskine
Attendance: 2,110

Albion	0	Stenhousemuir	0
Arbroath	2	Raith	1
Meadowbank	1	Queen's Park	1
Queen of South	2	Berwick	1
St Johnstone	1	East Stirling	1
Stirling	2	Stranraer	2

	P	W	D	L	F	A	Pts
Queen of South	27	18	6	3	52	20	42
DUNFERMLINE	26	16	8	2	61	34	40
Queen's Park	30	15	6	9	47	32	36
Arbroath	28	13	7	8	46	35	33
Meadowbank	28	11	10	7	47	36	32

Tuesday March 18 1986

MEADOWBANK (1) 2   DUNFERMLINE (1) 2
Lawrence (39, 86)   Campbell (34)
                      Watson (48)

MEADOWBANK: McQueen, Hendrie, Boyd, Clark (Scott), Tierney, Armstrong, Lawrence, Lawson, Jackson, Nisbet, McGachie
Sub: Smith

Bookings: Tierney, Lawrence

DUNFERMLINE: Westwater, Robertson, Forrest, McCathie, Young (Morrison), Gordon, Campbell, Moyes, Watson, Hamilton, Jenkins
Sub: Houston

Bookings: McCathie, Forrest, Gordon
Hamilton sent off

Referee: B. McGinlay, Balfron
Attendance: 1,200

Stenhousemuir	2	Arbroath	1
East Stirling	0	Berwick	2
Cowdenbeath	0	Albion	2
St Johnstone	0	Stirling	2

	P	W	D	L	F	A	Pts
Queen of South	27	18	6	3	52	20	42
DUNFERMLINE	27	16	9	2	63	36	41
Queen's Park	30	15	6	9	47	32	36
Meadowbank	29	11	11	7	49	38	33
Arbroath	29	13	7	9	47	37	33
St Johnstone	28	14	3	11	50	39	31

March 22 1986

DUNFERMLINE (0) 0   ARBROATH (0) 0

DUNFERMLINE: Westwater, Robertson, Forrest, McCathie, Young, Gordon, Campbell (Bowie), Houston, Watson, Morrison, Jenkins
Sub: Heddle

ARBROATH: Jackson, Lynch, Hill, Curran, Rodger, Jack, Fotheringham, Taylor (Mitchell), Torrance, McWalter (Kirkcaldy), Brannigan

Bookings: Brannigan, Torrance, Jack

Referee: A.N. Huett, Edinburgh
Attendance: 2,615
Mascot: Gordon Smith, 11 Hutchison Green

Berwick	1	St Johnstone	1
East Stirling	2	Meadowbank	3
Queen's Park	1	Stirling	0
Raith	2	Cowdenbeath	1
Stenhousemuir	1	Queen of South	2
Stranraer	2	Albion	3

	P	W	D	L	F	A	Pts
Queen of South	28	19	6	3	54	21	44
DUNFERMLINE	28	16	10	2	63	36	42
Queen's Park	31	16	6	9	48	32	38
Meadowbank	30	12	11	7	52	40	35
Arbroath	30	13	8	9	47	37	34

Midweek

Cowdenbeath	5	Stranraer	0
Albion	2	Queen of South	2
Stirling	2	Berwick	0
St Johnstone	1	Stenhousemuir	3
Raith	1	East Stirling	4

March 29 1986

DUNFERMLINE (2) 4   STRANRAER (0) 1
Hamilton (14)   Quinn (pen. 70)
Jenkins (41), Watson
(82), Morrison (88)

DUNFERMLINE: Westwater, Robertson, Forrest (Morrison), McCathie, Young, Gordon, Bowie (Campbell), Houston, Watson, Hamilton, Jenkins

STRANRAER: Thompson, O'Donnell, McCabe, McDaid, Filson, Quinn, Logan, Higgins, McGonigle, McCurdy, Innes
Sub: Smith

Booking: Filson

Referee: J. Duncan, Gorebridge
Attendance: 2,602
Mascot: Euan Hannah, 51 Forest Pl., Townhill

Albion	1	Queen's Park	1
Berwick	1	Raith	0
East Stirling	1	Stirling	0
Meadowbank	1	Queen of South	0
St Johnstone	4	Arbroath	1
Stenhousemuir	2	Cowdenbeath	1

	P	W	D	L	F	A	Pts
Queen of South	30	19	7	4	56	24	45
DUNFERMLINE	29	17	10	2	67	37	44
Queen's Park	32	16	7	9	49	33	39
Meadowbank	31	13	11	7	53	40	37
St Johnstone	31	15	4	12	56	44	34
Arbroath	31	13	8	10	48	41	34
Stirling	30	12	6	12	41	34	30
Raith	31	11	6	14	52	54	28

63

Monday March 31 1986
at Broomfield Park

ALBION ROVERS (0) 0   DUNFERMLINE (2) 3
Campbell (14, 85)
Hamilton (43)

ALBION ROVERS: McKeown, McArthur, Grant, Edgar, Gallagher, Deakin, Rodgers, Kasule, Nolan, Clelland, Conn
Subs: Paisley, Grant

Bookings: Kasule, Gallagher

DUNFERMLINE: Westwater, Robertson (Morrison), Gordon, McCathie, Young, Heddle, Bowie (Pryde), Houston, Watson, Hamilton, Campbell

Referee: J.D. Cumming, Carluke
Attendance: 1,500

Queen's Park	2	Stirling	0
St Johnstone	1	Meadowbank	0
East Stirling	4	Berwick	2
Stenhousemuir	1	Queen of South	0
Queen's Park	1	Stenhousemuir	1

	P	W	D	L	F	A	Pts
DUNFERMLINE	30	18	10	2	70	37	46
Queen of South	31	19	7	5	56	25	45
Queen's Park	34	17	8	9	52	34	42
Meadowbank	32	13	11	8	53	41	37

April 5 1986

QUEEN OF SOUTH   DUNFERMLINE (0) 1
(2) 3   Bowie (69)
Hetherington (15)
Cochrane (30, 64)

QUEEN OF SOUTH: Davidson, G. Robertson, Dick, Parker, Hetherington, Cloy, Reid, Cochrane, Bryce, McBride, J. Robertson
Subs: Forsyth, Maskrey

DUNFERMLINE: Westwater, Robertson, Gordon, Wilson, Young, Heddle, Bowie, Houston (Moyes), Watson, Hamilton, Campbell (Jenkins)

Bookings: Young, Hamilton, Gordon

Referee: A. Ferguson, Giffnock
Attendance: 5,000

Arbroath	2	Albion	0
Cowdenbeath	1	Meadowbank	0
Raith	2	East Stirling	0
Stirling	2	Berwick	2
Stranraer	1	St Johnstone	2

	P	W	D	L	F	A	Pts
Queen of South	32	20	7	5	59	26	47
DUNFERMLINE	31	18	10	3	71	40	46
Queen's Park	34	17	8	9	52	34	42
St Johnstone	33	17	4	12	59	45	38
Meadowbank	33	13	11	9	53	42	37

Tuesday April 8 1986

MEADOWBANK (2) 4   DUNFERMLINE (0) 0
Jackson (23),
Scott (26)
McGachie (53, 71)

MEADOWBANK: McQueen, Hendrie, Boyd, Scott, Tierney, Armstrong, Lawrence, Lawson, Jackson, Nisbet, McGachie
Subs: Stewart, Robertson

Booking: Tierney

DUNFERMLINE: McAlpine, Robertson, Forrest, Wilson (Moyes), Young, Gordon, Bowie, Thompson, Watson, Hamilton, Campbell (Jenkins)

Booking: Moyes

Referee: D.F.T. Syme, Rutherglen
Attendance: 1,756

Albion	0	Stirling	2
Arbroath	0	Queen's Park	2
Berwick	1	Stenhousemuir	1
Cowdenbeath	2	St Johnstone	1
East Stirling	1	Stranraer	2
Raith	0	Queen of South	2

	P	W	D	L	F	A	Pts
Queen of South	33	21	7	5	61	26	49
DUNFERMLINE	32	18	10	4	71	45	46
Queen's Park	35	18	8	9	54	34	44
Meadowbank	34	14	11	9	57	42	39
St Johnstone	34	17	4	13	60	47	38

April 12 1986

DUNFERMLINE (2) 4   ALBION ROVERS (0) 0
Watson (9, 45)
Thompson (49)
Campbell (90)

DUNFERMLINE: Westwater, Hamilton, Forrest, McCathie, Young, Gordon, Bowie, Moyes, Watson, Thompson, Campbell
Subs: Jenkins, Smith

ALBION ROVERS: McKeown, Conn, Deakin, Edgar, Gallacher, Greene, Kasule, Rodgers, Paisley, Morgan, Cleland
Subs: Nolan, Grant

Bookings: Paisley, Morgan

Referee: D.A. Yeats, Perth
Attendance: 2,657
Mascot: Carol Shepherd, 20 Orwell Place

Queen of South	3	East Stirling	1
Queen's Park	5	Berwick	0
St Johnstone	1	Meadowbank	3
Stenhousemuir	1	Raith	0
Stirling	1	Arbroath	0
Stranraer	1	Cowdenbeath	1

	P	W	D	L	F	A	Pts
Queen of South	34	22	7	5	64	27	51
DUNFERMLINE	33	19	10	4	75	44	48
Queen's Park	36	19	8	9	59	34	46
Meadowbank	35	15	11	9	60	43	41
St Johnstone	35	17	4	14	61	50	38
Arbroath	34	14	8	12	50	44	36
Stirling	34	14	7	13	46	38	35
Stenhousemuir	33	13	6	14	49	59	32
Cowdenbeath	34	12	7	15	46	48	31
Raith	34	12	6	16	54	57	30
East Stirling	34	11	4	19	43	57	26
Berwick	35	7	11	17	44	68	25
Albion	34	7	8	19	34	76	22
Stranraer	35	7	5	23	36	76	19

Wednesday April 16 1986

DUNFERMLINE (2) 4   ST JOHNSTONE (0) 0
Campbell (11), Moyes
(18), Watson (53)
Adam (o.g. 60)

DUNFERMLINE: Westwater, Hamilton, Forrest,
McCathie, Young, Gordon, Bowie (Smith),
Moyes, Watson, Thompson, Campbell
(Jenkins)

Booking: Gordon

ST JOHNSTONE: Balavage, Duffy, Paterson,
Millen, Liddell, Addison, Gibson, Johnston,
Lough, Thoms, Adam

Booking: Millen

Referee: I.R. Cathcart, Bridge of Allan
Attendance: 2,500
Mascot: Kerry Graham, 7 Loughborough Rd,
Kirkcaldy

Meadowbank	2	Arbroath	1
Stirling	1	Raith	1

	P	W	D	L	F	A	Pts
Queen of South	34	22	7	5	64	27	51
DUNFERMLINE	34	20	10	4	79	44	50
Queen's Park	36	19	8	9	59	34	46
Meadowbank	36	16	11	9	62	44	43

April 19 1986

DUNFERMLINE (2) 4   EAST STIRLING (0) 0
Thompson (37)
Hamilton (43)
Campbell (73)
Jenkins (84)

DUNFERMLINE: Westwater, Hamilton, Forrest,
McCathie, Young, Gordon, Bowie (Smith),
Moyes, Watson (Jenkins), Thompson,
Campbell

Booking: Watson

EAST STIRLING: Bowie, Laird, Leetion, Tollan,
McKay, Gilchrist, Doig, Wylde (McDonald),
Gaffney, McGonigal, McLindon (Barclay)

Booking: McKay

Referee: T. Muirhead, Stenhousemuir
Attendance: 3,298
Mascot: Barry Gow, 47 Rosebank

Arbroath	0	Queen of South	1
Meadowbank	3	Berwick	1
Queen's Park	0	Cowdenbeath	1
St Johnstone	1	Albion	0
Stirling	3	Raith	1
Stranraer	0	Stenhousemuir	1

	P	W	D	L	F	A	Pts
Queen of South	35	23	7	5	65	27	53
DUNFERMLINE	35	21	10	4	83	44	52
Queen's Park	37	19	8	10	59	35	46
Meadowbank	37	17	11	9	65	45	45
St Johnstone	37	18	4	15	62	54	40

Tuesday April 22 1986

DUNFERMLINE (0) 2   ARBROATH (0) 0
Mitchell (o.g. 46)
Young (65)

DUNFERMLINE: Westwater, Hamilton, Forrest,
McCathie, Young, Heddle, Bowie (Smith),
Moyes, Watson, Thompson, Campbell
(Jenkins)

ARBROATH: Jackson, Mitchell, Hill, Mackie
(Curran), Rodger, Lynch, Fotheringham, Bone,
Torrance, McWalter, Brannigan
Sub: Taylor

Bookings: Hill, Lynch

Referee: H.F. Williamson, Renfrew
Attendance: 3,000
Mascot: Moira Varndell, 55 Whinnyburn Pl.,
Rosyth

Stirling	3	Queen of South	1
Stenhousemuir	4	East Stirling	3
Cowdenbeath	1	Berwick	0
Raith	4	Stranraer	1

	P	W	D	L	F	A	Pts
DUNFERMLINE	36	22	10	4	85	44	54
Queen of South	36	23	7	6	65	50	53
Queen's Park	37	19	8	10	59	35	46
Meadowbank	37	17	11	9	65	45	45
Stirling	37	16	8	13	53	40	40

April 26 1986

BERWICK (0) 0   DUNFERMLINE (1) 4
Watson (44)
Campbell (50, 73)
Moyes (65)

BERWICK: Watson, Newman, O'Donnell, Gavine, Marshall, Muir, McGovern, Romaines, Newman, Hamilton (Conroy), Cavanagh
Sub: Dunn

DUNFERMLINE: Westwater, Hamilton, Forrest, McCathie, Young, Heddle, Bowie (Smith), Moyes, Watson (Jenkins), Thompson, Campbell

Referee: K.J. Hope, Clarkston
Attendance: 1,303

Albion	0	Meadowbank	2
Cowdenbeath	0	Stirling	1
East Stirling	1	Arbroath	1
Queen of South	1	Stranraer	2
Raith	2	Queen's Park	1
Stenhousemuir	0	St Johnstone	0

	P	W	D	L	F	A	Pts
DUNFERMLINE	37	23	10	4	89	44	56
Queen of South	37	23	7	7	67	32	53
Meadowbank	38	18	11	9	67	45	47
Queen's Park	38	19	8	11	60	37	46
Stirling	38	17	8	13	54	41	42
St Johnstone	38	18	5	15	62	54	41

Tuesday April 29 1986

STENHOUSEMUIR (0) 0   DUNFERMLINE (0) 0

STENHOUSEMUIR: Hamilton, Cairney, Meakin, Butler, Reid, Erwin, McComb, Bateman, Sinnet, McNaughton, Buchanan
Subs: Rodger, McIntosh

DUNFERMLINE: Westwater, Hamilton, Forrest, McCathie, Robertson, Heddle, Bowie (Smith), Moyes, Watson, Thompson, Campbell (Jenkins)

Referee: G.D. Cumming, Carluke
Attendance: 3,500

Cowdenbeath	3	Queen of South	3
Albion	2	East Stirling	1

	P	W	D	L	F	A	Pts
DUNFERMLINE	38	23	11	4	89	44	57
Queen of South	38	23	8	7	70	35	54
Meadowbank	38	18	11	9	67	45	47
Queen's Park	38	19	8	11	60	37	46
Stirling	38	17	8	13	54	41	42

May 3 1986

STIRLING (0) 3   DUNFERMLINE (1) 2
Irvine (52, 85)   Campbell (37)
McTeague (68)   McCathie (87)

STIRLING: Graham, Dawson, Spence, Aitchison, McTeague, Maxwell, Thompson, Ferguson, Irvine, Hoggan (Crawford), Ormond
Sub: Dwyer
Booking: Graham

DUNFERMLINE: Westwater, Hamilton, Forrest, McCathie, Young (Robertson), Gordon, Bowie (Smith), Moyes, Jenkins, Thompson, Campbell

Referee: L.B. Thow, Ayr
Attendance: 4,100

Berwick	0	Arbroath	4
Cowdenbeath	1	East Stirling	1
Meadowbank	1	Stenhousemuir	0
Stranraer	2	Queen's Park	1
Raith	5	Albion	2
St Johnstone	1	Queen of South	1

May 6 1986

Albion	0	Stenhousemuir	1

	P	W	D	L	F	A	Pts
DUNFERMLINE	39	23	11	5	91	47	57
Queen of South	39	23	9	7	71	36	55
Meadowbank	39	19	11	9	68	45	49
Queen's Park	39	19	8	12	61	39	46
Stirling	39	18	8	13	57	43	44
St Johnstone	39	18	6	15	63	55	42
Stenhousemuir	39	16	8	15	55	63	40
Arbroath	39	15	9	15	56	50	39
Raith	39	15	7	17	67	65	37
Cowdenbeath	39	14	9	16	52	53	37
East Stirling	39	11	6	22	49	69	28
Berwick	39	7	11	21	45	80	25
Albion	39	8	8	23	38	86	24
Stranraer	39	9	5	25	41	83	23

Season Analysis

HOME AND AWAY ANALYSIS

	HOME				AWAY					
	P	W	D	L	W	D	L	F	A	Pts
DUNFERMLINE	39	14	4	1	9	7	4	91	47	57
Queen of South	39	14	2	3	9	7	4	71	36	55
Meadowbank	39	11	7	2	8	4	7	68	45	49
Queen's Park	39	14	3	3	5	5	9	61	39	46
Stirling	39	10	6	4	8	2	9	57	43	44
St Johnstone	39	11	3	6	7	3	9	63	55	42
Stenhousemuir	39	11	4	4	5	4	11	55	63	40
Arbroath	39	9	5	5	6	4	10	56	50	39
Raith	39	11	3	6	4	4	11	67	65	37
Cowdenbeath	39	9	4	7	5	5	9	52	53	37
East Stirling	39	7	2	10	4	4	12	49	69	28
Berwick	39	5	9	6	2	2	15	45	80	25
Albion	39	4	5	10	4	3	13	39	86	24
Stranraer	39	5	1	13	4	4	12	41	83	23

Sunday May 4 1986
Fife Cup Semi Final

DUNFERMLINE (1) 1   EAST FIFE (1) 1
  Smith (18)   Stead (44)

East Fife 5-4 on penalties

DUNFERMLINE: Westwater, Hamilton (Jenkins), Forrest, McCathie, Robertson, Heddle, Smith, Connelly, Watson, Thompson, Pryde (Campbell)

EAST FIFE: Marshall, Inglis, Mitchell, Kirk, Halley, McCafferty, Burgess, Kirkwood, Hunter (Burns), Hill, Stead
Sub: Clarke

Albion Rovers	(H)	W 6-0
	(A)	W 3-0
	(H)	W 4-0
Arbroath	(A)	D 3-3
	(H)	D 0-0
	(H)	W 2-0
Berwick	(H)	W 4-2
	(A)	D 4-4
	(A)	W 4-0
Cowdenbeath	(H)	W 3-2
	(A)	W 1-0
	(A)	W 2-0
East Stirling	(A)	W 4-0
	(H)	W 2-1
	(H)	W 4-0
Meadowbank	(H)	D 1-1
	(A)	D 2-2
	(A)	L 0-4

Queen of South	(A)	D 0-0
	(H)	W 2-1
	(A)	L 1-3
Queen's Park	(A)	L 1-3
	(H)	W 3-2
	(H)	D 0-0
Raith Rovers	(H)	D 3-3
	(A)	W 2-1
	(A)	D 3-3
St Johnstone	(A)	W 2-1
	(H)	W 4-0
	(H)	W 4-0
Stenhousemuir	(H)	W 3-2
	(A)	D 1-1
	(A)	D 0-0
Stranraer	(A)	W 3-1
	(H)	W 1-0
	(H)	W 4-1
Stirling	(A)	W 1-0
	(H)	L 2-3
	(A)	L 2-3

Dunfermline recorded 5 hat-tricks of wins: over Albion Rovers, Cowdenbeath, East Stirling, Stranraer and St Johnstone. They failed to beat Meadowbank in any of the three meetings. On the other hand, nine of the thirteen teams failed on any of the three encounters to beat the Pars.

	P	W	D	L	F	A	Pts
Albion Rovers	3	3	0	0	13	0	6
East Stirling	3	3	0	0	10	1	6
St Johnstone	3	3	0	0	10	1	6
Stranraer	3	3	0	0	8	2	6
Cowdenbeath	3	3	0	0	6	2	6
Berwick	3	2	1	0	12	6	5
Arbroath	3	1	2	0	5	3	4
Raith Rovers	3	1	2	0	8	7	4
Stenhousemuir	3	1	2	0	4	3	4
Queen's Park	3	1	1	1	4	5	3
Queen of South	3	1	1	1	3	4	3
Stirling	3	1	0	2	5	6	2
Meadowbank	3	0	2	1	3	7	2
	39	23	11	5	91	47	57

Season 1985-86

Date	Opponents	F-A	Att.	League Position	Division Two
1985					
Aug 7	Aberdeen (H)	1-0	6,000	–	Centenary Challenge Cup
10	Arbroath (A)	3-3	1,100	7	
17	Berwick (H)	4-2	1,971	2	
19	Stenhousemuir (H)	4-0	2,581	–	Skol Cup, First Round
21	Morton (A)	2-2	1,386	–	3-4 penalties, Second Round
24	Queen's Park (A)	1-3	1,010	6	
31	Cowdenbeath (H)	3-2	2,953	5	
Sept 7	Queen of South (A)	0-0	1,102	5	
14	Raith Rovers (H)	3-3	3,119	6	
17	Hearts (H)	0-2		–	Benefit Match
24	St Johnstone (A)	2-1	1,562	4	
28	Stenhousemuir (H)	3-2	2,298	3	
Oct 5	Stranraer (A)	3-1	510	2	
12	Meadowbank (H)	1-1	2,612	2	
19	East Stirling (A)	4-0	1,100	2	
26	Albion Rovers (H)	6-0	2,386	2	
Nov 2	Stirling (A)	1-0	1,738	2	
9	Queen of South (H)	2-1	4,577	1	
16	Raith Rovers (A)	2-1	3,331	1	
23	St Johnstone (H)	4-0	4,245	1	
26	Rangers XI (H)	0-3	2,000	–	Friendly
Dec 3	Hibs (A)	3-5		–	Tom Hart Memorial Cup
7	Raith Rovers (H)	2-0	5,558	1	Scottish Cup, First Round
14	Stranraer (H)	1-0	2,835	1	
21	Berwick (A)	4-4	950	1	
1986					
Jan 4	Threave Rovers (A)	5-0	1,600	2	Scottish Cup, Second Round
11	Queen's Park (H)	3-2	2,772	2	
18	East Stirling (H)	2-1	2,663	2	
26	Hibs (A)	0-2	15,491	2	Scottish Cup, Third Round
Feb 1	Stirling (H)	2-3	2,541	2	
15	Raith (A)	3-3	3,200	2	
March 5	Cowdenbeath (A)	1-0	1,781	2	
8	Queen's Park (H)	0-0	3,112	2	
12	Stenhousemuir (A)	1-1	1,900	2	
15	Cowdenbeath (A)	2-0	2,110	2	
18	Meadowbank (A)	2-2	1,200	2	
22	Arbroath (H)	0-0	2,615	2	
29	Stranraer (H)	4-1	2,602	2	
31	Albion Rovers (A)	3-0	1,500	1	
April 5	Queen of South (A)	1-3	5,000	2	
8	Meadowbank (A)	0-4	1,756	2	
12	Albion Rovers (H)	4-0	2,657	2	
16	St Johnstone (H)	4-0	2,500	2	
19	East Stirling (H)	4-0	3,298	2	Promotion Won
22	Arbroath (H)	2-0	3,000	1	
26	Berwick (A)	4-0	1,303	1	
29	Stenhousemuir (A)	0-0	3,500	1	Championship Won
May 3	Stirling (A)	2-3	4,100	1	
4	East Fife (H)	1-1		–	4-5 Penalties, Fife Cup

68 One of the highlights of the season was the club's record run of 17 successive league games without defeat. The average home gate was just under 3,000.

Season 1985-86

	Appearances				Goals			
	League(39)	Skol (2)	Scottish (3)	Total(44)	League	Skol	Scottish	Total
Jim Bowie	21 (9)	1 (1)	2	24 (10)	2	–	–	2
Ian Campbell	24 (9)	2	1 (1)	27 (10)	15	3	0	18
Gordon Connelly	1	–	–	1	–	–	–	–
Bobby Forrest	36	2	3	41	2	–	–	2
Ian Gordon	15	–	0 (1)	15 (1)	–	–	–	–
Rowan Hamilton	32	–	2	34	5	–	–	5
Ian Heddle	25	2	3	30	3	–	2	5
Dave Houston	7 (8)	–	1	8 (8)	–	–	–	–
Grant Jenkins	23 (14)	– (2)	2	25 (16)	14	1	–	15
Norrie McCathie	37	2	3	42	8	–	–	8
Stevie Morrison	24 (5)	2	1 (2)	27 (7)	5	–	–	5
Davie Moyes	23 (2)	2	2	27 (2)	2	–	–	2
Ian Pryde	0 (2)	–	–	0 (2)	–	–	–	–
Bobby Robertson	27 (1)	2	3	32 (1)	–	–	–	–
Trevor Smith	10 (14)	1 (1)	1	12 (15)	3	–	–	3
Gary Thompson	8	–	–	8	2	–	–	2
John Watson	37	2	3	42	24	2	5	31
Ian Westwater	38	2	3	43	–	–	–	–
Gordon Wilson	2	–	–	2	–	–	–	–
Davie Young	38	2	3	43	3	–	–	3
Hamish McAlpine	1	–	–	1	–	–	–	–
Hugh Whyte	–	–	–	–	–	–	–	–

plus
3 o.g.   3 o.g.

91   104

Figures in brackets signify appearances as substitutes. In addition, a number of players were listed as substitutes, but did not appear: Houston (6), Campbell (5), Morrison (1), Jenkins (1), Smith (1), Moyes (1), Heddle (1). The League Championship was won with a squad of 21 players. Watson's total of 31 goals was the highest total since Alex Ferguson's season in 1965-66 in the old First Division.

A notable feature of the season was the struggle between Jenkins and Campbell for a first team place. Jenkins was listed as a substitute on 17 occasions, Campbell on 15 occasions.

To the Premier League Season 1986-87

There is really no 'close' season in a football club. Immediately after the last game of the championship-winning season, the tractors moved on to the hallowed, but rather tired, turf at East End Park, dug it up and planted new seed. For once, the ground staff prayed for rain and hoped the harvest would be rich and promising. The grass did grow (though not in time to permit the playing of many friendlies), the sale of season tickets went well, repairs to the ground were carried out and the new season was awaited with eager anticipation.

The World Cup Finals in Mexico provided the football fan with a healthy diet of his favourite sport and even if Scotland's performances were disappointing, there was the consolation of fine displays elsewhere. The other big footballing story was the imaginative capture by Rangers of Graeme Souness as player-manager. With a bulging, blank cheque book in his pocket, the internationalist drew on his considerable experience to build a team which had every look of restoring a tarnished Ibrox club to its former glories.

It was against this background that Jim Leishman, far removed from the glamour and riches of Mexico City and Govan, attempted to build up a side which would at least hold its own in the First Division from which it had been relegated in 1983. The problems facing Jim were there for all to see. All clubs up and down the country were looking out for players of exceptional talent and those who could offer full-time training, high wages, a large signing-on fee and the prospect of honours were at a considerable advantage. Dunfermline were not a rich club and could not afford to throw money away. While their achievement in winning the Second Division was immense, it did not cut a great deal of ice with footballers, especially those living in the West of Scotland who, though perhaps nearing the end of a distinguished career, still hankered after a club which would keep them in the public eye and in the style to which they were accustomed.

Like the frustrated angler, the manager could have written a book on the 'ones who got away'. Brian McNaughton, for instance, was known to be unsettled at Tynecastle but the prolific striker, who did wish to go part-time, received a more attractive offer from East Fife who had come within two points of promotion to the Premier League. Kenneth Brannigan, a solid centre half with Queen's Park, was another one who escaped the net, preferring to try his luck with Sheffield Wednesday.

The signings that Leishman did make, however, caused considerable interest in the town. His first transfer coup was to entice 21-year-old striker, Eric Ferguson, from Kincardine, to sign a two year contract. As a schoolboy he had played juvenile with Gairdoch F.C. and when he left Dunfermline High School in 1981 he went to Rangers. The Glasgow club, of course, did not have its troubles to seek then and Eric did not settle well. In 1983 he was loaned out to Clydebank for six months. The arrival of new manager

Souness saw the striker receive a free transfer and though he preferred full-time football, a position which several English clubs offered him, the persuasive tongue of Jim Leishman brought him to East End Park. Eric was impressed by the bustling atmosphere at the ground and referred to his new club as 'the sleeping giants of Scottish football,' a sentiment which was to be echoed by many commentators throughout the season.

Joining Ferguson was another attractive signing, the powerfully built Ian McCall (21), an amateur with Queen's Park. Pars' fans who watched the Spiders demolish their team at Hampden last season could not have been but impressed by the sparkling form of this tricky, versatile, left-footed player. Like Ferguson, he had originally been attracted by the Old Firm, signing on a schoolboy form with Celtic, but he too had moved on. In a recent competition in Germany, he was nominated 'Player of the Tournament' when the amateurs beat Fortuna Düsseldorf and Újpest Dozsa.

The third signing of note was the acquisition of Grant Reid (22) from Stenhousemuir for £10,000. The tall centre half had attracted Leishman's attention for some time, his defensive qualities having been noted by the manager. It was perhaps no coincidence that Reid had been absent from the two games between the rivals last season when Dunfermline scored seven goals. Although he had served one four-match suspension, he did not consider himself to be a 'hard man'. He had started his career with Norwich City in 1980 and then moved to Morton in 1982 before

Ian McCall in action against East Fife, August 30. (Dunfermline Press).

spending three seasons with the Warriors.

John Waddell (20), a 6'3" defender, was acquired on a free transfer from Dundee for whom he had played only a few games. He too had once been on the books of Norwich and would be good cover for Bobby Robertson whose medical duties continued to bite into his time.

On the outgoing side, midfielder Ian Gordon (25), who had made 23 league appearances over the past two seasons but had never been able to command a regular place in the team, was transferred to Raith Rovers for £3,000.

While most supporters were sunning themselves on holiday or relaxing in front of their T.V. enjoying a galaxy of sporting events, the players re-assembled at East End Park on July 3rd to begin their pre-season training and torturous battle to regain match fitness. Visits to Blairadam Forest, the beaches of Pettycur Bay and Portobello, Lochore

Country Park and Gleneagles left the players gasping for breath as the extra pounds were agonisingly shed. 'It's murder – I feel really sorry for them', grinned a malevolent manager.

On Monday evening, July 21 a friendly against Hearts was organised at Glenrothes Stadium in an attempt to sharpen up the players' footballing skills. A 2-1 defeat left Leishman to remark that 'we have a long way to go.' When further pressed to discuss the on-coming season, he elaborated: 'I will be pleased to consolidate our position. You won't catch me promising miracles, but I'm sure we will cause a few upsets and let other teams know who we are.' Prophetic words indeed.

More encouraging news came from the annual Musselburgh five-a-side tournament where the Pars' squad of Connelly, Smith, Heddle, Hamilton and Sharp won through to the final where they lost to Glasgow Rangers.

Before the month was out, chairman Jimmy Watters decided that the close season was the most opportune time to announce his intention to step down from 'the hot seat'. The statement did not come as a complete surprise as it was well known that he had been instructed by his doctor to take life easier and to lessen the stresses and strains which football administration undoubtedly carries. 'This meant', he explained, 'there was no way I could continue as chairman. I took my duties very seriously and we have a very important season coming up. I'm sorry to be leaving at this point because the club has something going. We have a great team on and off the park.'

Having served on the Board since 1970, he took immense pride in presiding over Dunfermline's centenary celebrations and in guiding the club back into the First Division. He was reluctantly persuaded to carry on as a director in an advisory capacity, the Board not wishing to lose his vast experience of the game which began as a goalkeeper with Hearts during the war.

His successor was vice-chairman, Mr. William Melbourne Rennie, who had joined the Board in 1971 when the club was going through a severe financial crisis. Mel Rennie, managing director of W.M. Rennie & Co., one of the biggest building contractors in the area, was responsible for several developments at East End Park, including the construction of the Paragon Social Club. The talents which had put him at the top of the business world would serve the club well. 'I take all things seriously', he said on his appointment. 'When I'm given a job to do, I do it to the best of my ability. Being chairman means a lot of pressure and a lot of hard work – and even that does not guarantee success. With my fellow directors, I look forward to Dunfermline recapturing the 'glory days' and, if possible, going full-time.'

Stepping up as vice-chairman was Mr. Bill Braisby, managing director of Braisby (Slaters and Plasterers) Fife Ltd. and a co-partner in Lin-Lor, a health and beauty salon. A life-long supporter of the club and a sponsor of the team for several seasons, Mr. Braisby joined the Board in 1982 when Pat Stanton was manager to replace, if anyone ever could, the legendary Andrew Watson who had just retired after 30 years of sterling service to the club.

One of the new chairman's first duties

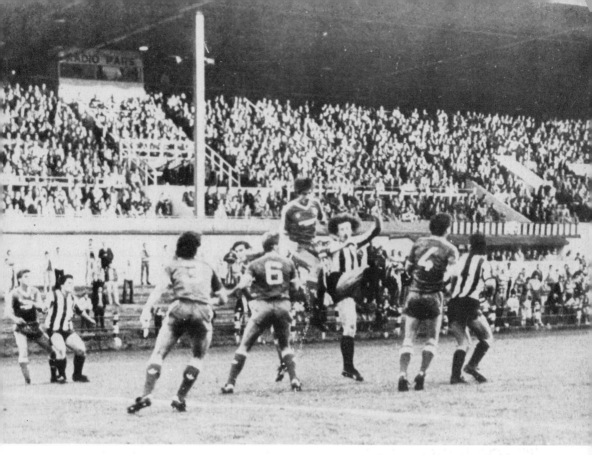

Action from Dunfermline's Skol Cup-Tie against St. Mirren on August 20, 1986. This was Dunfermline's largest home crowd of the season. (Enzo Mincella).

was to ensure that all the recommendations of the Popplewell enquiry, which was set up after the horrific fire at Bradford, were fully implemented at East End Park. Fortunately, largely due to the foresight of earlier directors, the ground required only a few modifications. A blacksmith was called in to install extra handrails, fire doors were redesigned to open outwards and safety exits were clearly marked with bold signs.

Underneath part of the stand, the old Patrons' lounge was gutted and under the guidance of art teacher and designer, Ken Forbes, the Jock Stein Lounge was created. The room was skilfully decorated to resemble a football ground, with a green carpet marked out with line markings re-inforcing that impression. One wall holds a long mural depicting Jock Stein jumping out of the dug-out at the Cup Final in 1961 in front of a massive crowd. Other walls feature blown-up photographs of the great man's career. The lounge, which has been fitted out with a bar and a T.V., is now used to entertain the ever-growing number of sponsors whose generosity helps to keep the club afloat. It was always the Board's intention to invite Mrs. Jean Stein and Celtic F.C. through

73

for an official opening but a crowded football programme has so far prevented this.

On the field, Jim Leishman had the first serious opportunity to examine how his new players would fit in when they took on Cowdenbeath in the first round of the Fife Cup at East End. On the evening of Wednesday July 30, the Pars got off to a cracking start. New boy, Eric Ferguson, opened the scoring after four minutes following good work from Watson, Waddell and McCall, and scored a second early in the second half. Thompson added a third when a perfectly flighted lob found the back of the net and fellow midfielder, McCathie, got the fourth with a fine header from Reid. Substitute Bowie scored his side's fifth with a thunderous shot which gave Allan no chance. Dunfermline: Westwater, Waddell, Forrest, McCathie, Reid, Heddle, Thompson, Moyes, Watson (Campbell), McCall (Bowie), Ferguson.

Dunfermline, however, were quickly brought back to earth on the Saturday when they travelled through to Kirkcaldy to play East Fife in the semi-final. Once again the East Enders found the men from Methil too hot to handle. With Watson, Bowie, Ferguson and Moyes all unable to play, a revamped Pars' side, backed by a strong support, was unable to equalise a first-half goal from a well organised Bayview side. They in turn, however, lost 3-1 to Raith Rovers in the final, sponsored for the first time by Kirkcaldy builder, Alex Penman.

Dunfermline: Westwater, Robertson, Forrest, McCathie, Reid, Heddle, Connelly, Hamilton (Waddell), Thompson, McCall, Campbell. Sub: Moyes.

Dunfermline restored some of their pride when, almost a year to the day, they took on Alex Ferguson's Aberdeen in a friendly at East End on Tuesday, August 5. The Cup holders, fielding a strong side, were shocked when the home side went one up through Smith after 32 minutes and were even more disgruntled when their shaky defence allowed Watson in to score a second. After a lambasting from Fergie at the interval, the visitors began to dominate the match, their full-time training allowing them to pull back the necessary two goals through Falconer and McLeish.

Dunfermline: Westwater, Robertson, Forrest, McCathie, Reid, Smith, Thompson, Moyes, Watson, McCall, Ferguson. Subs: Bowie, Morrison, Waddell.

With these preliminaries disposed of, the way was set for the season to begin in earnest. As a result of the promised league reconstruction, no Premier League teams had been relegated which meant that, unusually, the First Division comprised only 12 teams. To ensure fairness, all clubs would play each other four times, producing a stamina-sapping league programme of 44 games plus cup-ties. At the end of the season two clubs would be promoted and relegated as usual although for the following season, 1987-88, only one First Division club would go up. Clearly, a club's chances of promotion would be considerably greater in the coming season. In all honesty, few observers, least of all those most hard-headed men, the bookmakers, gave Dunfermline's prospects a second thought. Clubs like Morton, Dumbarton, Kilmarnock and Partick Thistle from the

Provost Robert Mill unveils the second division championship flag. Chairman Mel Rennie, ex-chairman Jimmy Watters and David Thomson of the Scottish League look on. (Dunfermline Press).

west of Scotland had experience of the Premier League and were considered amongst the favourites; country cousins like Dunfermline were expected to serve a longer apprenticeship.

With a difficult programme ahead, the manager appealed to the fans to be patient and to give the team their full support, while at the same time refraining from abusive remarks to players if the run of play went against them. Leishman remained quietly confident of doing well – 'my squad is raring to go!'

August 9 1986
DUNFERMLINE (1) 1   FORFAR (0) 0
  Watson (29)

Before the game began Provost Robert Mill, accompanied by chairman Mel Rennie and his predecessor, Jimmy Watters, unfurled the Scottish League Division Two championship flag to great acclaim from an emotional crowd of more than 3,000. As one remarkable

season was thus remembered, an even more momentous one was about to begin as the visitors from Angus cheered the champions on to the bright green turf.

The compliments finished then as Forfar, who had come within two points of promotion to the Premier League, gave the Pars a taste of what to expect during the next strenuous 39 weeks. With all his players fit, Leishman felt in confident mood, encouraging him to make a bold reflection in the match programme: 'There is nobody involved behind the scenes of the club who believes that Premier Division football would be impossible.'

A hard won 1-0 victory did nothing to blunt the manager's confidence. In the opening minutes of the game Trevor Smith and Eric Ferguson squandered good chances and Ian McCall showed early on what a promising player he might be, though the midfield provided their forwards with little service.

A controversial moment in the match against Forfar as John Watson puts the ball past Stewart Kennedy and into the net. (Dunfermline Press).

Dunfermline's goal came on the half hour mark and sparked off a controversy which saw two Forfar players booked for protesting. Former Dunfermline and Scotland 'keeper, Stewart Kennedy, caught a Thompson cross at the far post but collided with John Watson in the process. On falling to the ground he dropped the ball obligingly at the forward's foot for him to score easily.

Despite good efforts from the visitors through Ward, MacDonald and Clark, the home defence, inspired by Westwater, kept a clean score-sheet. Indeed, Dunfermline could well have added another when good efforts from defenders McCathie and Forrest, celebrating his 26th birthday, just missed.

With two points safely tucked away, Dunfermline could not have wished for a better baptism and though tired, the players realised that life could be sweet 'upstairs'.

DUNFERMLINE: Westwater, Robertson, Forrest, McCathie, Reid, Thompson, Smith (Bowie), Moyes, Watson, McCall, Ferguson (Campbell)

Booking: Moyes

FORFAR: Kennedy, Bennet (Farningham), McPhee, Morris, McKillop, Lennox (MacDonald), Ward, Lorimer, Scott, Brewster, Clark

Bookings: Clark, McPhee

Referee: I.R. Cathcart, Bridge of Allan
Attendance: 3,294
Mascot: Duncan Stewart, 68 Wardlaw Way, Oakley.

Brechin	0	Montrose	0
East Fife	1	Kilmarnock	4
Morton	3	Clyde	0
Partick	1	Dumbarton	2
Queen of South	0	Airdrie	0

Wednesday August 13 1986

DUMBARTON (0) 0   DUNFERMLINE (0) 1
                  Clougherty (o.g. 65)

Dunfermline made this midweek visit to Boghead expecting a tough encounter, and so it turned out to be. Dumbarton, under the new management team of former Pars' stars Alex Totten and Bert Paton, were strong favourites to regain their Premier League berth which they had relinquished two seasons earlier, though their match programme did acknowledge that 'it is an Everest ambition. Will the 'Sons have enough Sherpas?' A 1-0 defeat at home was certainly a set-back for them; Dunfermline were delighted to be undefeated and top of the league!

The first half, which the visitors won on points, was played at a tremendous pace and kept the fans on tenter hooks throughout. The second half was 20 minutes old when John Watson engineered the only goal of the night. Skipper Robertson sent a well-struck pass down the right wing for Watson to chase, a familiar enough move in any Pars' build up. The striker homed in on goal, beating off a challenge from

McCahill, and shot low into the corner. Although 'keeper Arthur did well to palm the ball out, it fell to defender Clougherty who succeeded only in chipping his pass-back into his own net.

As expected, Dumbarton began to pile on the pressure, forcing the visiting full backs to clear off their goal line while the central defenders, McCathie and Reid, found themselves toiling to beat out the determined sorties launched by the despairing home side. The aggressive midfield duo of Moyes and Thompson worked away relentlessly in the middle of the park and helped to set up good chances for substitutes Morrison and Campbell whose efforts were goalbound but for the woodwork.

Leishman admitted to being "definitely well pleased with a great game, a good performance" though he cautioned about "not getting carried away" at the club's lofty position.

DUMBARTON: Arthur, Montgomerie, Curran, Clougherty, McCahill, T. Coyle, Moore, McGowan, Bourke, McIvor, Grant
Subs: McCoy, J. Coyle

Booking: Montgomerie

DUNFERMLINE: Westwater, Robertson, Forrest, McCathie, Reid, Thompson, Smith (Morrison), Moyes, Watson, McCall, Ferguson (Campbell)

Booking: Thompson

Referee: G.A. Evans, Bishopbriggs
Attendance: 1,600

Airdrie	4	Brechin	0
Clyde	0	Queen of South	0
Forfar	1	Partick	1
Kilmarnock	2	Morton	2
Montrose	2	East Fife	2

A training session at East End Park showing the players enjoying themselves.

August 16 1986

MORTON (0) 0   DUNFERMLINE (0) 1
                                   McCathie (76)

The convoy of buses and cars again headed west from Fife, this time to the other side of the Clyde, to Greenock. Like Dumbarton, Morton were the last team to be relegated from the Premier League and were strongly fancied for promotion. With former record goal scorer, Allan McGraw, at the helm, aided by player-coach, Jackie McNamara, formerly of Celtic and Hibs, Morton had fine players in goalkeeper David Wylie, new signing Rowan Alexander, ex-'Ger Alex O'Hara and Ian Clinging.

On their last visit to Cappielow one year earlier, Dunfermline came away aggrieved that lady luck had not smiled more favourably on their tremendous efforts; on this occasion, it was no doubt a skilful, well-organised Morton side which felt that good fortune had deserted them when they counted up their missed opportunities.

In the first half, the home side could well have been several goals up as Robertson, Clinging and Turner all came

dangerously close but found goalkeeper Westwater in excellent form. Indeed, but for a vigorous and brave save by him from Simpson just before the interval, Morton could well have gone into a not undeserved lead. For their part, the Dunfermline attack was quiet with only McCall seriously troubling the very capable Wylie.

After the interval, Smith, McCall and Ferguson all might have made more of their few chances but it was left to Norrie McCathie to snatch the only goal of the game. In the 76th minute the powerful defender towered above the home defence to head in the winner.

Leishman paid tribute to a fine Morton side while also praising the character and attitude of his side. "I'm making sure they don't get carried away. There are 41 games to go after all," he solemnly remarked.

MORTON: Wylie, O'Hara, Holmes, Hunter, Doak, Turner, Robertson, Clinging, McNeil (Coyle), Alexander, Simpson (Boag)

Bookings: Alexander, O'Hara

DUNFERMLINE: Westwater, Robertson, Forrest, McCathie, Reid, Thompson, Smith, Moyes, Watson, McCall, Ferguson
Subs: Campbell, Morrison

Bookings: Watson, Ferguson

Referee: M. Delaney, Cleland
Attendance: 3,000

Airdrie	1	Dumbarton	0
Clyde	3	East Fife	3
Forfar	3	Kilmarnock	1
Montrose	3	Partick	1
Queen of South	2	Brechin	0

	P	W	D	L	F	A	Pts
DUNFERMLINE	3	3	0	0	3	0	6
Airdrie	3	2	1	0	5	0	5
Montrose	3	1	2	0	5	3	4
Queen of South	3	1	2	0	2	0	4
Morton	3	1	1	1	5	3	3
Kilmarnock	3	1	1	1	7	6	3

Wednesday August 20 1986
Skol Cup Second Round
DUNFERMLINE (0) 0   ST. MIRREN (1) 2
                      McGarvey (33, 63)

A welcome break from the tension of league football was provided by the arrival of St. Mirren for this second round tie in the highly popular Skol Cup with its generous incentives. At the same time the home fans had the opportunity to measure how their favourites compared with a Premier League side enjoying full-time training.

Although St. Mirren had made a poor start to the season and were without injured captain, Tony Fitzpatrick, their side nonetheless contained a number of very experienced players: 'keeper Campbell Money and striker Frank McGarvey who had experience of the international scene and Dougie Bell, on loan from Rangers. Dunfermline were unchanged for the fourth successive game which meant that there were still no places in the line-up for rebels Young and Jenkins who had yet to re-sign.

A large crowd of 6,161, who held the kick-off up for 10 minutes, turned up to see if another Fife team could repeat the result of last season when Cowdenbeath sent the Love Street side tumbling out of this competition. For the first half hour Dunfermline gave as good as they got against a side which was far from impressive at times. McCall and Watson were both unlucky not to open the scoring.

The departure of skipper Bobby Robertson with a hamstring injury after only 18 minutes unsettled the home defence and his cover, Davie Moyes, gifted the opening goal. His back-heeler to Westwater was woefully short and was picked up by Gallacher who centred for McGarvey to score. Gallacher himself should have made it number two a few minutes later.

Dunfermline opened the second half in determined mood and looked as though they might grab the equaliser. The enterprising McCall almost tucked away a cross from substitute Morrison and a brave run from Smith was only ended by a sharp tackle from Cooper. Too often, however, Dunfermline's forwards found themselves victims of the visitors' off-side traps. Just after Morrison had narrowly headed the ball over Money's bar, a lapse in concentration from Forrest let St. Mirren clinch the tie. His poor pass-back to Westwater put the keeper in trouble and though he saved Gallacher's initial shot, he was unable to prevent McGarvey from scoring an easy goal. Apart from these two blunders, there was little to separate the two sides.

DUNFERMLINE: Westwater, Robertson (Morrison), Forrest, McCathie, Reid, Thompson, Smith, Moyes, Watson, McCall (Campbell), Ferguson

Booking: Morrison

ST. MIRREN: Money, Clarke, Abercromby, Bell, Godfrey, Cooper, Hamilton (Winnie), Lambert, McGarvey (McDougall), Speirs, Gallacher

Bookings: Godfrey, Cooper

Referee: D.A. Yeats, Perth
Attendance: 6,161
Mascot: Mark Bennet, 33 Old Kirk Rd.

August 23 1986

DUNFERMLINE (2) 2   CLYDE (0) 0
  McCall (3) Watson (12)

With Robertson unfit after Wednesday night's injury, Rowan Hamilton was **79**

Keeper Atkins of Clyde fails to hold a pass-back and John Watson moves in to score the second goal. (Dunfermline Press).

recalled for his first league game and fitted well into the full-back position, though it has to be said that a lack-lustre Clyde side did little to trouble the home defence. Jim Leishman had paid his opponents, under new manager John Clark who had replaced Craig Brown, the compliment of watching them in their home cup-tie against Falkirk which they won 2-1 after being a goal behind.

After only three minutes, Dunfermline brought the giant killers down to earth. Good build-up work from Ferguson and Watson gave McCall an excellent

through ball which he drove home for his first goal for his new club. Nine minutes later Evans panicked when put under pressure in his own box and his fierce pass-back was only palmed away to Watson who rounded the 'keeper on the ground and scored from a narrow angle. Inexplicably, Dunfermline eased up, the midweek struggle perhaps taking its toll. Though Ferguson and Hamilton both came close, the crowd had to be satisfied with two goals at the interval.

With the points seemingly tied up, Dunfermline failed to capitalise on their early lead and the game degenerated into a scrappy affair. Grant Reid did have the ball in the net but his effort was adjudged off-side. With 10 minutes to go Ian McCall, nominated Man of the Match by sponsors Aluglaze, brought out the save of the game from Atkins. The Dunfermline defence, with little to trouble them, easily recorded their fourth successive shut-out to keep the team firmly at the top of the table.

DUNFERMLINE: Westwater, Hamilton, Forrest, McCathie, Reid, Thompson, Smith (Morrison), Moyes, Watson, McCall, Ferguson (Campbell)

CLYDE: Atkins, Napier, Dickson, I. Ferguson, Flexney, Murray, Reilly, Logan (Millar), Watters, Evans, Murphy (Willock)

Referee: R.B. Valentine, Dundee
Attendance: 3,530
Mascot: Scott Rylance, 16 Newhouse Ave, Dunbar

Rapt attention from new signing, Grant Reid. (Ian Malcolm)

Brechin	2	Morton	5
Dumbarton	3	Forfar	2
East Fife	1	Airdrie	1
Kilmarnock	3	Montrose	0
Partick	1	Queen of South	1

	P	W	D	L	F	A	Pts
DUNFERMLINE	4	4	0	0	5	0	8
Airdrie	4	2	2	0	6	1	6
Morton	4	2	1	1	10	5	5
Kilmarnock	4	2	1	1	10	6	5
Queen of South	4	1	3	0	3	1	6
Dumbarton	4	2	0	2	5	5	4

August 30 1986

DUNFERMLINE (0) 2	EAST FIFE (3) 4
Morrison (85)	McNaughton (21, 33)
Watson (87)	Burgess (43)
	Hill (84)

Any expectation that Dunfermline harboured that East Fife would be exhausted after their sapping midweek tussle against Rangers in the Skol Cup which the Ibrox side won narrowly on penalties, was quickly dispelled by the side which almost became Fife's first representatives in the Premier League last season. Under the guiding hand of long-serving manager, Dave Clark, East Fife comprehensively beat the team which they had twice knocked out of the Fife Cup in recent months.

The league leaders, who had yet to lose a goal in the championship, suddenly found themselves four goals behind with only six minutes, left to a team which totally belied their fourth bottom position. The calming influence of skipper Robertson was certainly missed and centre half Reid looked less than match fit. Grant Jenkins, the last of the re-signing rebels, made his peace with the club and later came on as a substitute.

Ironically, the main thorn in Dunfermline's flesh was the player whom they had unsuccessfully tried to sign, Brian McNaughton, who sealed the Pars' fate with two opening goals in the first half hour. Just before half-time, Burgess scored via a deflection from a free kick after Thompson had upended

McNaughton. Few of the home side, apart from Westwater, McCathie and Thompson, showed anything like their true form and found the visitors' tight defence difficult to break down despite good efforts from McCall and Forrest.

In the second half, Dunfermline stepped up the pressure but East Fife showed themselves to be dangerous on the break and on one such occasion, Hill completed the humiliation with a long range effort going in off the post. To Dunfermline's credit they made the score respectable and a better reflection of events by recording late strikes from Morrison and Watson. Thompson was nominated Man of the Match by sponsors, A.S. Pitblado.

With Airdrie beating Montrose, the Pars now dropped into second position by virtue of goal difference.

DUNFERMLINE: Westwater, Hamilton, Forrest, McCathie, Reid, Thompson, Smith (Morrison), Moyes (Jenkins), Watson, McCall, Campbell

Booking: Thompson

EAST FIFE: Marshall, Connor, Gray, Hill, Burgess, McLaren, Blair, McCafferty, McNaughton, Kirkwood, Hunter (Mitchell)
Sub: Burns

Referee: G.D. Cumming, Carluke
Attendance: 4,448
Mascot: Stewart Hughes, 24 St. Fillans Cres, Aberdour

Brechin	0	Forfar	1
Montrose	1	Airdrie	2
Morton	0	Dumbarton	3
Partick	0	Clyde	0
Queen of South	2	Kilmarnock	1

	P	W	D	L	F	A	Pts
Airdrie	5	3	2	0	8	2	8
DUNFERMLINE	5	4	0	1	7	4	8
Queen of South	5	2	3	0	5	2	7
Dumbarton	5	3	0	2	8	5	6
Kilmarnock	5	2	1	2	11	8	5
Morton	5	2	1	2	10	8	5

September 6 1986

KILMARNOCK (1) 1   DUNFERMLINE (1) 2
Cook (45)   Jenkins (15)
                                    Forrest (87)

Any mature Pars' supporter travelling to Rugby Park cannot but help recall the good old days of the 1960s when both clubs were at their peak, dominating not only the Scottish scene, but also performing well in Europe. Both teams now nursed hopes of a return of this golden age of soccer. The record books showed that historically there was little to separate the two teams: in 63 league encounters Killie had won 24 to Dunfermline's 23, the rest being draws.

Leishman rang the changes after last week's disappointing display, giving his most recent signing, John Waddell, the chance to stake his claim at full back. Ian Heddle and Stevie Morrison were brought in to sharpen up the midfield. Dunfermline started well, weathering an initial bout of pressure before going into the lead through Jenkins after 15 minutes when he took advantage of a poor save by McCulloch from McCall to slam the ball home.

The visitors then seem to have put themselves at a considerable disadvantage when first of all new boy Waddell picked up his second booking in the 26th minute and was duly ordered off. Then, just on the stroke of half-time, Cook struck home the equaliser.

As is often the case, a 10 man side, with their tails up and with a goalkeeper in inspired form, can be exceedingly difficult to beat. Killie failed to capitalise on their apparent advantage and, in the words of their manager, "stopped playing." To the great delight of the large travelling support, Dunfermline clinched

Action from the Kilmarnock game as McCathie, Morrison and Reid race for the ball. (Ian Malcolm).

a late and not undeserved winner. McCall picked up the ball in the centre circle, threaded it through to the overlapping Forrest on the wing who boldly strode in to the box and unleashed a drive over McCulloch, courtesy of a deflection. Forrest's 17th goal for his club kept it joint top of the league.

KILMARNOCK: McCulloch, McLean, McLeod, Robertson, Martin, R. Clarke, McGivern, McCafferty (McGuire), Cook, J. Clarke, Bryson (Miller)

Booking: Bryson

DUNFERMLINE: Westwater, Waddell, Forrest, McCathie, Reid, Heddle, Morrison, Thompson, Watson, McCall (Smith), Jenkins (Campbell)

Sent off: Waddell (26 min)

Referee: D. Syme, Rutherglen
Attendance: 2,700

Airdrie	1	Partick	0
Clyde	1	Montrose	1
Dumbarton	3	Brechin	1
East Fife	1	Morton	0
Forfar	1	Queen of South	1

83

	P	W	D	L	F	A	Pts
Airdrie	6	4	2	0	9	2	10
DUNFERMLINE	6	5	0	1	9	5	10
Dumbarton	6	4	0	2	11	6	8
Queen of South	6	2	4	0	6	3	8
East Fife	6	2	3	1	12	12	7
Forfar	6	2	2	2	8	7	6
Kilmarnock	6	2	1	3	12	10	5
Morton	6	2	1	3	10	9	5
Montrose	6	1	3	2	7	9	5
Clyde	6	0	4	2	4	9	4
Partick	6	0	3	3	4	8	3
Brechin	6	0	1	5	3	15	1

September 13 1986

BRECHIN (1) 1   DUNFERMLINE (2) 4
  Kennedy (13)   Heddle (16, 71)
                        McCall (34), Watson
                        (82)

Though unfashionable Brechin had shocked the footballing world by winning the Second Division Championship three years earlier, their current, dismal record of failing to win a game out of six attempts suggested to the visitors that they had little to fear. Yet, the home side, which had only three goals to their credit, shocked Dunfermline by going into an early lead in 13 minutes through Kennedy.

This was the incentive the visitors needed and they promptly went on to put four goals past a defence which had already lost fifteen. Player-manager Ian Fleming failed to scythe down McCall who pushed the ball on to Heddle. The young midfielder did what he had been doing so well in the reserves – beating goalkeepers, in this instance with a low right foot shot into the net.

Heddle clearing the ball during the match against Brechin on September 13. McCathie, Thompson and Reid look on. (Ian Malcolm).

An own goal from John Donnelly of Partick Thistle is watched by Ian McCall (Enzo Mincella).

After misses at both ends, a move familiar to Pars' fans put Dunfermline into the lead. Forrest crossed the ball to Watson who nodded it down for his colleagues and in this case McCall obligingly blasted the ball home.

Ian Campbell, who knew Glebe Park as well as anyone on the field, replaced Smith and was unlucky not to add to the scoring with a ball that came off the crossbar. The killer-goal came in the 71st minute when Jenkins picked up a ball from Morrison, ran half the length of the field and crossed it to the unmarked Heddle to score his second goal. By way of formality, Watson completed a satisfactory outing by netting his side's fourth.

BRECHIN: Martin, Watt, Scott, Brown, Fleming, Taylor, Gallacher, Kennedy (D. Lees), Powell, Lyall, Crawley (G. Lees)

Bookings: Lyall, Taylor, Fleming

DUNFERMLINE: Westwater, Thompson, Forrest, McCathie, Reid, Heddle, Smith (Campbell), Morrison, Watson (Bowie), McCall, Jenkins

Bookings: Forrest, Smith

Referee: A.M. Roy, Aberdeen
Attendance: 1,000

Airdrie	3	Kilmarnock	2
Dumbarton	1	Montrose	0
Forfar	2	Clyde	1
Partick	2	Morton	5
Queen of South	2	East Fife	0

	P	W	D	L	F	A	Pts
Airdrie	7	5	2	0	12	4	12
DUNFERMLINE	7	6	0	1	13	6	12
Dumbarton	7	5	0	2	12	6	10
Queen of South	7	3	4	0	8	3	10
Forfar	7	3	2	2	10	8	8
Morton	7	3	1	3	15	11	7

Tuesday September 16 1986

DUNFERMLINE (1) 2   PARTICK THISTLE (0) 0
Jenkins (18)
Donnelly (o.g. 60)

Visitors Partick Thistle, under new manager Derek Johnstone, the famous Rangers' star, were singled out by manager Leishman as likely promotion contenders though their 5-2 defeat at home on Saturday to Morton did not suggest a great side. The Pars did not play particularly well yet they still won, a sign of true promotion contenders.

A large crowd of almost 4,000 found themselves viewing a rather dour struggle with little sign of inventiveness from either side. The *Press* reporter thought the visiting side was "as uncompromising as a Maryhill tenement."

On the positive side, Jenkins took one of the few chances of the evening and opened the scoring in 18 minutes with a well struck half-volley from outside the box. Leishman later referred to the player, who had been on the verge of leaving the club, as "a real trouper."

Patrick's expected fight-back did not materialise though they were unfortunate after the interval to have a goal disallowed for off-side. With almost an hour gone and the home fans desperately looking for another goal, up stepped Maryhill midfielder John Donnelly, whom Dunfermline had tried unsuccessfully to sign from Leeds, to send a cracking pass-back into his own net with his goalkeeper unable to do anything.

The most pleasing news of the night came when it was announced that Clyde had held Airdrie to a draw, thus restoring Dunfermline to the top of the table.

DUNFERMLINE: Westwater, Thompson, Forrest, McCathie, Reid, Heddle, Hamilton, Morrison, Watson, McCall, Jenkins
Subs: Campbell, Bowie

PARTICK: Brough, Spittal, Walker, McIntyre, Carson, Watson, Mackie (Gallacher), Newman, Smith (Mullin), McDonald, Donnelly

Referee: D. Miller, Garrowhill
Attendance: 3,852
Mascot: Ross McPherson, 15 Cleveland Dr., Inverkeithing

Clyde	1	Airdrie	1
East Fife	1	Brechin	0
Kilmarnock	2	Dumbarton	1
Montrose	1	Forfar	1
Morton	5	Queen of South	2

	P	W	D	L	F	A	Pts
DUNFERMLINE	8	7	0	1	15	6	14
Airdrie	8	5	3	0	13	5	13
Dumbarton	8	5	0	3	13	8	10
Queen of South	8	3	4	1	10	8	10

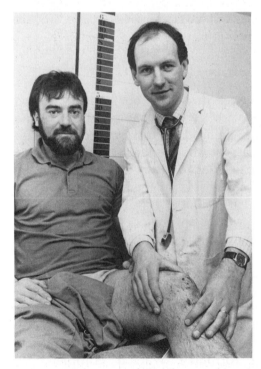

Doctor Bobby Robertson, Team Captain, examines Gary Thompson's injuries. (Dunfermline Press).

September 20 1986

QUEEN OF SOUTH (1) 1   DUNFERMLINE (0) 1
Robertson (pen. 11)   Morrison (54)

This top-of-the table clash between the newly promoted clubs from the Second Division certainly lived up to its billing and provided great entertainment for the crowd of 4,000, the fourth largest gate in Scotland that sunny afternoon. Like Dunfermline, Queen of the South had made an excellent start to the season under new manager Mike Jackson and were undefeated until midweek when Morton put five goals past them.

Fears that there might be a repeat of last season's crowd trouble when segregation was not imposed, happily proved unfounded. Queens were out for revenge for having been pipped for the championship and if the gods had smiled more favourably, they might have achieved their ambition. They did not reckon on a mere mortal, the ever dependable Ian Westwater in the Dunfermline goal, who put up a tremendous performance to virtually steal a point for the visitors. It even took a penalty to beat him, awarded in the 10th minute when McCathie, in no apparent danger, fouled Bryce. Winger Robertson converted the kick and he and fellow winger Willie Reid gave the Dunfermline defence a roasting, aided by generous gifts in front of goal. Only Morrison and Thompson, apart from the 'keeper, could take much credit out of the game for the visitors.

Dunfermline continued to struggle in the second half and most of their long range, speculative shots were easily dealt with by Englishman Alex Williams, on loan from Manchester City. It was left to

John Donnelly, signed in September, pauses for breath during the Montrose match, September 30. (Enzo Mincella).

the fierce shooting power of midfielder Morrison to level the score in the 54th minute, much against the run of play, when he volleyed home a weak clearance from outside the box. The Pars held on to win a precious point and might even have stolen two if Williams had not been alert to another Morrison shot near the end.

QUEEN OF SOUTH: Williams, G. Robertson, Sim, Hetherington, Anderson, McBride, Reid, Cochrane, Bryce, Cloy, J. Robertson
Subs: Maskrey, Mills

DUNFERMLINE: Westwater, Hamilton, Forrest, McCathie, Reid, Heddle (Waddell), Morrison, Thompson, Campbell, McCall, Jenkins (Ferguson)

Referee: J. McCluskey, Stewarton
Attendance: 4,000

Airdrie	3	Forfar	1
Brechin	2	Kilmarnock	2
Clyde	2	Dumbarton	1
East Fife	2	Partick	0
Morton	0	Montrose	2

	P	W	D	L	F	A	Pts
Airdrie	9	6	3	0	16	6	15
DUNFERMLINE	9	7	1	1	16	7	15
Queen of South	9	3	5	1	11	9	11
East Fife	9	4	3	2	15	14	11

Some of the full-time squad enjoying a game of pool in the players' lounge.

September 27 1986
DUNFERMLINE (0) 0   AIRDRIE (0) 0

At such an early stage in the season both managers rightly agreed that it was premature to talk of a championship decider between two sides who were joint top of the league, four points clear of the field and separated by only one goal.

For the home support, it was their first opportunity to view new player, John Donnelly, signed in midweek from Partick Thistle. Leishman had his eye on this creative midfielder for some time but had been scared off when Leeds United were reportedly asking around £20,000. He went instead to the Glasgow club last season when they appeared to be in a more promising position than Dunfermline. Leishman hoped he would add to his goal tally of 11 last season, give some imagination to the midfield and quickly repay his £5,000 transfer fee.

The game failed to live up to its billing. Neither side wanted to lose this vital game and the large crowd of almost 6,000, a record for East End Park in the new First Division, was treated to a rather drab struggle with little about which to enthuse. The free-scoring side of last season were now beginning to painfully realise that experienced First Division defenders could stifle, by fair means or foul, ponderous build-ups.

Ian Heddle took over as left back, not his natural role, and Bobby Forrest became the fifth incumbent so far of the right back position. Reid and McCathie, later nominated Man of the Match by Autocentre, held firm at the back but the forwards seldom seriously troubled the visitors' goal. Donnelly had a quiet debut but showed enough delicate touches on and off the ball to suggest that he might be the sort of talented play-maker that the Pars required.

If Dunfermline felt aggrieved at not opening the scoring in the first half, they were relieved after the interval to see shots from Frye and Flood rebound harmlessly off the woodwork. Indeed, it was Westwater – again – who was called upon to make the save of the match when he brilliantly caught a fierce header from Frye. A pelvic cartilage strain, however, which had been niggling him for several weeks, often prevented him from clearing his line properly.

The goalless draw, however, did not particularly displease either side.

DUNFERMLINE: Westwater, Forrest, Heddle, McCathie, Reid, Donnelly, Thompson, Morrison, Watson, McCall (Bowie), Jenkins
Sub: Ferguson

Booking: Heddle

AIRDRIE: Martin, McKinnon, Black, McKeown, McCormack, Lindsay, Frye, Fairlie, Flood, Walker, Christie
Subs: Rodger, Templeton

Booking: McKinnon

Referee: L.B. Thow, Ayr
Attendance: 5,877
Mascot: Barry Foster, 57 Robertson Rd

Panic in the Montrose penalty box during this corner kick from Dunfermline. (Enzo Mincella).

Dumbarton	2	East Fife		1
Forfar	2	Morton		2
Kilmarnock	0	Clyde		0
Montrose	3	Queen of South		4
Partick	1	Brechin		0

	P	W	D	L	F	A	Pts
Airdrie	10	6	4	0	16	6	16
DUNFERMLINE	10	7	2	1	16	7	16
Queen of South	10	4	5	1	15	12	13
Dumbarton	10	6	0	4	16	11	12
East Fife	10	4	3	3	16	16	11
Morton	10	4	2	4	22	17	10

Tuesday September 30 1986

DUNFERMLINE (1) 1   MONTROSE (0) 0
  Watson (33)

To complete the first quarter of the league fixtures, Dunfermline encountered a Montrose side which, under the guidance of manager Ian Stewart, was lying joint third bottom in the league with only two wins to their credit although they had recently knocked Hearts out of the Skol Cup. Such was Dunfermline's impact on the footballing scene that the stand was full of scouts from other clubs – Crystal Palace, Spurs, Luton, Hibs, Hearts, Motherwell and Dundee. Thankfully for the home support, their interest did not materialise.

They saw Dunfermline beat the visitors by only one goal when the margin would have been greater but for the goalkeeping skills of Ray Charles whose talents had also attracted attention. Though only one goal was scored, it was of the highest quality. In the 33rd minute, Jim Bowie, in the team from the start, took off on a bold run into the visitors' half. His early cross was met head on by the diving Watson who

89

crashed it past a despairing goalkeeper. If the T.V. cameras had been there it would surely have been a candidate for 'goal of the season.'

Several more excellent chances came Dunfermline's way but a mixture of inspired goalkeeping and poor finishing kept the home crowd of almost 3,500 on edge right till the end, though Montrose never looked like equalising. This greatly pleased reserve 'keeper, Hugh Whyte, who was drafted into the team for the first time since March 1985 to allow Westwater's groin strain time to heal.

With Airdrie losing on the same night at Cappielow, Dunfermline now regained top spot, leaving everyone at East End very content with a magnificent start to the league campaign.

DUNFERMLINE: Whyte, Forrest, Heddle, McCathie, Reid, Donnelly, Bowie (McCall), Hamilton, Watson, Thompson, Jenkins
Sub: Ferguson

MONTROSE: Charles, Barr, McLelland, Brown, Sheran, Lyons, Allan (Forbes), Bennett, Paterson, Wright, McDonald (Murray)

Bookings: Brown, Sheran, Wright

Referee: M. McGinley, Clydebank
Attendance: 3,498
Mascot: Colin Feeney, 72 Burnside Cres., Rosyth

Brechin	2	Clyde	1
East Fife	1	Forfar	2
Morton	2	Airdrie	1
Partick	1	Kilmarnock	0
Queen of South	1	Dumbarton	3

	P	W	D	L	F	A	Pts
DUNFERMLINE	11	8	2	1	17	7	18
Airdrie	11	6	4	1	17	8	16
Dumbarton	11	7	0	4	19	12	14
Queen of South	11	4	5	2	16	15	13
Morton	11	5	2	4	24	18	12
Forfar	11	4	4	3	16	15	12

October 4 1986

FORFAR (2) 3   DUNFERMLINE (2) 3
MacDonald (pen. 19,   Hamilton (29)
44, 76)   Watson (40)
                     McCathie (83)

Dunfermline were unchanged for the return visit to Station Park, which meant another outing for Hugh Whyte and Jim Bowie, two of the club's longest serving players. Jim Moffat, another former Dunfermline player, took over in goal for the home side though he was not to give away any presents to his former mates.

Although Forfar were six points behind the leaders, a recent victory at Bayview and a share of the points at Cappielow reminded the visitors that this would not be an easy trip, and so it turned out to be.

In the 16th minute Dunfermline received a fright when a partially saved shot from Whyte had to be cleared off the line by Heddle. Three minutes later McCathie conceded a penalty and MacDonald converted from the spot. With Dunfermline's midfield for once firing on all cylinders, the visitors got back into the game with Hamilton heading a Donnelly chip into the net for the equaliser. Five minutes before half-time, Donnelly was again the architect for his side's second goal when he laid on a perfect pass for Watson to score. A mistake by the Dunfermline defence on the stroke of half-time let Forfar in to grasp the equaliser.

The second half continued at a cracking pace and Dunfermline seemed to have thrown the game away 14 minutes from time when a large gap appeared in their defence to let MacDonald in to complete his hat-trick. To their credit, Dunfermline continued

"The Three Musketeers": Rowan Hamilton, Jim Bowie and Stevie Morrison congratulate each other after Dunfermline's equaliser against Forfar. (An award-winning photograph by Ian Malcolm).

to battle away and with only seven minutes left were duly rewarded. Jenkins crossed to McCathie who beat the 'keeper with a firm, diving header.

The fans certainly received value for money and the visitors could not complain too much at the loss of a point, especially when they heard that Airdrie had lost at home to Queen of the South.

FORFAR: Moffat, Bennett, McPhee, Morris, McKillop, Clark, Brewster, Lorimer (Ward), Scott, Bell, MacDonald
Sub: Lennox

Booking: MacDonald

DUNFERMLINE: Whyte, Forrest, Heddle, McCathie, Reid, Donnelly, Bowie (McCall), Thompson, Watson, Hamilton, Jenkins
Sub: Ferguson

Booking: Heddle

Referee: K.J. Hope, Clarkston
Attendance: 1,892

Airdrie	1	Queen of South	3				
Clyde	1	Morton	2				
Dumbarton	2	Partick	2				
Kilmarnock	1	East Fife	1				
Montrose	0	Brechin	2				

	P	W	D	L	F	A	Pts
DUNFERMLINE	12	8	3	1	20	10	19
Airdrie	12	6	4	2	18	11	16
Dumbarton	12	7	1	4	21	14	15
Queen of South	12	5	5	2	19	16	15
Morton	12	6	2	4	26	19	14
Forfar	12	4	5	3	19	18	13
East Fife	12	4	4	4	18	19	12
Kilmarnock	12	3	4	5	19	18	10
Montrose	12	2	4	6	13	18	8
Clyde	12	1	6	5	10	17	8
Partick	12	2	4	6	10	19	8
Brechin	12	2	2	8	10	24	6

Wednesday October 8 1986

DUNFERMLINE (0) 0   DUMBARTON (0) 1
McCoy (71)

With Dunfermline sitting three points clear at the top of the First Division, they were certainly becoming the team to beat. Visitors Dumbarton were still smarting from their narrow defeat in August and had since climbed menacingly into third top spot, only four points behind.

Sadly for the large support of more than 4,000, Dunfermline chose to have an off-night when little went right for them. Leishman settled for the same side that drew with Forfar except that a fitter Westwater was recalled to goal. Few of his colleagues played anything like their normal form and found that the close-marking, fierce-tackling and cautious approach of the visitors put them off their stride. Jenkins and Watson, who was reportedly the subject of an unsuccessful bid by Crystal Palace, squandered chances which they might otherwise have converted.

It took until after the interval for Hamilton to force the visiting 'keeper to make his first real save of the match. As a no-scoring draw looked increasingly likely, right winger Moore, who had played a good game, broke away from Heddle and touched the ball on to the advancing McCoy for him to beat Westwater with a low drive, 19 minutes from time. Try as they might Dunfermline could not reply, and it was no surprise when, in the dying minutes, centre half Reid kicked past a Bowie corner when it seemed easier to score.

The defeat, only Dunfermline's second of the programme, was a timely reminder that they could not expect an easy passage at the top of the division.

DUNFERMLINE: Westwater, Forrest, Heddle, McCathie, Reid, Donnelly, Bowie (McCall), Thompson (Ferguson), Watson, Hamilton, Jenkins

Bookings: Watson, Reid

John Watson is sandwiched between two Dumbarton players. Such close marking prevented Dunfermline from scoring throughout the game. (Enzo Mincella).

DUMBARTON: Stevenson, Docherty, Montgomerie, Martin, McCahill, T. Coyle, Moore, Kay, Houston, McCoy, O. Coyle
Subs: Grant, McGowan

Booking: McCahill

Referee: J. Duncan, Gorebridge
Attendance: 4,161
Mascot: Darryl Falls, 4 Beck Cres.

Brechin	1	Airdrie	2
East Fife	2	Montrose	1
Morton	2	Kilmarnock	0
Partick	1	Forfar	1
Queen of South	1	Clyde	1

	P	W	D	L	F	A	Pts
DUNFERMLINE	13	8	3	2	20	11	19
Airdrie	13	7	4	2	20	12	18
Dumbarton	13	8	1	4	22	14	17
Morton	13	7	2	4	28	19	16
Queen of South	13	5	6	2	20	17	16
Forfar	13	4	6	3	20	19	14

October 11 1986

CLYDE (1) 1   DUNFERMLINE (0) 0
  Murphy (41)

With the 'Bully Wee' obliged to vacate their stadium at Shawfield and to move in with Partick Thistle, Dunfermline made the first of four visits to Firhill in search of points against a team which had only one victory to their credit. Centre half Reid, who did not realise that he had broken his nose at Forfar, was obliged to drop out and give Davie Young, who had been a pillar of strength last season, his first taste of action.

He must have wished he was still in the reserves as his mates, previously unbeaten away from home, slumped to their second successive defeat. Although Dunfermline started well enough with Jenkins figuring well in the early action,

Action from the Pars' game against Forfar on October 4. (Ian Malcolm).

it was the home side which called the shots against a defence which looked none too solid. Near the half-hour mark, Clyde came desperately close on two occasions to opening the scoring and justice seemed to be done when, four minutes from half-time, Murphy sent a free kick round the defensive wall and into the net. Ironically, Leishman had earlier shown an interest in this forward. Minutes later, Watters could have killed the game if he had capitalised on a rare McCathie error.

After the interval, Dunfermline had another narrow escape before the introduction of the substitutes gave the large visiting support some hope. However, despite efforts from Watson and Ferguson, Dunfermline had to resign themselves to the loss of another two valuable points.

Jim Leishman, though bitterly disappointed, accepted the defeat philosophically. "We didn't seem to have any cohesion," he remarked. "It was more a number of individual contributions rather than a collective effort. We have to keep battling away and things will begin to happen."

CLYDE: Atkins, McFarlane, Napier, Tait, Flexney, McDowall, Murphy (Miller), Logan, Watters, Evans, Lloyd
Sub: Willock

DUNFERMLINE: Westwater, Forrest, Heddle (McCall), McCathie, Young, Donnelly, Bowie (Ferguson), Thompson, Watson, Hamilton, Jenkins

Referee: A. Ferguson, Giffnock
Attendance: 1,665

Airdrie	0	East Fife	3
Forfar	3	Dumbarton	5
Montrose	0	Kilmarnock	2
Morton	2	Brechin	3
Queen of South	1	Partick	1

	P	W	D	L	F	A	Pts
Dumbarton	14	9	1	4	27	17	19
DUNFERMLINE	14	8	3	3	20	12	19
Airdrie	14	7	4	3	20	15	18
Queen of South	14	5	7	2	21	18	17
Morton	14	7	2	5	30	22	16
East Fife	14	5	5	4	23	21	15

October 18 1986

DUNFERMLINE (1) 1   MORTON (1) 1
    Donnelly (29)   Clinging (21)

Midfielder John Donnelly leaves his Morton marker behind. (Dunfermline Press).

The return of captain Bobby Robertson at full back, his first appearance since August 20, helped to steady his team which desperately sought to return to the winning path against a side which was already the highest-scoring side in the Division. After being cautioned in the East Fife match earlier and spoken to in a reserve match later, Jim Leishman now found himself forced to watch the rest of the season from the tranquility of the Directors' Box.

Dunfermline found it difficult to break down a well organised defence which gave the high scoring partnership of last season – Watson and Jenkins – little chance to shine. Indeed, the whole forward line spent a most frustrating afternoon as attack after attack resulted in off-side decisions, though some were certainly dubious, and referee McGilvray found his ears ringing throughout.

Although Dunfermline opened the match well with Watson and Young both coming close, it was the visitors who surprisingly took an early lead when lapses in the home defence let Clinging in to slot the ball past Westwater. An error at the other end midway through the half, however, gave Donnelly an excellent opportunity to show how fine a striker of the ball he can be when he accepted a pass from McCathie and blasted a cracking shot past the Morton 'keeper.

In the second half Morton stepped up the pressure and looked the likelier side to grasp the winner had not Westwater pulled off several fine saves. However, as the minutes ticked away, McCathie ran on to a through ball and looked certain to score when the advancing 'keeper, noticing he was outside the box, cynically hauled him to the ground. **95**

A proud mascot leads out his team onto the park.

Bruce's booking for "a professional foul" was little consolation when a goal, or even a penalty kick, would have been a more just reward.

Neither manager was dissatisfied with the result, knowing full well that the day of reckoning could be postponed till a later date.

On a sadder note, as history would later demonstrate, this would be Jim Bowie's last first-team appearance for Dunfermline, the club he had joined in 1976.

DUNFERMLINE: Westwater, Robertson, Forrest, McCathie, Young, Donnelly, Thompson (Bowie), Morrison, Watson, McCall (Ferguson), Jenkins

Booking: Watson

MORTON: Bruce, O'Hara, Holmes, Hunter, Doak, Clinging, Robertson, Richardson, Alexander, Turner, McNeill
Subs: Coyle, Boag

Bookings: Hunter, Bruce

Referee: J.F. McGilvray, Edinburgh
Attendance: 3,741
Mascot: Graeme Inglis, 74 Scotland Dr.

Brechin	2	Queen of South	1
Dumbarton	2	Airdrie	1
East Fife	1	Clyde	1
Kilmarnock	3	Forfar	0
Partick	5	Montrose	0

	P	W	D	L	F	A	Pts
Dumbarton	15	10	1	4	29	18	21
DUNFERMLINE	15	8	4	3	21	13	20
Airdrie	15	7	4	4	21	17	18
Morton	15	7	3	5	31	23	17
Queen of South	15	5	7	3	22	20	17
East Fife	15	5	6	4	24	22	16

October 25 1986

DUNFERMLINE (1) 4   BRECHIN (0) 0
    Jenkins (6)
    Watson (46, 73)
    Ferguson (77)

The men from Glebe Park who lost four goals in the first league encounter with Dunfermline, obligingly conceded another four to give the Pars their first win in five outings. Brechin, who had ex-Ranger Gregor Stevens at the heart of their defence, lay second bottom in the table.

Centre half Davie Young kept his place while Reid struggled with a complication to his injury; young Gordon Connelly made his first appearance of the season in midfield and became the 22nd player that Leishman had used; midfielder Thompson and full back Robertson swapped roles while Eric Ferguson, whose early form had been bedevilled by injury and illness, was restored to the line-up. Leishman's tactical changes, not

Though Watson fails to connect with the ball, Eric Ferguson makes no mistake in scoring Dunfermline's fourth goal against Brechin. (Dunfermline Press.)

to mention his pre-match encouragement, paid off as Dunfermline ran out comfortable winners.

Though the visitors mounted the first serious attack, it was Dunfermline who opened the scoring in the sixth minute when Jenkins calmed everyone's nerves by crashing home a fine shot from 25 yards. Whilst the visitors did cause the odd moment of panic, Dunfermline were well in control and after the interval a quick goal from Watson, after ex-Par Perry gave the ball away, settled the issue.

Thereafter, the visitors, who had won four of their last five games, crumbled as an eager forward line tore into them. Further goals by Watson and Ferguson and a near miss by Man of the Match, Jenkins, capped a good night's work which was enough to send Dunfermline back to the top of the league.

"I thought we played some excellent stuff" enthused a delighted manager.

DUNFERMLINE: Westwater, Thompson, Forrest, McCathie, Young, Donnelly, Robertson, Connelly (McCall), Watson, Ferguson, Jenkins
Sub: Bowie

BRECHIN: Martin, Watt, Fleming (Lees), Brown, Stevens, Lyall, Lytwyn, Adam (Gallacher), Powell, Scott, Perry

Bookings: Lyall, Stevens

Referee: P. Hanley, Coatbridge
Attendance: 3,159
Mascot: James Penman, 28 Nith St.

Clyde	2	Forfar	3
East Fife	3	Queen of South	2
Kilmarnock	2	Airdrie	0
Montrose	1	Dumbarton	0
Morton	1	Partick	2

	P	W	D	L	F	A	Pts
DUNFERMLINE	16	9	4	3	25	13	22
Dumbarton	16	10	1	5	29	19	21
East Fife	16	6	6	4	27	24	18
Airdrie	16	7	4	5	21	18	18
Morton	16	7	3	6	32	25	17
Queen of South	16	5	7	4	24	23	17

Wednesday October 29 1986

PARTICK THISTLE   DUNFERMLINE (0) 1
   (0) 0   Watson (75)

The last time Dunfermline played Partick at Firhill was in September 1982 following the Glasgow club's relegation from the Premier League when a missed penalty by a certain Mo Johnston kept the score at 1-1. Of that Pars' team only Robertson, McCathie, Jenkins and (left

Popular full back, Bobby Forrest, in full-flight. (Dunfermline Press).

98

winger) Forrest turned out for this evening fixture. Dunfermline fielded the same formation which had demolished Brechin at the weekend against a side which had not lost in seven matches.

The game, watched by a crowd of just over 2,500, was marred by the torrential rain which had fallen during the day to leave the pitch resembling a quagmire. After 11 minutes Ferguson had the ball in the net, only for the referee to rule that he had fouled the 'keeper in kicking the ball out of his hands. Minutes later, Watson was unfortunate not to score at two attempts from Dunfermline's first corner.

As the second half wore on, the heavy pitch sapped the players' energies and the game, watched by Ken Bates, the Chelsea chairman who had bailed Thistle out financially, seemed to be heading for a draw. That is, until a brilliant move involving Robertson, Watson, Ferguson and Connelly ended up with Watson diving to score with a fine header. Mackie, Herd and West, on loan from sister club, Chelsea, all had good efforts but failed to convert their chances to goals and found Ian Westwater more than equal to anything they threw at him.

PARTICK: Brough, Spittal, Workman, Cairns, Carson, Watson, Law, Herd, West, Mackie, McDonald
Subs: Gallacher, Kelly
Booking: Herd

DUNFERMLINE: Westwater, Thompson, Forrest, McCathie, Young, Donnelly, Robertson, Connelly (Campbell), Watson, Ferguson, Jenkins
Sub: McCall

Referee: W.N. Crombie, Edinburgh
Attendance: 2,579

Airdrie	P	Clyde	P
Brechin	2	East Fife	2

			Dumbarton	2	Kilmarnock			0
			Forfar	3	Montrose			0
			Queen of South	0	Morton			2

	P	W	D	L	F	A	Pts
DUNFERMLINE	17	10	4	3	26	13	24
Dumbarton	17	11	1	5	31	19	23
Morton	17	8	3	6	34	25	19
East Fife	17	6	7	4	29	26	19
Airdrie	16	7	4	5	21	19	18
Forfar	17	6	6	5	29	29	18
Queen of South	17	5	7	5	24	25	17
Kilmarnock	17	6	4	7	26	22	16
Partick	17	4	6	7	19	23	14
Clyde	16	2	8	6	15	22	12
Montrose	17	3	5	9	16	30	11
Brechin	17	4	3	10	18	35	11

Norrie McCathie feels the full brunt of the Killie defence. Watson and Jenkins try to assist. (Dunfermline Press).

November 1 1986

DUNFERMLINE (1) 1   KILMARNOCK (0) 0
  Donnelly (pen. 31)

Dunfermline could feel well satisfied at recording a 'double' over an unlucky Ayrshire side whose poor finishing – and excellent goalkeeping from Westwater – prevented them from scoring. McCathie and Jenkins both made their 200th appearance for the team since joining the club in 1981.

The scoreline might have been different if first Harkness and then McGuire had not squandered good chances for the visitors in the opening minutes. Jenkins could have celebrated his notable anniversary in style if he had not blasted the ball over from 15 yards after good work from Watson and Ferguson in the 26th minute. Minutes later, however, Ferguson was bundled off the ball as he darted for the bye-line and from the resultant penalty, the first of the season for Dunfermline, the deadly John Donnelly made no mistake as he recorded his second, vital goal for his new club. It was also his 50th goal in senior football, his 17th from the spot.

Killie struck back with a vengeance and Westwater did extremely well with two fine one-handed saves to deny the visitors.

Early in the second half, play-maker Donnelly went off with a groin strain and Dunfermline struggled to mount attacks. Although Killie continued to play some good football, Dunfermline's commitment and drive won them the two points to dispel the gloom of the previous month. Westwater, who had now recorded his third successive shut-out, was correctly judged the Man of the Match by sponsors, Gray's Power Tools.

For Jim Leishman, the game marked the completion of three years at East End Park as manager. As he saw his side sit proudly at the top of the First Division, he could look back with no small measure of satisfaction at the transformation he had brought about.

Master of the penalty kick, John Donnelly, scores from the spot against Kilmarnock. (Enzo Mincella).

DUNFERMLINE: Westwater, Robertson, Forrest, McCathie, Young, Donnelly (Morrison), Thompson, Connelly, Watson, Ferguson, Jenkins (McCall)

KILMARNOCK: Holland, Miller, Robertson, Clark, Martin, Docherty (MacLeod), J. Clark (McConville), McLean, Harkness, McGivern, McGuire

Bookings: R. Clark, Docherty

Referee: W.P. Knowles, Inverurie
Attendance: 4,179
Mascot: Anne Shepherd, 20 Orwell Place

Brechin	3	Dumbarton	1
Montrose	0	Clyde	1
Morton	1	East Fife	1
Partick	2	Airdrie	0
Queen of South	2	Forfar	1

	P	W	D	L	F	A	Pts
DUNFERMLINE	18	11	4	3	27	13	26
Dumbarton	18	11	1	6	32	22	23
Morton	18	8	4	6	35	26	20
East Fife	18	6	8	4	30	27	20
Queen of South	18	6	7	5	26	26	19

Midweek

| Airdrie | 0 | Clyde | 2 |

November 8 1986

EAST FIFE (1) 2	DUNFERMLINE (0) 1
McCafferty (37)	Young (79)
Blair (64)	

Dunfermline travelled to Bayview for this important derby fixture with an unchanged team for the fourth successive time which meant a continued run for young midfielder Gordon Connelly. The visitors were seeking revenge for a 4-2 drubbing inflicted in August and were hoping to secure their first victory at Methil since season 1973-74. East Fife, fourth top in the league, could not afford to see the six-point gap widen any further.

On a bitterly cold November

Skipper Bobby Robertson showing that he is never one to shirk a tackle, against Kilmarnock, November 1. (Dunfermline Press).

afternoon, Bayview's largest crowd of the season was treated to an exciting, flowing game, full of end-to-end action. As early as the ninth minute Dunfermline suffered a set-back when full back Forrest had to withdraw after receiving a nasty hip injury, though the visitors have to look elsewhere for their excuses.

After 15 minutes goalkeeper Marshall had to act smartly to foil first Jenkins and then Morrison from opening the scoring: on the half-hour mark. Watson too was frustrated by a goalkeeper in excellent form. Against the run of play, however, seven minutes later, the smallest figure on the field, McCafferty, hit a swerving drive from 30 yards over the visitors' defence and into the net.

Although Dunfermline continued to play with composure and skill in the second half, a loose pass from Connelly in his own half found Blair who rushed on to the error and scored at his second **101** attempt. Mitchell should have made it number three, minutes later, but an excellent save by Westwater, celebrating his 23rd birthday, denied him.

Dunfermline received a richly deserved consolation goal in the 79th minute when McCathie's header for goal was only cleared off the line for Young to pick his spot. Westwater brought off two other magnificent saves but try as they might, his forwards failed to beat Marshall for a second time.

Though losing two points, Dunfermline remained at the top of the table with Dumbarton's home defeat of Morton putting them only one point behind. Former leaders Airdrie were now six points adrift.

EAST FIFE: Marshall, Connor, Conroy, Kirkwood, Inglis, Burgess, McNaughton (Hunter), Mitchell, Smith, McCafferty, Blair
Sub: Pitman

Bookings: McCafferty, Conroy

DUNFERMLINE: Westwater, Robertson, Forrest (Morrison), McCathie, Young, Donnelly, Thompson, Connelly (McCall), Watson, Ferguson, Jenkins

Booking: Watson

Referee: H. Gould, Markinch
Attendance: 3,843

Airdrie	3	Montrose	0
Clyde	3	Partick	3
Dumbarton	2	Morton	1
Forfar	0	Brechin	1
Kilmarnock	3	Queen of South	2

	P	W	D	L	F	A	Pts
DUNFERMLINE	19	11	4	4	28	15	26
Dumbarton	19	12	1	6	34	23	25
East Fife	19	7	8	4	32	28	22
Morton	19	8	4	7	36	28	20
Airdrie	19	8	4	7	24	23	20
Queen of South	19	6	7	6	28	29	19

November 15 1986

DUNFERMLINE (1) 2   QUEEN OF SOUTH
   Watson (90 secs)   (2) 2
   Ferguson (75)   Bryce (9, 20)

The absence of Bobby Forrest through injury allowed Ian Heddle back into the team and it was the young player who set up Dunfermline's opening goal. With the crowd still streaming in through the turnstiles, the full back raced into the penalty box and crossed for the ever alert John Watson to head home.

This early strike should have settled Dunfermline but it was the visitors who were pepped up by the set-back as their lively forwards took the game into Dunfermline's half. After only nine minutes Queens equalised through Bryce when his shot from inside the box slipped in under the 'keeper's body. Ten minutes later the centre forward struck again, this time connecting with a cross to fire a powerful header into the net. The same player almost scored his hat-trick on the half-hour mark when only quick intervention from Westwater denied him while the visitors' fast running forwards, Reid and Robertson, had a field day.

Queens started the second half in the same fashion and looked as though they might increase their lead although Heddle was desperately unlucky to see a fiercely struck free kick rebound off the bar. The introduction of the Dunfermline substitutes brought fresh legs, if not ideas, to the home attack and with the visitors beginning to wilt, the Pars snatched the equaliser. Morrison's corner kick was only partially cleared by goalkeeper Davidson as McCathie challenged him and the bouncing ball came off Ferguson's legs and into the net.

Grant Jenkins finding the tackling tougher in the First Division. Action from the game against Queen of the South. (Enzo Mincella).

Though either side might have grabbed the winner, the game ended in a draw, a result about which the home fans could hardly complain. For Jim Leishman, celebrating his 33rd birthday, though the performance must have aged him considerably, it was a point which still kept his side at the top of the division.

The Man of the Match award from Blyth and Blyth went to John Watson.

DUNFERMLINE: Westwater, Robertson, Heddle, McCathie, Young, Donnelly, Thompson, Connelly (Morrison), Watson, Ferguson, Jenkins (McCall)

Booking: Thompson

QUEEN OF SOUTH: Davidson, G. Robertson, Sim, Mills, Anderson, McBride, Reid, Cochrane (Maskrey), Bryce, Cloy, J. Robertson
Sub: Hetherington

Bookings: Cloy, Sim

Referee: D.D. Hope, Erskine
Attendance: 4,013
Mascot: Stewart Moyes, 34 Moncur St., Townhill

Dumbarton	1	Clyde	1
Forfar	3	Airdrie	1
Kilmarnock	0	Brechin	1
Montrose	0	Morton	3
Partick	3	East Fife	3

	P	W	D	L	F	A	Pts
DUNFERMLINE	20	11	5	4	30	17	27
Dumbarton	20	12	2	6	35	24	26
East Fife	20	7	9	4	35	31	23
Morton	20	9	4	7	39	28	22
Forfar	20	7	6	7	33	33	20

103

Centre half Davie Young beating his opponent, as usual, in the air. Eric Ferguson is behind him. (Dunfermline Press).

November 22 1986

AIRDRIE (2) 3   DUNFERMLINE (0) 0
Flood (14, 43)
McCabe (71)

When Airdrie had visited East End in September they sat confidently at the top of the league; only two months on, a series of poor results had sunk them to seventh position, seven points behind the Pars. With Forrest restored to the team after making an amazingly quick recovery, Dunfermline fielded a strong team to deal with opponents who had only won one of their last seven games.

It was an outing which Dunfermline will want to forget, suffering their worst defeat of the whole season. While Dunfermline could manufacture only one real chance, the home side rattled in three goals and missed as many. Without doubt, the atrocious weather and playing surface killed the game off as a spectacle and made good, flowing football a rarity but it has to be said that Airdrie adapted better to the conditions.

The Diamonds made excellent use of the strong wind in their backs in the first half and knocked in two goals from the aptly named Flood before half-time. Dunfermline managed only one clear-cut chance at goal after good build-up work from Ferguson, Morrison and McCathie. Dunfermline found it difficult to clear their lines when goal kicks by

A break from training: W. Irvine, B. Robertson, D. Young, S. Morrison, I. Westwater, N. McCathie, B. Forrest.

Westwater, still not fully recovered from his groin strain, struggled to go anywhere near the centre circle.

Although the Pars had the benefit of the wind in the second half, the game was beyond them as a confident Lanarkshire side contained the sporadic attacks which were mounted. McCabe squandered two excellent chances to kill the game before finally beating Westy to let the disgruntled visiting supporters leave much earlier than they would otherwise have anticipated.

Rivals East Fife and Dumbarton could only share the points in their game but the single point was enough to allow the 'Sons to leap-frog back into pole position.

AIRDRIE: Martin, McEwan, Black, McCormack (Walker), Lawrie, Lindsay, Hughes, Docherty, McCabe, Templeton (Marshall), Flood

Bookings: McCormack, Lawrie

DUNFERMLINE: Westwater, Robertson, Forrest, McCathie, Young, Donnelly, Thompson, Morrison, Watson, Ferguson (Connelly), Jenkins (Smith)

Referee: A.M. Roy, Aberdeen
Attendance: 1,800

Brechin	0	Partick	1
Clyde	0	Kilmarnock	0
East Fife	0	Dumbarton	0
Morton	0	Forfar	0
Queen of South	1	Montrose	0

	P	W	D	L	F	A	Pts
Dumbarton	21	12	3	6	35	24	27
DUNFERMLINE	21	11	5	5	30	20	27
East Fife	21	7	10	4	35	31	24
Morton	21	9	5	7	39	28	23
Airdrie	21	9	4	8	28	26	22
Queen of South	21	7	8	6	31	31	22

November 29 1986

MONTROSE (0) 0   DUNFERMLINE (1) 2
Watson (42)
Hamilton (70)

To complete the first round of return fixtures, Dunfermline went to Montrose, the team they had already beaten 1-0 at home in September. While the Pars lay joint top of the table, the Angus club lay at the foot of the table, six points adrift of the second bottom club.

After last week's drubbing, Leishman left out one of his three strikers, the injured Ferguson, and brought in left winger Ian McCall to give the attack more width. Rowan Hamilton was drafted into the midfield, with Gary Thompson relegated to the substitutes' bench for the first time. Although the revamped team did not produce one of their better performances against a determined home side, the Pars did enough to wrap up the two points.

Montrose had much of the play in the first half with winger McDonald in particular in fine form and their attacks outnumbered the visitors'. The home side could consider themselves rather unlucky to be a goal down at half-time. In the 42nd minute, Jenkins and Watson combined well outside the box to enable the red-haired striker to shoot low and hard under Charles. Minutes later Montrose might have equalised if they has capitalized on a poor pass-back from centre half Young who called on his keeper to make a good save.

After a lambasting from a disgruntled manager at the interval, the Pars at last began to assert themselves as league leaders, with Donnelly especially making his mark. They were aided in no small way by Montrose full back Wright who

cut down the galloping Morrison in full flight and was duly ordered off for his second booking. Soon afterwards, with the Montrose defence in disarray, Hamilton picked up a quickly taken free-kick, ran right through the defence and beat the goalkeeper at the second attempt.

This victory, the 12th of the season, was one more than the best total Dunfermline had ever recorded in a whole season, previously 1979-80, in the new First Division.

With Dumbarton dropping a point at home, Dunfermline's hard earned victory put them one point clear at the top as the competition now reached its half-way mark. Who would have dreamed of that situation at the beginning of the campaign?

MONTROSE: Charles, Wright, McLelland, Brown, Sheran, Wallace, Allan, Lyons, Paterson (Murray), Duffy (Forbes), McDonald

Booking: Allan
Wright sent off

DUNFERMLINE: Westwater, Robertson, Forrest, McCathie, Young, Donnelly, Hamilton (Thompson), Morrison, Watson, McCall, Jenkins (Smith)

Referee: K.F. O'Donnell, Airdrie
Attendance: 1,200

Airdrie	1	Morton	2
Clyde	4	Brechin	1
Dumbarton	1	Queen of South	1
Forfar	1	East Fife	1
Kilmarnock	3	Partick	2

	P	W	D	L	F	A	Pts
DUNFERMLINE	22	12	5	5	32	20	29
Dumbarton	22	12	4	6	36	25	28
Morton	22	10	5	7	41	29	25
East Fife	22	7	11	4	36	32	25
Queen of South	22	7	9	6	32	32	23
Airdrie	22	9	4	9	29	28	22
Forfar	22	7	8	7	34	34	22
Kilmarnock	22	8	5	9	32	28	21
Clyde	22	5	11	6	26	27	21
Partick	22	6	8	8	30	32	20

December 6 1986

DUNFERMLINE (0) 2   FORFAR (0) 0
Watson (65)
Morrison (88)

Having already taken three points out of four from the Sky Blues, Dunfermline added another two as a result of a powerful second half performance when the league leaders showed something like true form.

Both goalkeepers were in the thick of the action in the first half and it was largely their fine efforts — and poor quality finishing — which kept the scoreline blank at half-time. Bennett and MacDonald both came close for the Loons while strikers Jenkins and Watson should have done better for Dunfermline on numerous occasions.

Early in the second half, Forfar belied their middle-of-the-table position by coming dangerously close on two occasions. With the fans becoming increasingly frustrated it was left to the darling of the crowd, John Watson, to spare his side's blushes. In the 65th minute, Hamilton touched on a Morrison cross and there was the striker in the six-yard box to nod home the opening goal.

Despite their lead, Dunfermline continued to live dangerously and were lucky not to concede a penalty when Hamill was uprooted in the box. Westwater was called upon again to make two excellent saves from eager forwards searching for the equaliser. In the dying minutes, however, substitute Ferguson capitalised on hesitation in the visiting defence and ran down the wing away from his markers. His perfect cross was met superbly by Morrison who gave Kennedy absolutely no chance with a tremendous shot from 20 yards.

Morrison, in fact, was probably the

One of the new full-timers, Stevie Morrison, trying to train in the snow. (Dunfermline Press).

best player on the park and showed how much he was thriving on full-time training. He received the Man of the Match award for his outstanding contribution. For Ian Westwater this was his 12th shut-out of the season, a figure which only Billy Thompson of Dundee United could better.

107

DUNFERMLINE: Westwater, Robertson, Forrest, McCathie, Young, Donnelly, Hamilton, Morrison, Watson, McCall (Ferguson), Jenkins (Thompson)

FORFAR: Kennedy, Lorimer, McPhee, Morris, Smith, Hamill, Ward, Bennett, Clark, Bell (Cormack), MacDonald
Sub: Brewster

Bookings: Lorimer, Smith

Referee: D. Syme, Rutherglen
Attendance: 3,353
Mascot: Barry Duffy, 61 Gilfillan Rd.

Brechin	2	Montrose	3
East Fife	2	Kilmarnock	1
Morton	3	Clyde	2
Partick	0	Dumbarton	2
Queen of South	0	Airdrie	1

	P	W	D	L	F	A	Pts
DUNFERMLINE	23	13	5	5	34	20	31
Dumbarton	23	13	4	6	38	25	30
Morton	23	11	5	7	44	31	27
East Fife	23	8	11	4	38	33	27
Airdrie	23	10	4	9	30	28	24
Queen of South	23	7	9	7	32	33	23

December 13 1986

DUMBARTON (1) 1   DUNFERMLINE (1) 2
Houston (41)   McCall (9)
                        McCathie (81)

There was no doubting the importance of this fixture at Boghead. For several months the two combatants had jostled for top spot and with Dunfermline just one point ahead it was vital for the home side to prevent the gap from widening. Although both managers played down the game as a "make-or-break" contest, hindsight would prove that this indeed would be a 'crunch' game, a real 'four-pointer.' A confident Dunfermline remained unchanged from the previous week, remembering that they had been the only team to win at Boghead.

With both teams playing a 4-3-3 system, the 4,000 fans were treated to a "match of endless excitement and incidents, fast, vigorous, earnest,

unpolished, occasionally feverish, never vindictive" as the *Sunday Times* correspondent put it. The media were also represented by John Greig and David Francey who covered the second half live for Radio Scotland and who were most impressed by what the two candidates for promotion had to offer.

Dumbarton's big defenders, McCahill and Coyle, were less than sophisticated and time and again Watson's head flicks had them spinning. His diving header after seven minutes went very close and two minutes later another header moved a free kick on to Jenkins, whose quick pass to McCall left him clear to shoot home. The 'Sons came back into the game, never losing their spirit, and were rewarded near half-time when a 20-yard shot from Houston was deflected enough to lob over Westwater and into the net.

Dumbarton continued well after the interval and only the exceptional skills of Westwater denied Coyle, Rooney and Houston. Dunfermline's substitutes helped turn the game for them and they climaxed a superb afternoon with a winner nine minutes from time. 'Keeper Arthur mispunched a Morrison free kick from the right and McCathie rose above everyone to head in from close range to give Dumbarton their first defeat in five games.

With Morton losing at Rugby Park, the Pars now had a comfortable lead at the top of the table.

DUMBARTON: Arthur, Kay, Traynor, Martin (Docherty), McCahill, T. Coyle, McGowan, Rooney, Houston, McCoy, O. Coyle (Grant)

DUNFERMLINE: Westwater, Robertson, Forrest, McCathie, Young, Donnelly, Hamilton (Thompson), Morrison, Watson, McCall (Ferguson), Jenkins

Referee: K. O'Donnell, Airdrie
Attendance: 4,000

Airdrie	3	Brechin	1
Clyde	2	Queen of South	1
Forfar	1	Partick	2
Kilmarnock	2	Morton	0
Montrose	2	East Fife	1

	P	W	D	L	F	A	Pts
DUNFERMLINE	24	14	5	5	36	21	33
Dumbarton	24	13	4	7	39	27	30
Morton	24	11	5	8	44	33	27
East Fife	24	8	11	5	39	35	27
Airdrie	24	11	4	9	33	29	26
Kilmarnock	24	9	5	10	35	30	23

December 20 1986

Brechin	1	Morton	3
Dumbarton	0	Forfar	1
Dunfermline	P	Clyde	P
East Fife	0	Airdrie	0
Kilmarnock	1	Montrose	0
Partick	P	Queen of South	P

December 27 1986

MORTON (2) 2	DUNFERMLINE (1) 2
Cowie (31)	McCall (43)
McNeil (45)	McCathie (89)

Bad weather before Christmas prevented Dunfermline from fulfilling their fixture against Clyde which allowed the host side to close the gap by two points by winning at Glebe Park. Dunfermline were without Watson, suspended for two games, but were able to dip into their strong pool to find Eric Ferguson to replace him. Two players certainly not considered were local lad, Ian Heddle, who was transferred to St Johnstone before Christmas to allow him to play first-team football and recent signing, John Waddell, who was given a free transfer.

The Cappielow side had yet to beat the Pars this season and a most commendable performance by the Fifers kept it like that, with a draw very much to the liking of Jim Leishman. Dunfermline began the game well with McCathie and Donnelly both coming close. McNeil at the other end was only prevented from scoring by a magnificent, diving save from Westwater. Jackie McNamara had to draw on his considerable experience to

Limbering up under the floodlights during a training session are E. Ferguson, B. Forrest, G. Reid and R. Hamilton.

109

stop McCall from opening the scoring.

It was Morton, however, who took the lead first. On the half-hour mark a nod down from the division's top scorer, Rowan Alexander, found Cowie, on loan from Hearts, who bundled the ball over the line. Dunfermline fought back and following good dribbling from Thompson, McCall grabbed on to a rebound from Wylie in the 43rd minute to level the score. While the Pars were still congratulating themselves, a free kick from 20 yards out from McNeil deceived Westwater and ended up in the net. There was no time to centre the ball.

The visitors put the Morton goal under considerable pressure in the second half and disappointingly shot wide on two occasions. After a tremendous save by Wylie in the 75th minute, Morton found themselves a man down when Doak received his marching orders for a foul on Ferguson. It looked as though the 10 men were going to hang on to record a famous victory but they had not reckoned on the versatility of Dunfermline's central defender, Norrie McCathie. In the dying seconds, after Jenkins had squandered a good chance to equalise by shooting straight at the 'keeper, McCathie latched on to a rebound from the bar and headed home a glorious equaliser.

Dunfermline's Christmas present had come late, but it was well worth waiting for.

MORTON: Wylie, Cowie, Holmes, Hunter, Doak, McNamara, Robertson, O'Hara, Alexander, McNeil (Turner), Clinging
Sub: Boag

Booking: O'Hara
Doak sent off

110

DUNFERMLINE: Westwater, Robertson, Forrest, McCathie, Young, Donnelly, Morrison, Thompson, Ferguson, McCall (Campbell), Jenkins
Sub: Hamilton

Bookings: Forrest, Thompson, Morrison

Referee: D.D. Hope, Erskine
Attendance: 3,200

Airdrie	1	Dumbarton	0
Clyde	0	East Fife	1
Forfar	1	Kilmarnock	1
Montrose	0	Partick	0
Queen of South	2	Brechin	0

	P	W	D	L	F	A	Pts
DUNFERMLINE	25	14	6	5	38	23	34
Morton	26	12	6	8	49	36	30
Dumbarton	26	13	4	9	39	29	30
East Fife	26	9	12	5	40	35	30
Airdrie	26	12	5	9	34	29	29
Kilmarnock	26	10	6	10	37	31	26

January 1 1987

DUNFERMLINE (1) 1   EAST FIFE (0) 1
   Jenkins (28)   Jenkins (o.g. 49)

The opening of the New Year brought a great deal of promise and hope to East End – as well as enough rainwater to have filled the Carnegie Pool several times over! East Fife, lying joint second just four points behind, were determined to maintain their excellent record over their rivals.

It was a game which many referees would never have contemplated starting, so swamped was the playing surface, but go ahead it did and, amazingly, the 5,000 crowd were treated to a far more entertaining game than they had any right to expect. In scenes more reminiscent of the recent pantomime in Carnegie Hall, both sides battled out a 1-1 draw in sub-zero temperatures amidst driving snow and rain. On the terracing side, massive puddles made football a farce with the ball often stuck unceremoniously in the mud as the

Grant Jenkins opens the scoring against East Fife in the Ne'erday fixture. This was his 50th goal for Dunfermline. (Dunfermline Press).

players ran past it. It was little wonder that John Donnelly went down with hypothermia at half-time and that Bobby Forrest almost followed him. The players re-appeared after the break wearing two strips to keep out the cold!

It would have been a cruel blow for either side to have lost such a contest though Dunfermline could consider themselves unlucky not to win, especially as it took an own goal from Jenkins to bring the visitors back into the game.

It was the bearded striker who had put his side ahead after 28 minutes when he accepted a clever back-heeler from Donnelly, put the ball through a defender's legs and then rammed the ball home to score his 50th goal with the Pars. Immediately after the interval, the same striker should have sewn up the points when a mis-kick from the opposing defence let him through but the ball stuck in the mud, giving Marshall time to block the shot. Three minutes later, he was once again the victim of the quagmire when he turned the ball into his own net.

Elsewhere, Morton trounced Dumbarton 4-1 which not only set back **111**

Hunter of East Fife challenges McCathie (Dunfermline Press).

their challenge but confirmed the Cappielow side as major contenders for promotion.

DUNFERMLINE: Westwater, Robertson, Forrest, McCathie, Young, Donnelly (Hamilton), Thompson, Morrison, Ferguson, McCall, Jenkins
Sub: Campbell

Bookings: McCathie, Thompson, Westwater, Ferguson

EAST FIFE: Marshall, Conroy, Connor (McLaren), McCafferty, Halley, Burgess, Perry (Stead), Kirkwood, Hunter, Mitchell, Blair

Bookings: Perry, Burgess, McCafferty

Referee: D.T. McVicar, Carluke
Attendance: 4,956
Mascot: Alan Partick, 8 St. Peter's Port, Inverkeithing

Brechin	1	Forfar	1
Montrose	0	Airdrie	1
Morton	4	Dumbarton	1
Partick	P	Clyde	P
Queen of South	1	Kilmarnock	2

	P	W	D	L	F	A	Pts
DUNFERMLINE	26	14	7	5	39	24	35
Morton	27	13	6	8	53	37	32
Airdrie	27	13	5	9	35	29	31
East Fife	27	9	13	5	41	36	31
Dumbarton	27	13	4	10	40	33	30
Kilmarnock	27	11	6	10	39	32	28
Forfar	27	8	10	9	38	40	26
Queen of South	26	8	9	9	36	37	25
Clyde	25	6	11	8	30	32	23
Partick	25	7	9	9	32	35	23
Brechin	27	7	4	16	29	53	18
Montrose	27	5	6	16	21	45	16

January 3 1987

KILMARNOCK (0) 2
McGuire (48),
Reid (89)

DUNFERMLINE (1) 2
Donnelly (pen. 26),
Ferguson (88)

Three days later, Dunfermline were Kilmarnock's first-foots at Rugby Park, hoping to complete a hat-trick of wins over the Ayrshire club. Killie's promotion hopes had taken a bruising in recent weeks and the break of the ball against the Pars suggested that their luck was still out. For Bobby Forrest, this was his 200th appearance for the club since joining in 1981.

The game, watched by a large holiday crowd of almost 5,000, was fairly evenly balanced until the 26th minute when referee Paterson judged that Cockburn's challenge on Morrison in the box was unfair. Penalty claims have been rejected for more blatant fouls, but John Donnelly put these thoughts from his mind as he expertly converted the award. Immediately afterwards, central defender Paul Martin and John Watson clashed going for a high ball. The forward fell on his back and was apparently kicked in the face by Martin whom the referee promptly ordered off. Just before the interval, Morrison should have killed off the home side but his teed-up volley screamed over the bar.

In the second half, the 10 men rallied and took the game to Dunfermline. In 48 minutes they got back on level terms when McGuire thundered home a volley following a nod-down from a free-kick. Killie held on grimly and, indeed, with a bit of luck, might have scored five minutes from time if substitute Reid had not headed over.

The fans, however, were to be treated to a grandstand finish. In 88 minutes, Ferguson received a lovely chip from Thompson, beat two defenders and the 'keeper, before side-footing home what looked like a glorious winner. While the visiting fans were still celebrating, newcomer Reid, playing in his first home game, had better fortune when the ball rebounded nicely for him to pivot round and slam home the equaliser past Westwater.

KILMARNOCK: McCulloch, G. Millar, Cockburn, Clark, Martin, McVeigh, McLean, Cook (Reid), Harkness, McGuire (Cuthbertson), Bryson

Bookings: Cockburn, Bryson. Martin sent off

DUNFERMLINE: Westwater, Robertson, Forrest, McCathie, Young, Donnelly, Thompson (Hamilton), Morrison, Ferguson, Watson (McCall), Jenkins

Booking: Watson

Referee: R.W. Paterson, Neilston
Attendance: 4,900

Airdrie	1	Partick					0
Clyde	P	Montrose					P
Dumbarton	P	Brechin					P
East Fife	P	Morton					P
Forfar	1	Queen of South					1

	P	W	D	L	F	A	Pts
DUNFERMLINE	27	14	8	5	41	26	36
Airdrie	28	14	5	9	36	29	33
Morton	27	13	6	8	53	37	32
East Fife	27	9	13	5	41	36	31
Dumbarton	27	13	4	10	40	33	30
Kilmarnock	28	11	7	10	41	34	29

Always a tense moment for the players as they come down the steps from the dressing room.

Midweek

East Fife	2	Morton	1

January 10 1987

Airdrie	P	Kilmarnock	P
Brechin	P	Dunfermline	P
Dumbarton	P	Montrose	P
Forfar	P	Clyde	P
Partick	P	Morton	P
Queen of South	P	East Fife	P

January 17 1987

Clyde	P	Airdrie	P
Dunfermline	P	Partick	P
East Fife	P	Brechin	P
Kilmarnock	P	Dumbarton	P
Montrose	P	Forfar	P
Morton	2	Queen of South	0

January 24 1987

QUEEN OF SOUTH   DUNFERMLINE (1) 2
 (0) 1   Ferguson (10)
 Bryce (48)   Jenkins (46)

Following the snowy bout of Arctic **113**

A big day out for many young fans at Easter Road. (Dunfermline Press).

weather in mid-January, this was Dunfermline's first game for three weeks during which Jim Leishman had frantically tried to organise match practice in indoor games halls. Queen of the South, who had enjoyed the benefit of a match the previous week, had slumped well down the table but Leishman was still paying them the utmost of respect now that promotion seemed more than the pipe dream it had once been.

A late call-off from an injured Forrest allowed Grant Reid back into the side for

the first time since October 8, in the unaccustomed role of left back. Gary Thompson was just beginning a four-match suspension and his role was taken over by Hamilton. Davie Young was making his 200th appearance since joining in 1984.

Dunfermline, despite their enforced lay-off, opened well and Ferguson in particular had two good scoring chances before he finally found the net in the 10th minute following a nod-on from McCathie from a Donnelly corner. The visitors continued to threaten the home defence with Jenkins and McCathie the main architects of danger.

Just after the break, a refreshed Dunfermline came out and scored another goal. Jenkins accepted a pass from Hamilton and drove an unstoppable shot from outside the box into the top left-hand corner of Davidson's goal. Almost immediately Queen's replied with a similar goal. Bryce, their top scorer for the past two seasons, smacked a powerful left-foot shot into the visitors' net. The home side pressed for the equaliser and Westwater did well to save from Maskrey, Mills and Robertson although Dunfermline also had opportunities through Morrison and Ferguson to extend their lead; indeed a more match-fit Fife side might have converted at least one of these chances.

Dunfermline held on to record their first victory since December 13 to give the side a great tonic for the forthcoming Scottish Cup-tie against Hibs.

QUEEN OF SOUTH: Davidson, G. Robertson, Sim, Hetherington, Mills, McIntyre, Reid, Maskrey, Bryce, Cloy (Telfer), J. Robertson

Booking: Sim

A small section of the dedicated crowd of 5,000 Pars fans who went to cheer on their side against Hibs in the Scottish Cup-tie. (Dunfermline Press).

DUNFERMLINE: Westwater, Robertson, Reid, McCathie, Young, Donnelly, Hamilton, Morrison, Watson (McCall), Ferguson, Jenkins.
Sub: Smith
Booking: Young

Referee: J. Duncan, Gorebridge
Attendance: 2,900

Airdrie	p	Forfar	P
Brechin	P	Kilmarnock	P
Clyde	1	Dumbarton	2
East Fife	1	Partick	1
Morton	6	Montrose	1
Kilmarnock	0	Airdrie	0

	P	W	D	L	F	A	Pts
DUNFERMLINE	28	15	8	5	43	27	38
Morton	30	15	6	9	62	40	36
Airdrie	29	14	6	9	36	29	34
East Fife	29	10	14	5	44	38	34
Dumbarton	28	14	4	10	42	34	32
Kilmarnock	29	11	8	10	41	34	30

Midweek

East Fife	2	Brechin	2
Kilmarnock	1	Dumbarton	2
Partick	3	Queen of South	0

January 31 1987

HIBS (1) 2   DUNFERMLINE (0) 0
  Weir (42), Kane (82)

Though Dunfermline had to look back to the semi-final tie at Tynecastle in 1965 to find their last victory over Hibs in the Scottish Cup – the ties in 1976, 1979, 1981 and 1986 all eventually being lost – the Fifers this time went as leaders of the First Division and with an ever growing confidence. Hibs for their part were but pale shadows of their former selves and had not enjoyed the best of seasons. John Blackley had recently resigned and his successor, Alex Miller, was still in the process of re-building the morale of the Edinburgh club.

Ironically, it was Miller's St. Mirren which had earlier eliminated Dunfermline from the Skol Cup. By chance, Leishman had watched Hibs during one of his blank Saturdays and had singled out, with remarkable **115**

A fine example of the aerial power of John Watson. (Dunfermline Press).

foresight, new signing Dougie Bell and diminutive Micky Weir as the danger men. He was equally aware of the talents of Roughie, Steve Cowan, Joe McBride, George McCluskey and Paul Kane. Saying grace at a Burns Supper a few days earlier, Leishman beseeched:

"Oh Lord, I'll tell ye nae' mair fibs
If ye'll only let me beat the Hibs"

Thanks to undersoil heating at Easter Road, this was one tie which was assured of beating the weather and over 5,000 Fifers, whether by coach, special train or car, made the short trip on a beautifully sunny afternoon. Archie McPherson and the B.B.C. cameras were also there to put the Premier League pretenders under the microscope.

Hibs, on a hiding to nothing, began in lively fashion with Bell and Weir combining well on the right wing and only poor finishing and good defensive work from Dunfermline kept the scoreline blank. The Pars, suffering either stage-fright or still lacking in match practice, found it difficult to make openings against the side from the top division although Ferguson came the closest with an acrobatic kick which Rough, looking less than fully fit after his lay-off, did well to push over.

When it seemed as though the visitors might hold out for a well earned breather, they needlessly conceded a corner. The ball broke to Weir who coolly drove it past the unsighted Westwater. The Pars were then unfortunate not to have a penalty when Jenkins was pushed to the ground before the interval.

Grant Reid came on in place of the injured Robertson and Dunfermline stepped up a gear in the second half, as they had to. Davie Young came close, forcing Rough to make a brave save on the ground after he had initially dropped

Centre forward Watson again in the thick of the action at Easter Road. (Dunfermline Press).

It's that man Watson again. The Hibs' defence found him a handful. (Dunfermline Press).

the ball. Unfortunately, the boot of the on-rushing Ferguson caught him on the head (for which he was booked) and for the rest of the match the internationalist looked partially concussed. Tactically, Dunfermline should have bombarded him from long range but the Hibs' defence manfully protected him as the minutes ticked away.

While Dunfermline were pressing forward, a defensive blunder presented Hibs with the decisive goal eight minutes from time. Forrest was woefully short with his pass-back and Kane punished it to the full, lobbing it over the stranded Westwater. To complete Dunfermline's misery, Ferguson was stretchered off near the end.

As the T.V. recording illustrated, Dunfermline were not disgraced,

perhaps only outclassed. Even an ordinary Premier League side, with the benefit of full-time training and the experience of big crowds, could make life uncomfortable for aspiring candidates from a lower division. As Alex Miller said, "The only real difference between the teams was that we took two of the chances we created and Dunfermline didn't take any."

HIBS: Rough, Hunter, Mitchell, Bell, Rae, McIntyre, Weir, Kane, Cowan, Collins (May), McBride (Tortolano)

Bookings: Cowan, McIntyre

DUNFERMLINE: Westwater, Robertson (Reid), Forrest, McCathie, Young, Donnelly, Hamilton (McCall), Morrison, Watson, Ferguson, Jenkins

Bookings: Young, Ferguson

Referee: I.R. Cathcart, Bridge of Allan
Attendance: 16,500
Mascot: Alan Hunter, 2 Broomhead Park

117

February 7 1987

DUNFERMLINE (1) 1   AIRDRIE (0) 1
   Donnelly (45)   Lindsay (75)

The Easter Road tie was quickly forgotten about as Dunfermline, with three successive matches at home, took on a much improved Airdrie who had hauled themselves back to within four points of the leaders. The fans were boosted by the news that winger Billy Mackay (26), whose career at Ibrox had been shattered when he sustained a damaging knee injury, had been signed on a month's loan from Hearts with the option of buying him thereafter.

Having taken Dundee United to a replay in the Scottish Cup and having inflicted a 3-0 defeat on the Pars earlier, Airdrie received the full respect of the Dunfermline squad. Eric Ferguson had recovered sufficiently well from last week's injury to start the game. Grant Reid continued to deputise, however, for Robertson.

The young fans certainly enjoyed the match. Before the kick-off, match sponsors Riley's Crisps gave away 1,500 free packets. The first half was full of end-to-end play, reminiscent of a cup-tie. Morrison almost put Dunfermline ahead after two minutes while at the other end Reid had to clear off his own goal line. Watson and Morrison both had good chances as had Templeton for the visitors. With half-time approaching, it was Dunfermline who made the vital breakthrough. In a goalmouth mêlée, 'keeper Martin could only push a diving header from Ferguson against the bar and the clearance fell neatly to Donnelly, 18 yards out, who cleanly struck the ball home.

After the break, Dunfermline looked very comfortable and Watson and substitute McCall both narrowly missed. Then, much to the crowd's delight, Leishman sent on Mackay to show an expectant crowd what he could do. The darting winger certainly showed quick acceleration down the right flank but his debut will unfortunately be remembered for a hesitant pass-back 15 minutes from time which let in Lindsay to accept the gift and lob Westwater to give Airdrie a point which they never looked like acquiring.

John Watson, who put in a tremendous performance, especially in the air, was selected as Man of the Match — for a crisp display?

DUNFERMLINE: Westwater, Reid, Forrest, McCathie, Young, Donnelly, Hamilton, Morrison, Watson, Ferguson (MacKay), Jenkins (McCall)

Booking: Reid

AIRDRIE: Martin, McKeown, Lindsay, McCormack, Lawrie, O'Neill, Walker, Moore, Templeton, McCabe (Reilly), Flood

Booking: McKeown

Referee: D Miller, Garrowhill
Attendance: 4,272
Mascot: Ian Barber 77 Leadside Cr, Wellwood

Dumbarton	1	East Fife				1
Forfar	3	Morton				3
Kilmarnock	1	Clyde				1
Montrose	3	Queen of South				0
Partick	0	Brechin				0

	P	W	D	L	F	A	Pts
DUNFERMLINE	29	15	9	5	44	28	39
Morton	31	15	7	9	65	43	37
East Fife	31	10	16	5	47	41	36
Dumbarton	30	15	5	10	45	36	35
Airdrie	30	14	7	9	37	30	35
Kilmarnock	31	11	9	11	43	37	31
Forfar	29	8	12	9	42	44	28
Partick	29	8	11	10	36	37	27
Queen of South	31	8	10	13	38	48	26
Clyde	27	6	12	9	32	35	24
Brechin	29	7	6	16	31	55	20
Montrose	29	6	6	17	25	51	18

John Watson's clever flick troubles the Airdrie defence. (Dunfermline Press).

Tuesday February 10 1987
DUNFERMLINE (1) 2   CLYDE (0) 0
   Ferguson (14)
   Donnelly (pen. 55)

Though Dunfermline were consoled by the fact that rivals Morton, Dumbarton and East Fife had all dropped a point on Saturday, they were in determined mood not to slip up against the team which lay third bottom and which had beaten them in October.

Clyde must have departed thinking it might have been better to have played this match on its original date, December 20, because nothing went right for them on the night. Playing on a rain-soaked surface and before a large, partisan crowd, Clyde were never allowed to settle and as early as the 14th minute found themselves a goal behind.

Left back Reid dispossessed McGlashan and sent a harmless ball up field. The Clyde defence casually turned the ball back to their 'keeper, not allowing for the quick thinking Watson to latch on to it. Though his shot was blocked by Atkins, Ferguson was on hand to net the rebound.

The visitors' defence fell apart as first Tait limped off injured and then Flexney was twice booked and then sent off. George Smith ruled the game with an iron fist, not tolerating the least sign of dissent or foul play, which was one reason why long-throw expert, Reid, booked once, was brought off to give Mackay another run.

Thus handicapped, Clyde withdrew their embattled troops to defend their own half, allowing Dunfermline plenty of **119** scope. It was, however, another defensive error which gifted the Pars their second goal in the 55th minute. Forrest collected the ball when Atkins dropped it and hovered harmlessly over it near the bye-line. Docherty needlessly scythed him down and Donnelly converted clinically once more from the resultant spot kick. Watson and Ferguson might have added number three near the end but for poor finishing and good goalkeeping. Shots from Millar and McGlashan for the visitors reminded Dunfermline that they were not a spent force.

Leishman was well pleased with the two points which kept Dunfermline at the top and extended their unbeaten run to nine games.

DUNFERMLINE: Westwater, Reid (MacKay), Forrest, McCathie, Young, Donnelly, Hamilton (McCall), Morrison, Watson, Ferguson, Jenkins

Bookings: Reid

CLYDE: Atkins, McFarlane, Napier, Tait, Flexney, McDowall, Murphy, Docherty, McGlashan, Millar, Willock.
Subs: Watters, Logan. Sent off: Flexney

Referee: G.B. Smith, Edinburgh
Attendance: 3,489
Mascot: Jordan Richards, 41 Davaar Dr, Kirkcaldy

Montrose	0	Forfar			1
Partick	0	Morton			1

	P	W	D	L	F	A	Pts
DUNFERMLINE	30	16	5	9	46	28	41
Morton	32	16	9	7	66	43	39
DUNFERMLINE	31	10	5	16	47	41	36
Dumbarton	30	15	10	5	45	36	35
Airdrie	30	14	9	7	37	30	35
Killie	31	11	11	9	43	37	31

February 14 1987

Brechin	0	Clyde	1
Dunfermline	P	Montrose	P
East Fife	0	Forfar	0
Morton	2	Airdrie	1
Partick	P	Kilmarnock	P
Queen of South	0	Dumbarton	1

	P	W	D	L	F	A	Pts
Morton	33	17	7	9	68	44	41
DUNFERMLINE	30	16	9	5	46	28	41
Dumbarton	31	16	5	10	46	36	37
East Fife	32	10	17	5	47	41	37
Airdrie	31	14	7	10	38	32	35
Kilmarnock	31	11	9	11	43	37	31

February 21 1987

DUNFERMLINE (1) 2   PARTICK THISTLE (1) 1
Ferguson (25)   Donnelly (o.g. 40)
McCall (75)

Dunfermline's home game against Montrose on February 14 was surprisingly called off because of a frosty pitch. Morton's home game against Airdrie went ahead and by winning 2-1, the Greenock side went to the top of the league on goal difference and with three more games played.

With February 21 reserved for cup action, Dunfermline played their postponed fixture against Partick Thistle. Bobby Robertson, fully recovered from injury, was recalled to the side as was Gary Thompson, his suspension over. There was still no place for the errant Moyes, who was now back in training after absenting himself from the club for several months.

Dunfermline won both points but made heavy weather of it. It would have been a tragedy if the Pars had dented their promotion hopes by dropping a point to a side which really did not merit one. The home side dominated the first half and deserved to go into the lead when a Morrison cross was not properly cleared and striker Ferguson, lying on the ground, struck the ball home through Brough's legs.

Disaster struck for the Pars five minutes before half-time when John Donnelly, under no real pressure from

Rowan Hamilton makes a brave tackle for the ball against Clyde on February 10, 1987. (Enzo Mincella).

the advancing Colin McAdam, headed the ball into his own net. Ironically, it was the same player who had scored an own goal while visiting East End with the Jags in September.

The appearance of substitute Ian McCall pepped the game up for Dunfermline in the second half as his darting runs put the visitors under pressure. It was fitting that he should be the one to score a deserved winner when he curled a left-foot shot past Brough 15 minutes from time.

Thompson made a good come-back, Morrison and Watson played well and the defence easily dealt with anything that the visitors could throw at them. The poor performance from Partick was soon to cost Derek Johnstone his job.

With Morton having a rest day, Dunfermline were once again re-established at the top of the table, a position from which they were not to be dislodged until the penultimate game of the season.

DUNFERMLINE: Westwater, Robertson, Forrest, McCathie, Young, Donnelly (MacKay), Thompson, Morrison, Watson, Ferguson, Jenkins (McCall)

Bookings: Robertson, Donnelly

PARTICK THISTLE: Brough, Spittal, Workman (Cairns), Law, J. Carson, Watson, Mackie, A. Carson, McAdam (Gallacher), West, McDonald

Bookings: J. Carson, Spittal, A. Carson

Referee: D. Yates, Perth
Attendance: 3,795
Mascots: Martin and Dominic Corrigan.

Clyde	1	Airdrie				0
Dumbarton	2	Montrose				1
Queen of South	0	East Fife				1
Brechin	1	Kilmarnock				0

	P	W	D	L	F	A	Pts
DUNFERMLINE	31	17	9	5	48	29	43
Morton	33	17	7	9	68	44	41
Dumbarton	32	17	5	10	48	37	39
East Fife	33	11	17	5	48	41	39
Airdrie	32	14	7	11	38	33	35
Kilmarnock	32	11	9	12	43	38	31
Forfar	31	9	13	9	43	44	31
Clyde	30	8	12	10	34	37	28
Partick	31	8	11	12	37	40	27
Queen of South	33	8	10	15	38	50	26
Brechin	31	8	6	17	32	56	22
Montrose	31	6	6	19	26	54	18

Tuesday February 24 1987

BRECHIN (0) 0   DUNFERMLINE (1) 2
                       Donnelly (43)
                       McCall (66)

This re-arranged match against second bottom Brechin left Dunfermline undefeated in 11 matches. Ian McCall, who had played well as substitute in recent outings, was deservedly in the line-up from the start and played well in front of a disappointingly low crowd of around 1,000, most of them visitors.

It was a game in which the Pars did as much as was required of them, fading out of the match for long periods of time. The midfield of Thompson, Morrison and Donnelly took most of the credit for the hard graft which they put in and for stifling any imagination that Brechin dared show.

Although Dunfermline had several good chances to go into the lead in the first half, it was Brechin who brought out the very best of Westwater in the 42nd minute. However, almost immediately afterwards it was the cultured left foot of John Donnelly which put the visitors ahead when he drove in a superb shot through a puzzled defensive wall.

In the 66th minute Ian McCall tied up the points by slipping the ball under the 'keeper after good play from the midfield. In the final stages, Watson was desperately unfortuante not to score his side's third goal.

In the dying minutes, as the crowds began to trickle away, referee Smith stunned the large travelling support by awarding a penalty against Thompson for a foul which everyone thought was well outside the box. Justice was done when Westy dived the correct way to first of all parry the spot kick and then to safely gather the ball from the feet of the advancing Gallacher. His heroic action gave him another clean sheet and increased his side's healthy goal difference over other challengers.

BRECHIN: Neilson, Watt, Scrimgeour, Brown, Stevens, Adam, Gallacher, Taylor, Powell, Scott, Lees (Lyall)

Bookings: Lees, Scott

DUNFERMLINE: Westwater, Robertson, Forrest, McCathie, Young, Donnelly, Morrison (Jenkins), Thompson, Watson, Ferguson (MacKay), McCall

Bookings: Morrison, Donnelly, Forrest

Referee: G.B. Smith, Edinburgh
Attendance: 1,000

Airdrie		0	Forfar			0
Clyde		0	Montrose			0

	P	W	D	L	F	A	Pts
DUNFERMLINE	32	18	9	5	50	29	45
Morton	33	17	7	9	68	44	41
Dumbarton	32	17	5	10	48	37	39
East Fife	33	11	17	5	48	41	39

February 28 1987

FORFAR (2) 3   DUNFERMLINE (1) 1
  Lorimer (18)   McCall (3)
  Cormack (26)
  MacDonald (pen. 81)

The Pars' final visit to Station Park this

Gary Thompson, as ever, is never far from the thick of the action, in this case against Partick on February 21 at East End Park. (Dunfermline Press).

season brought them back to earth with a bump against a side which had just won their way through to the quarter-finals of the Scottish Cup where, history would show, they would give Dundee United the fright of their lives. In season 1961-62 Dunfermline had manged to go for a record-breaking 12 games without defeat in what was, admittedly, the more rarified atmosphere of the old First Division. Losses of concentration at vital stages of the game ensured that this high flying Pars team of the late '80s would not emulate the exploits of their more illustrious predecessors. It was, co-incidentally, Forfar's 11th match without defeat.

Yet, everything seemed to be going Dunfermline's way when they went into an early lead through McCall, his third goal in as many games. Dunfermline could have gone two up if Watson had connected with a fiery shot across the goal from Morrison.

A rare error, however, by the normally dependable Westwater gave full back Lorimer the chance to steal his side's equaliser in the 18th minute. Eight minutes later another mis-judgement from the keeper saw a hopeful effort from Cormack deceive him and trickle over the line.

The turning point of the game came in the second half when Dunfermline were given a splendid chance to equalise in the 70th minute after being awarded a penalty, although it seemed to many that Watson had simply run into his marker. In any event, Donnelly missed his first penalty for the Pars by blasting the ball wide.

In the 81st minute McCathie found himself dispossessed in front of goal and the luckless Westwater was forced to give away a penalty to prevent Cormack from scoring. The goal was only delayed for seconds – Kenny MacDonald made no mistake with his gift, sending the 'keeper the wrong way.

By way of a footnote it should be mentioned that the crowd of 2,039 was Forfar's biggest of the season and produced record receipts for them for a league match. A sign of the times?

FORFAR: Kennedy, Lorimer, Hamill, Morris, Smith, McPhee, Brewster, W. Bennett, Clark, Cormack (Ward), MacDonald
Sub: M. Bennett
Booking: Lorimer

DUNFERMLINE: Westwater, Robertson, Forrest, McCathie, Young, Donnelly, Thompson, Morrison (Jenkins), Watson, McCall, Ferguson (MacKay)
Bookings: Watson, Morrison

Referee: W.E. Knowles, Inverurie
Attendance: 2,039

Airdrie	0	Queen of South	1
Clyde	0	Morton	0
Dumbarton	1	Partick	0
Kilmarnock	3	East Fife	1
Montrose	1	Brechin	1

	P	W	D	L	F	A	Pts
DUNFERMLINE	33	18	9	6	51	32	45
Morton	34	17	8	9	68	44	42
Dumbarton	33	18	5	10	49	37	41
East Fife	34	11	17	6	49	44	39
Airdrie	34	14	8	12	38	34	36
Forfar	33	10	14	9	46	45	34
Kilmarnock	33	12	9	12	46	39	33
Clyde	32	8	14	10	34	37	30
Queen of South	34	9	10	15	39	50	28
Partick	32	8	11	13	37	41	27
Brechin	33	8	7	18	33	59	23

Tuesday March 3 1987

DUNFERMLINE (0) 2   MONTROSE (0) 0
Watson (64)
Jenkins (81)

Last Saturday's match saw three quarters of the league programme completed and though the result was disappointing, Dunfermline were still in a strong position. As the team entered the home straight, the talk of the town increasingly turned on Dunfermline's chances of making the Premier League for the first time ever.

It was very much against this background that the Pars entertained Montrose on Shrove Tuesday, desperate to please an anxious and demanding support but very conscious of the mounting pressures on them. "I wouldn't even admit we are on the path to promotion," maintained a tight-lipped Leishman. "We will continue to take each game as it comes."

Bottom-of-the-table Montrose threw up a tight defence which a jaded home team found difficult to break down, so much so that it was not until the 41st minute that Donnelly gave Charles the opportunity to make his first direct save. Montrose did not look like lambs going to the slaughter and showed a remarkable confidence. The home crowd were not slow to vent their frustration.

After a nondescript first half, Dunfermline showed more enterprise after the break and both Donnelly and Ferguson should have done better when they saw goal. It was left to substitute Billy Mackay to show Dunfermline the way. After coming narrowly close himself, he drove a long ball into the six-yard box which was flicked on by

Mackay's cross is touched on by the diving McCathie for Watson to open the scoring against Montrose. (Dunfermline Press).

McCathie to Watson who gleefully accepted the golden opportunity to record his first goal since early December. The coup de grace was delivered nine minutes from time when the other substitute, Grant Jenkins, found the net with a blistering shot.

DUNFERMLINE: Westwater, Robertson, Forrest, McCathie, Young, Donnelly, Thompson, Morrison (MacKay), Watson, Ferguson (Jenkins), McCall

Booking: Donnelly

MONTROSE: Charles, Durno, McClelland, Barr, Sheran, Forbes, Wright, Lyons (McManus), Paterson (Martin), Wallace, McDonald

Bookings: Forbes, Wright, McManus

Referee: A. Ferguson, Giffnock
Attendance: 3,539
Mascot: Stewart Rodaks, 26 Dymond Grove

Partick		1	Kilmarnock				2

	P	W	D	L	F	A	Pts
DUNFERMLINE	34	19	9	6	53	32	47
Morton	34	17	8	9	68	44	42
Dumbarton	33	18	5	10	49	37	41
East Fife	34	11	17	6	49	44	39
Airdrie	34	14	8	12	38	34	36
Kilmarnock	34	13	9	12	48	40	35

March 7 1987
DUNFERMLINE (1) 1   DUMBARTON (0) 0
Morrison (11)

125

Jim Leishman had no need to emphasise to his players how important this match was in the countdown towards promotion. His side were unbeaten at home since October 8 when none other than Dumbarton won 1-0. Dunfermline led the visitors by six points and another two, or even one, would surely kill off their stubborn challenge.

The manager looked forward "to a good attacking game because Dumbarton will come here looking for both points" and he and a crowd of over 4,000 were not to be let down. Rather disappointingly for a team doing so well, Dumbarton's supporters were rather thin on the ground. The game was righly forecast as "Match of the Day" and S.T.V., foregoing the glamour of the Premier League, paid a welcome return to East End. The last time they were there was in January 1981 when Hibs narrowly won a Scottish Cup-tie replay.

One player certainly missing from the Dunfermline squad was Billy Mackay whose projected transfer from an injury-stricken Hearts did not materialise.

Dunfermline got off to a dream start by scoring what turned out to be the only goal of the match in the 11th minute. Watson received a wonderful through pass from McCall and raced for goal but in rounding the 'keeper, he strayed too far to his left. A greedier player might have rushed a shot from an ever-narrowing angle but the selfless striker turned it back for the on-rushing Morrison to send in a fierce drive. This was blocked but he made no mistake from the rebound.

McCathie would have killed the game off near the end of the half if the strong wind had not kept out his looping header, with 'keeper Arthur beaten.

Dumbarton fought back fiercely in the second half and neutrals might have claimed they were unlucky not to snatch a point. Their best chance fell to Houston whose point-blank header was miraculously saved by Westwater.

McCathie deserved the Man of the Match award but he was run close by John Watson and Ian Westwater. "I hope to see you again next season," were the parting words of commentator Jock Brown, "in the Premier League!" Dunfermline's victory was certainly a milestone on that path.

The organisers of the Centenary Club Cabaret night in the Glen Pavilion could not have chosen a better evening; the wine certainly did flow as the celebrations continued well into the night.

DUNFERMLINE: Westwater, Robertson, Forrest, McCathie, Young, Donnelly, Thompson, Morrison (MacKay), Watson, Ferguson (Jenkins), McCall

DUMBARTON: Arthur, Montgomerie, Docherty, Clougherty, Martin, Coyle, McGowan, Rooney, McIver, Houston, Coyle
Subs: McLeod, Rafferty

Referee: P. Hanley, Coatbridge
Attendance: 4,366
Mascot: Darren Westwater, 23 Aberdour Rd

Brechin	0	Airdrie	2
East Fife	3	Montrose	1
Morton	P	Kilmarnock	P
Partick	2	Forfar	1
Queen of South	P	Clyde	P

	P	W	D	L	F	A	Pts
DUNFERMLINE	35	20	9	6	54	32	49
Morton	34	17	8	9	68	44	42
Dumbarton	34	18	5	11	49	38	41
East Fife	35	12	17	6	52	45	41
Airdrie	35	15	8	12	40	34	38
Kilmarnock	34	13	9	12	48	40	35
Forfar	34	10	14	10	47	47	34

One of the most important goals of the season — Morrison scores the only goal of the game against Dumbarton. (Enzo Mincella).

Midweek

Queen of South	4	Clyde	1
Morton	2	Kilmarnock	1

March 14 1987

CLYDE (0) 0   DUNFERMLINE (0) 1
                              McCathie (90)

The countdown was definitely on. There was a rush to buy calculators in local shops as permutations and goal differences were meticulously worked out. One thing was certain — Dunfermline could only throw away promotion, such was their lead. Although Morton had done well in midweek to defeat Kilmarnock (a match which Jim Leishman commentated on live for B.B.C. SportSound), they were seven points behind Dunfermline albeit with a game in hand, encouraging otherwise sane folk in the Auld Grey Toun to think even of the championship. Dumbarton and East Fife were both eight points behind.

Before such lofty thoughts became reality, there was the business of defeating fifth bottom Clyde at Firhill. Dame Fortune stayed with Dunfermline to enable Norrie McCathie to scramble the only goal of the game in the dying seconds. 'Keeper Atkins failed to hold a cross from Donnelly and the big defender was on hand to collect two more precious points. "They got the goal," commented a delighted Leishman, "at a time when Clyde couldn't possibly come back."

Up until then, the game had the makings of a no-score draw although chances had fallen to either side. **127**

Robertson, Watson and McCall all might have scored in the first half as might Willock for Clyde.

In the second half McGlashan brought out the save of the match from Westwater. Paul Flexney also came close. Then McCathie snatched the all important winner to keep Dunfermline bang on course for promotion.

CLYDE: Atkins, Doherty, Napier, Tait, Flexney, McFarlane, Willock, Logan (Ahern), McGlashan, Millar, Murphy (Watters)

DUNFERMLINE: Westwater, Robertson, Forrest, McCathie, Young, Donnelly, Thompson, Morrison (Smith), Watson, McCall, Ferguson (Jenkins)

Booking: McCall

Referee: K. O'Donnell, Airdrie
Attendance: 1,500

Airdrie	0	East Fife	0
Forfar	P	Dumbarton	P
Montrose	1	Kilmarnock	1
Morton	1	Brechin	0
Queen of South	0	Partick	1

	P	W	D	L	F	A	Pts
DUNFERMLINE	36	21	9	6	55	32	51
Morton	36	19	8	9	71	45	46
East Fife	36	12	18	6	52	45	42
Dumbarton	34	18	5	11	49	38	41
Airdrie	36	15	9	12	40	34	39
Kilmarnock	36	13	10	13	50	43	36

Midweek

| Forfar | 0 | Dumbarton | 2 |
| Partick | 0 | Clyde | 2 |

March 21 1987

DUNFERMLINE (0) 1   MORTON (1) 2
   McCathie (58)   Turner (30)
                McNeil (pen. 66)

For the second home game in succession, the T.V. cameras paid a visit to East End, surely an unprecedented occurrence for a First Division side, but so much was at stake that their presence

was fully warranted. Earlier in the week Archie MacPherson and his crew had been filming Dundee United's marvellous performance in the Nou Camp Stadium against Barcelona. As older Dunfermline supporters admiringly watched the transmission, their minds travelled back to the 1960s when it was their own club which had acquitted itself so well against the might of Valencia, Zaragoza and Bilbao. If these days were ever to return, then a small step in that direction would be the destruction of the main contenders for promotion, nay for the championship itself, Morton.

In a 44-match league, every team is bound to go through a sticky patch at some time and Dunfermline were now about to enter such a worrying stage. Morton were the highest-scoring side in the league and soon showed why this was so in a game which resembled the spirit of a cup-tie. It was fought out in front of a crowd just under 6,000, the fourth largest in Scotland on a day when there was live international rugby on the T.V. The crowd set a new record for a First Division game at East End since league reconstruction.

It might have turned out much differently if Watson had capitalised on an excellent chance early on. A low McCall cross was missed by Jenkins and came through to Watson who could not control it as the ball spun off his shin.

The first goal came at the other end. In the 30th minute, Turner latched on to a pass from Robertson, stepped away from his cover and struck the ball past Westwater. Dunfermline hardly deserved to be a goal down at the interval but the experience and skills of McNamara, Holmes and Wylie kept the Greenock

Norrie McCathie is desperate to equalise the score against championship contenders, Morton. (Dunfermline Press).

side just out in front.

Dunfermline plugged away at the Morton defence after the break and were rewarded in 58 minutes when the scourge of Morton, Norrie McCathie, chested down a cross from McCall, turned beautifully and calmly drilled the ball home. This was his third goal against Morton.

Just as Dunfermline were settling down to play with more assurance, a devastating blow befell them in the 66th minute when Dougie Robertson, "turning with the speed of a tanker in the Forth," as *The Scotsman* phrased it, toppled over the outstretched leg of Forrest. A penalty was awarded which McNeil converted with ease and his

team held out to win an important fixture.

For Dunfermline it was certainly an unfortunate setback, a missed opportunity to clinch the division's honours. Archie MacPherson thought Dunfermline were "a bit stage conscious". A delighted Allan McGraw was more forthcoming: "It makes it tight. It makes sure the race will go to the end of the season." How right he was.

DUNFERMLINE: Westwater, Robertson, Forrest, McCathie, Young, Donnelly (Smith), Thompson, Morrison, Watson, McCall, Jenkins (Ferguson)

Bookings: Jenkins, Smith

Ian McCall shows the Morton defence a clean pair of heels. (Dunfermline Press).

MORTON: Wylie, O'Hara, Holmes, Hunter, Doak, McNamara, Robertson (Boag), Clinging, Alexander, McNeil (Arthur), Turner

Booking: O'Hara

Referee: T Muirhead, Stenhousemuir
Attendance: 5,959
Mascot: Dianne Storrie, 69 Durleydene Cres., Bridge of Earn

Brechin	1	Queen of South	2
Dumbarton	2	Airdrie	2
East Fife	1	Clyde	1
Kilmarnock	2	Forfar	0
Partick	0	Montrose	0

	P	W	D	L	F	A	Pts
DUNFERMLINE	37	21	9	7	56	34	51
Morton	37	20	8	9	73	46	48
Dumbarton	36	19	6	11	53	40	44
East Fife	37	12	19	6	53	46	43
Airdrie	37	15	10	12	42	36	40
Kilmarnock	37	14	10	13	52	43	38
Forfar	36	10	14	12	47	51	34
Clyde	36	9	15	12	38	43	33
Partick	37	10	12	15	41	46	32
Queen of South	37	11	10	16	45	53	32
Brechin	36	8	7	21	34	64	23
Montrose	37	6	10	21	29	61	22

March 28 1987

EAST FIFE (1) 1　　　DUNFERMLINE (0) 1
　McNaughton (36)　　　Irvine (pen. 58)

The Bayview side which Dunfermline faced showed several important changes in personnel from the last encounter. Manager Dave Clark, one of the division's longest serving bosses, had earlier left to go full-time with Falkirk and was replaced by player Gavin Murray. More recently, 'keeper Gordon Marshall was transferred to Falkirk with Ray Charles purchased from Montrose to fill the gap. Talented youngster David Kirkwood was snapped up by Rangers who in turn sent out on loan midfielder Scott Nisbet.

The Pars had also rung the changes. The long-serving Jim Bowie joined his former team-mate, Ian Heddle, at St. Johnstone while Willie Irvine (23) was signed from Hibs for £15,000 and went straight into the team. As a Stirling Albion player he had scored more than 60 goals but had never settled at Easter Road since his £35,000 transfer there last year.

On a bitterly cold and windy afternoon, Dunfermline adopted a cautious approach, conceding corners where necessary and firing in long-range efforts to test the home 'keeper. It was somewhat against the run of play when East Fife opened the scoring in the 36th minute. Paul Hunter picked up a long clearance, turned neatly and fired in a shot from the edge of the box which Westwater could only parry out to the on-rushing McNaughton to score yet again against Dunfermline to bring his season's total to 21 goals.

Dunfermline worked patiently for the equaliser with Watson, McCall and new boy Irvine all combining well. After ignoring one good penalty claim after the interval when McCall was bundled to the ground, the referee saw justice done when he granted one in the 58th minute. Full back Conroy was adjudged to have fouled Irvine in the box as they both chased a long, wind-assisted kick from Westwater. Without consultation, the debutant, with all the coolness in the world, put the ball on the spot and to the immense relief of the large travelling support, he scored with ease.

If Irvine was the hero, Westwater was not far behind as he pulled off two excellent saves from Burgess and Blair to earn his side a precious point. Thus, Dunfermline's dismal record of failing to record a win over their rivals in five encounters this season continued. However, as a not too disappointed Jim Leishman remarked, "Winning promotion is about beating every team in the league, not just East Fife. The wind spoiled the game a bit, but I thought we thoroughly deserved the draw because we created more chances." There was further consolation for the fans as they journeyed home when the radio announced that Morton had all but killed off Dumbarton's challenge by beating them 3-2 at Boghead.

This was East Fife's 20th draw and the Bayview side needed to look no further than this statistic to see why promotion so cruelly eluded them once again.

EAST FIFE: Charles, Connor, Conroy, McCafferty, Halley, Burgess, Blair, Nisbet, Hunter, Perry, McNaughton
Subs: Smith, Pitman

DUNFERMLINE: Westwater, Robertson, Forrest, McCathie, Young, Smith (Jenkins), Thompson, Morrison, Watson, McCall (Ferguson), Irvine

Booking: Forrest

The ever dependable Ian Westwater, worthily voted "Player of the Year"

Referee: I.R. Cathcart, Bridge of Allan
Attendance: 2,730

Airdrie	4	Montrose	1
Clyde	1	Partick	1
Dumbarton	2	Morton	3
Forfar	0	Brechin	0
Kilmarnock	2	Queen of South	2

	P	W	D	L	F	A	Pts
DUNFERMLINE	38	21	7	10	57	35	52
Morton	38	21	9	8	76	48	50
Dumbarton	38	19	12	7	56	44	45
East Fife	38	12	6	20	54	47	44
Airdrie	38	16	12	10	46	37	42
Kilmarnock	38	14	13	11	54	45	39

Midweek

Dumbarton	1	Brechin	1
Forfar	1	Clyde	2

April 4 1987

DUNFERMLINE (0) 0   KILMARNOCK (1) 1
Harkness (5)

The Dunfermline support was keen to view the Pars' latest recruit, the 26-year- **131** old Stuart Beedie, signed earlier in the week for £35,000 from Hibs. The midfielder had begun his professional career with Montrose before going to Muirton Park for £15,000 and helping St. Johnstone into the Premier League. He was transferred to Dundee United in 1984 and then moved in 1986 to Hibs with whom he never really settled, partly because of a serious knee injury. He made his debut in the right midfield, pushing Morrison to the left in favour of Donnelly whose form had slumped in recent games.

Dunfermline were encouraged by Dumbarton surprisingly dropping a point at home to Brechin during the week and sought to consolidate their own position at the expense of Kilmarnock who had only won four away games and languished in mid-table. The most critical factor of the afternoon turned out to be the gale-force wind which blew across the park from the east. The Pars had the misfortune to battle against it in the first half and the loss of a careless goal after only five minutes presented them with an uphill struggle from which they never recovered.

Clark of Kilmarnock sent over a harmless ball to the terracing side which the defence dreamily thought was off-side. As the defenders stood rooted to the spot with hands held protestingly high, Colin Harkness raced in on goal and put the ball past the advancing Westwater. Dunfermline found it difficult to regain their composure and found many of their attempted clearances swirling menacingly back towards them. Shortly afterwards, Westwater kept the game going as a contest when he denied Reid from scoring what looked like a certain goal.

As the half progressed, Dunfermline did manage to string one or two good moves together and were unfortunte not to be rewarded from good efforts from Morrison and McCall who hit the post.

In the second half, it was all one-way traffic as Dunfermline desperately sought to salvage a deserved point but on numerous occasions they found that their luck was out or else 33-year-old, experienced keeper Alan McCulloch was in the right spot to clutch at a netbound shot. McCathie in particular was unlucky to see his header from a Morrison corner hit the upright in 65 minutes. As the minutes ticked away, the crowd realised that the elusive equaliser was not going to materialise, and Killie held out to record their first win of the season over a luckless Dunfermline.

Fortunately, East Fife had taken a point from Morton at Cappielow and Dunfermline's position as league leaders, though more under threat, was safe for another week. Coach Gregor Abel, dismayed at the side picking up only one point out of the last six, refused to be pushed into rash, tactical changes. "We lost an early, stupid goal," he explained, "and from then on we were left chasing the game. Frustration inevitably builds up in these circumstances."

The Pars' Man of the Match award went to captain Bobby Robertson.

DUNFERMLINE: Westwater, Robertson, Forrest, McCathie, Young, Morrison (Smith), Thompson, Beedie, Watson (Jenkins), McCall, Irvine

Booking: Thompson

A concerned Dunfermline dug-out during the Kilmarnock game: G. Abel, J. Jobson, T. Smith, J. Nelson.

KILMARNOCK: McCulloch, Millar, Cockburn, Clark, Martin, McVeigh, Houston, Reid, Harkness (Cuthbertson), McGuire, Bryson (Docherty)

Bookings: Bryson, McVeigh

Referee: G.A. Evans, Bishopbriggs
Attendance: 3,704
Mascot: Paul Holliday, 11 St John's Place

Brechin	1	Dumbarton	2
Montrose	2	Clyde	1
Morton	1	East Fife	1
Partick	2	Airdrie	2
Queen of South	1	Forfar	4

	P	W	D	L	F	A	Pts
DUNFERMLINE	39	21	8	10	57	36	52
Morton	39	21	9	9	77	49	51
Dumbarton	39	20	12	7	58	45	47
East Fife	39	12	6	21	55	48	45
Airdrie	39	16	12	11	48	39	43
Kilmarnock	39	15	13	11	55	45	41
Forfar	39	11	13	15	52	54	37
Clyde	39	10	13	16	42	47	36
Partick	39	10	15	14	44	49	34
Queen of South	39	11	17	11	48	59	33

April 11 1987
PARTICK THISTLE (0) 0 DUNFERMLINE (1) 2
Morrison (3)
Donnelly (53)

The Pars answered their critics in the best possible way — with a resounding 2-0 victory at Firhill against a demoralised Thistle side still without a manager. Dunfermline had already taken full points from previous encounters and found that two more came surprisingly easily. Leishman shrugged off last week's defeat and kept faith with the players who had taken the club to the top.

The experienced John Donnelly was restored to play against his former mates and managed, for once, to score for the right side. Gary Thompson, his beard shorn off, resumed his former role of right back, and skipper Robertson was

133

slotted in at left back which meant that, for the first time, Bobby Forrest was relegated to the substitutes' bench.

A strong wind was again to play a crucial role, this time in Dunfermline's favour. The game was only a few minutes old when Stevie Morrison reminded everyone what a lethal left foot he possesses. He controlled a difficult ball from Irvine and let loose a cracking 35-yarder which, with the assistance of the wind, left goalkeeper Brough with absolutely no chance. Leishman called it the best goal of the season, although in truth any goal would have been welcome at this jittery stage in the Pars' history.

This was the early goal the Pars needed and they then proceeded to give a notably composed performance against which Thistle had no answer. The midfield of Morrison, Beedie and Donnelly controlled the game and gave excellent service to Irvine, Watson and McCall, the last of whom tormented the Jags' defence. Indeed, ten minutes before half-time, McCall went off on a blistering run and Watson should have given the move a better finish than he managed. On one of their rare sorties up-field, Thistle were denied an undeserved equaliser when centre half Young had to clear a shot from McDonald off the line.

Early in the second half, Dunfermline scored the goal which ensured them victory. John Donnelly, having an impressive return to first-team action, beat three defenders before delicately chipping the ball over Brough's head. Thanks to the strong head wind, the ball was prevented from going over the bar and landed neatly in the goal.

Partick, watched by their Chelsea saviour Ken Bates, were forced to throw everything into attack and in doing so, presented Dunfermline with chances which should have led to further goals as first Watson and then Irvine both hit the woodwork. McCall too had an excellent chance to add to his goal tally of seven in the dying minutes but he again overplayed the ball.

Statistically, Dunfermline had taken another momentous step towards the Premier League. With only four games left, they now required a maximum of four points, perhaps less, to be assured of promotion.

PARTICK: Brough, Walker, Cairns, McAdam, Spittal, Watson, McQuade (Gallacher), Mitchell, Logan, McDonald, Kelly (Carson)

Booking: Spittal

DUNFERMLINE: Westwater, Thompson, Robertson, McCathie, Young, Morrison, Donnelly, Beedie, Watson, McCall, Irvine (Jenkins)
Sub: Forrest

Referee: M. McGinley, Clydebank
Attendance: 2,633

Airdrie	3	Clyde	2
Brechin	3	East Fife	2
Dumbarton	3	Kilmarnock	2
Forfar	4	Montrose	1
Queen of South	2	Morton	3

	P	W	D	L	F	A	Pts
DUNFERMLINE	40	22	10	8	59	36	54
Morton	40	22	9	9	80	51	53
Dumbarton	40	21	7	12	61	47	49
Airdrie	40	17	11	12	51	42	45
East Fife	40	12	21	7	57	52	45
Kilmarnock	40	15	11	14	57	48	41
Forfar	40	12	15	13	56	55	39
Clyde	40	10	16	14	44	50	36
Partick	40	10	14	16	44	51	34
Queen of South	40	11	11	18	50	62	33
Brechin	40	9	9	22	39	69	27
Montrose	40	7	10	23	33	70	24

April 18 1987

DUNFERMLINE (0) 0   BRECHIN (0) 2
                      Brown (48), Lyall (72)

With only four games left, the town of Dunfermline was well and truly in the grip of promotion fever. If Dumbarton lost at Montrose, which seemed unlikely, and if Dunfermline could beat Brechin, whom they had trounced three times earlier in the season, then the Pars would be all but there.

The pundits, however, had forgotten about poor old Brechin, lying second bottom of the league, who had relegation staring them in the face unless they could stage their own miracle. Under new manager, John Richie, who had replaced Ian Fleming in

February, they had just beaten East Fife, a feat which Dunfermline had been unable to produce.

A large Easter holiday crowd, almost 5,000 strong, turned out to see if their heroes could carve a niche in Dunfermline's proud history. Dunfermline were unchanged after their highly successful outing to Firhill the previous week.

The game itself was a massive disappointment to the home fans and the least said about it the better. The bone-hard pitch made it difficult for the players to control the high bouncing ball but no-one would doubt that the visitors adapted better to the conditions. The end of season nerves which had affected

Willie Irvine scores the goal that clinches Dunfermline's promotion into the Premier League. John Watson looks on admiringly. (Dunfermline Press).

135

Rangers in midweek against Dundee were certainly in evidence at East End Park. Passes went astray, free kicks were needlessly conceded and no pattern could be detected in the play. There was more interest in the Junior Supporters' Club penalty competition during the interval than throughout the first half. It was Brechin who came out in the second half determined to salvage something from the game. Just a few minutes after the re-start, Brechin stunned the home crowd by going into the lead when a cross from Charlie Adam found defender Brown who headed forcibly past Ian Westwater. Indeed, the visitors might have gone two up, minutes later, when an overhead kick from Kennedy bounced dangerously off Westwater's bar.

It took until midway through the second half for Dunfermline to win their first corner, a measure of how out of touch they were. McCall and Morrison were substituted – but it could have been anyone. Dunfermline pushed men forward in a bid to grasp at least an equaliser, but in doing so allowed Lyall through with 18 minutes left to side-foot the ball past the diving Westwater.

In the closing stages, Dunfermline came close to snatching at least a consolation goal and Watson should have done better when the ball fell at his feet a few yards out. It was simply not Dunfermline's day as they slumped to their third home defeat in a row and some fans were not slow to let the manager know it. "When the Dunfermline team needed their fans most", explained a relieved Brechin manager, "they deserted them. That is a tragic thing". Norrie McCathie was

nominated Man of the Match by sponsors, Asphaltic, who must have wished for a better outcome to the day.

The only consolation came when the results announced that Morton and Dumbarton had also surprisingly lost. While Dunfermline were kicking themselves for not thus having wrapped up promotion and taken a step nearer the championship, there was the realisation that only one victory, even a draw, was all that was now required to ensure promotion.

DUNFERMLINE: Westwater, Thompson, Robertson, McCathie, Young, Donnelly, Beedie, Morrison (Forrest), Watson, McCall (Jenkins), Irvine

BRECHIN: Neilson, Watt, Stevens, Brown, Inglis (Gallacher), Adam, Kennedy (Lytwyn), Taylor, Bourke, Scott, Lyall

Referee: T. Muirhead, Stenhousemuir
Attendance: 4,645
Mascots: Colin & Connor McCaul, 21 Whinhill

Clyde	1	Forfar	2
East Fife	5	Queen of South	0
Airdrie	4	Kilmarnock	3
Montrose	2	Dumbarton	0
Morton	1	Partick	2

	P	W	D	L	F	A	Pts
DUNFERMLINE	41	22	10	9	59	38	54
Morton	41	22	9	10	81	53	53
Dumbarton	41	21	7	13	61	49	49
East Fife	41	13	21	7	62	51	47
Airdrie	41	18	11	12	55	44	47
Kilmarnock	41	15	11	15	60	52	41

April 25 1987

DUNFERMLINE (1) 1   QUEEN OF SOUTH
   Irvine (12)   (0) 0

For this critical game. Bobby Forrest was restored to the full-back position with John Donnelly dropping out of the side. The fixture brought back memories of last season's clashes between these two clubs when they had fought out the championship. While Dunfermline had gone on to complete their rags-to-riches fairy story, Queen of the South were floundering dangerously near the relegation zone, aggravated by Brechin's shock win the week before. The Palmerston side, who had failed to beat Dunfermline this season, could be expected to put up a stout challenge.

The kick-off was held up for more than five minutes to allow in the big crowd which expected to see Dunfermline clinch their place in the Premier League. The sun shone brightly, the fans got firmly behind their team and a defiant manager, bedecked in a scarf discarded the previous week by a disgruntled fan, took his seat in the stand as the match kicked off.

The play on the field will never be remembered for the football. Dunfermline got off to a perfect start when, after an early scare at Westwater's goal, new signing Willie Irvine calmed everyone's nerves in the 12th minute by opening the scoring, his second crucial goal for the club. Morrison's drive from the right wing was only parried by the goalkeeper and the former Hibs' forward was on hand to score at his second attempt.

Dunfermline, however, failed to put the issue beyond doubt with a second goal, try as they might. John Watson was particularly unfortunate in the second half when he found himself clear with only the 'keeper to beat, but was unable to capitalise on his good fortune.

Queen of the South were not a bad side, especially down their right flank, and they produced enough chances, particularly at the end of the second half, to have grabbed at least an equaliser. Westwater, as he had done all season, produced two fine saves in the closing

stages to maintain Dunfermline's narrow lead. Centre half Young, who worthily received the Man of the Match award from the sponsors, Ford Autocentre, was outstanding in defence and in driving his colleagues on.

As the minutes ticked away and as the nails were bitten to the quick, the fans urged their team on and begged the referee to sound the final whistle. When it finally came at 4.53 p.m., the stadium erupted like the volcano it had threatened to become. Thousands of fans spilled on to the pitch to greet their heroes; in the Directors' Box, normally an oasis of sedate behaviour, an exhausted but jubilant manager was almost smothered amidst delighted supporters.

The players and the coaching staff, when they had fought their way through the ecstatic crowd, made their way up to the stand to add their congratulations to the man who had engineered the whole campaign. The day these fans had waited so long for had finally arrived and they were determined to make the most of this unique occasion. Referee Cumming knew what to expect – he had seen it all at Stenhousemuir a year earlier when the championship was won.

In the dressing room, the champagne was opened and the celebrations began in earnest. The manager and chairman, who had previously announced that as a reward the club had arranged a holiday in Majorca, were unceremoniously dumped into the bath as the tension of the day quickly evaporated. Minutes later, the players washed the match ball, autographed it and presented it to Mel Rennie as a token of their appreciation.

In the Paragon Club and later in the **137**

The tension is unbearable for everyone as the minutes of the game against Queen of the South slowly tick away.

East Port Bar, the players and fans continued the celebrations well into the night, at times unable to take in exactly what had been achieved in such a short space of time.

DUNFERMLINE: Westwater, Robertson, Forrest, McCathie, Young, Beedie, Thompson, Morrison, Watson, McCall (Jenkins), Irvine (Ferguson)

Booking: Beedie

QUEEN OF SOUTH: Davidson, G. Robertson, Sim, Hetherington, Gray, McBride, Reid (McIntyre), Telfer, Bryce (Maskrey), Cloy, J. Robertson

Booking: Sim

Referee: G.D. Cumming, Carluke
Attendance: 5,482
Mascot: Fiona Sims, 2 Trondheim Place

Dumbarton	2	Clyde	1
Forfar	1	Airdrie	0
Kilmarnock	0	Brechin	1
Montrose	1	Morton	4
Partick	2	East Fife	0

	P	W	D	L	F	A	Pts
DUNFERMLINE	42	23	10	9	60	38	56
Morton	42	23	9	10	85	54	55
Dumbarton	42	22	7	13	63	50	51
Airdrie	42	18	11	13	55	45	47
East Fife	42	13	21	8	62	53	47
Forfar	42	14	15	13	59	56	43

May 2 1987

AIRDRIE (0) 2   DUNFERMLINE (0) 1
  Flood (78, 82)   McCall (pen. 70)

Once the celebrations had died down (and that took some time!), there was still the question of the Championship to consider. Morton had kept the pressure up by winning 4-1 at Montrose, securing their own place in the Premier League. Dunfermline still led the race by one point and were clearly in the driving seat, not having to rely on other teams doing them any favours.

It was with this in mind that a large

Premier Bound — at last, after a wait of 12 years.

Dunfermline support made the trip to Airdrie, a side whom they had never beaten this season. Airdrie's early promise had faltered and recent poor results had seen the departure of manager Derek Whiteford with no replacement as yet made. While Dunfermline had the incentive of going for the Championship, Airdrie had their pride at stake. Dunfermline fielded the same side which had triumphed last week, but failed to show any of the fire which had driven them on then. Watson, elbowed in the face in the opening minutes, was out of touch and was replaced on the half-hour mark by Jenkins. Westwater had little to do in the Dunfermline goal.

The game came alive in the second half. In the opening minutes, Jenkins was unlucky to see a shot rebound off the post when the visiting support was willing the ball to go in. Dunfermline finally made the breakthrough in the 70th minute when Airdrie failed to clear a Morrison corner. Forrest sent the ball back to Young who passed it on to McCall. The tricky forward bored his way into the home defence before being edged off the ball in the box. The referee, to the great delight and relief of the visitors, awarded a penalty and McCall scored by sending the 'keeper the wrong way. At that point, the Pars looked home and dry and appeared to be coasting to the required victory against a lack-lustre side. That is until Jamie Flood replaced Christie in the home attack. This player, who had sunk the Pars with two goals in November, now proceeded to repeat the act when he capitalised on two lapses in the Dunfermline defence. In the 78th minute, he ran on to a pass from

139

The joyous scenes of celebration – and relief – require no further comment!

Lindsay to score an equaliser which stunned the fans; worse was to come a few minutes later when Frye picked up a badly cleared ball and crossed for Flood to volley home the winner.

In the dressing room, the Dunfermline players rued the loss of two points against a side which, apart from the goals, never really threatened their defence. More depressing was the news from Greenock which announced that Morton, by beating Forfar, had gone back to the top of the league for the first time since February.

AIRDRIE: Martin, Lawrie, Black, McKeown, McCormack (Doherty), Lindsay, Hughes, McCabe, Frye, Moore, Christie (Flood)

Bookings: McKeown, Frye

DUNFERMLINE: Westwater, Robertson, Forrest, McCathie, Young, Beedie, Thompson, Morrison, Watson (Jenkins), McCall, Irvine (Ferguson)

Booking: Thompson

Referee: C.C. Sinclair, Forfar
Attendance: 2,759

Brechin	1	Partick	1
Clyde	0	Kilmarnock	1
East Fife	2	Dumbarton	1
Morton	3	Forfar	1
Queen of South	0	Montrose	0

	P	W	D	L	F	A	Pts
Morton	43	24	9	10	88	55	57
DUNFERMLINE	43	23	10	10	61	40	56
Dumbarton	43	22	7	14	64	52	51
Airdrie	43	19	11	13	57	47	49
East Fife	43	14	21	8	64	55	49
Kilmarnock	43	16	11	16	61	53	43
Forfar	43	14	15	14	60	59	43
Partick	43	12	15	16	49	43	39
Clyde	43	10	16	17	46	55	36
Queen of South	43	11	12	20	50	68	34
Brechin	43	11	10	22	43	70	32
Montrose	43	8	11	24	36	74	27

May 9 1987

MONTROSE (1) 1   DUNFERMLINE (0) 0
  Paterson (41)

The end of a long, hard season brought

140

Members of the Brucefield supporters' club brought a truly carnival atmosphere to the last game of the season at Montrose.

the Pars to Links Park for their final game with the outcome of the Championship still in the balance. As Jim Leishman had often predicted, the contest had gone to the last game. There was a whole division separating the two teams — Dunfermline were bound for the Premier League while Montrose, who had won only eight games, were destined for the Second Division, and yet the game was to make a travesty of that situation. Dunfermline had already taken full points from Montrose — without the loss of a goal — and were looking for another two in the expectation of Morton slipping up at Broomfield where they themselves had stumbled the previous week. "While we have a little chance," proclaimed Jim, "we will go for it with all our strength."

Ever hopeful, more than 2,000 fans made the journey north and the appearance of forty of the Brucefield Supporters' Club in fancy dress brought a carnival atmosphere to the normally quiet, Angus ground. John Watson, still suffering from a groin strain, watched the game from the dug-out as did Willie Irvine, relegated to the substitutes' bench. Jenkins and Ferguson led the attack.

Alas, just when Dunfermline were required to produce a scintillating performance to have any hope of winning the Championship, the fans were treated to a rather indifferent display against a team which contained two trialists. Yet, it might have been completely different if McCall had enjoyed better luck in the opening **141** minute when his shot at goal rebounded off the stand-in keeper before being finally saved. Dunfermline played their best football in the opening twenty minutes, forcing several corners, and putting Montrose under some pressure.

Montrose, however, were not slow to let it be known that they were not there to make up the numbers as they started to threaten the Pars' goal. In the 41st minute, they sneaked a goal which stunned both the visiting players and support. Durno crossed the ball from the left and Ian Paterson, scorer of ten goals already, added another with a glancing header which gave Westwater no chance.

Dunfermline started the second half in determined mood and were soon to receive the news from delirious fans that Morton had fallen a goal behind at Airdrie. Sadly, the harder the players battled away, the less progress they made. Indeed, the home side were unlucky on several occasions not to add to their lead as gaps at the back of the Dunfermline defence let in the Montrose attack. In a last throw, Leishman sent on Irvine for Forrest and Hamilton for Morrison, but to no avail. As the precious minutes ticked away, it became all too clear that the fans would not even see one goal, far less two.

The final whistle brought Dunfermline's fifth defeat in eight games. When the result from Broomfield confirmed that Airdrie had in fact beaten Morton, the disappointment in the Dunfermline camp was all the greater. Montrose had certainly spoiled the party; yet, the fans were still in good cheer and gave the players and manager a resounding ovation, remembering that the main goal, promotion, had been achieved.

MONTROSE: Buchan, Barr, McLelland, Brown, Sheran, Forbes, Allan, Durno, Paterson, Robertson, McDonald

Booking: Sheran

DUNFERMLINE: Westwater, Robertson, Forrest (Irvine), McCathie, Young, Beedie, Thomson, Morrison (Hamilton), Ferguson, McCall, Jenkins

Referee: D. Syme, Rutherglen
Attendance: 2,500

Airdrie	1	Morton	0
Clyde	2	Brechin	1
Dumbarton	3	Queen of South	0
Forfar	1	East Fife	4
Kilmarnock	1	Partick	0

	P	W	D	L	F	A	Pts
Morton	44	24	9	11	88	56	57
DUNFERMLINE	44	23	10	11	61	41	56
Dumbarton	44	23	7	14	67	52	53
East Fife	44	15	21	8	68	55	51
Airdrie	44	20	11	13	58	46	51
Kilmarnock	44	17	11	16	62	53	45
Forfar	44	14	15	15	61	63	43
Partick	44	12	15	17	49	54	39
Clyde	44	11	16	17	48	56	38
Queen of South	44	11	12	21	50	71	34
Brechin	44	11	10	23	44	72	32
Montrose	44	9	11	24	37	74	29

HOME AND AWAY ANALYSIS

		Home			Away			Goals		
	P	W	D	L	W	D	L	F	A	Pts
Morton	44	12	4	6	12	5	5	88	56	57
DUNFERMLINE	44	12	5	5	11	5	6	61	41	56
Dumbarton	44	12	6	4	11	1	10	67	52	53
East Fife	44	10	10	2	5	11	6	68	55	51
Airdrie	44	15	2	5	5	9	8	58	46	51
Kilmarnock	44	11	7	4	6	4	12	62	53	45
Forfar	44	7	9	6	7	6	9	61	63	43
Partick	44	7	7	8	5	8	9	49	54	39
Clyde	44	6	9	7	5	7	10	48	56	38
Queen of South	44	7	5	10	4	7	11	50	71	34
Brechin	44	5	5	12	6	5	11	44	72	32
Montrose	44	7	5	10	2	6	14	37	74	29

Dunfermline were thus only joint fifth in the table when it came to scoring goals. A few more goals at the end of the season would have won them the championship. However, they did have the best defence.

Dunfermline's gates were again the healthiest in the division and the best outwith the Premier League. Over the season, 91,223 fans went through the turnstiles to view 22 league matches – an average of 4146 per game. In addition, 6161 paid to watch the Skol Cup-tie, making a grand total of just under the 100,000 mark.

Dumfermline were never out of the top two berths in the league throughout the season and led the table for three-quarters of the way.

Ian Westwater had 19 shut-outs in the league, about one every two games.

Disappointingly, the Pars failed to win any major cup-ties or score any goals.

Their best run of victories was four successive league wins at the start of the programme in August. Their best spell in the league came either side of Christmas when they went eleven games without defeat.

Dunfermline managed to take full points from only one team – Partick Thistle. They also never lost to Queen of the South. Conversely, they failed to beat both East Fife and Airdrie at four attempts. With league champions Morton, they shared the points and the goals scored.

John Watson was again top scorer – but with the much diminished total of 13 goals. New signings Ian McCall and John Donnelly, who both went full-time during the season, scored eight and seven goals respectively. Ferguson, Jenkins and midfielder McCathie each grabbed six goals.

Norrie McCathie appeared in all 46 major games, a remarkable performance. Ian Westwater, John Watson and Bobby Forrest came close on 44, 42 and 42 appearances, respectively.

Ten players made less than eight appearances each, giving Dunfermline a promotion-winning squad of essentially 17 players. McCall and Jenkins made most appearances as substitute on the field – 13 and 12 respectively.

Thus, the curtain came down on a momentous season for Dunfermline Athletic. On Sunday May 10, an open day was held at East End Park and proved to be very successful. Hundreds of season tickets were sold; the players signed dozens of autograph books; Provost Mill presented the Reserve League Trophy (East) to the club; Radio Forth announced the latest winner of the Centenary Club's £500 draw; not too serious five-a-side matches were played and hundreds of fans

A never-to-be-forgotten day in the 102 year history of Dunfermline Athletic F.C.

and their families wandered round the boardroom, the Jock Stein Lounge and the dressing rooms, soaking up the atmosphere.

The following night, a far from full-strength Athletic side took on Raith Rovers at Stark's Park in a testimonial match for Chris Candlish, and narrowly lost 2-1.

Although the season ended on a rather low note at Montrose, it should not be forgotten what Dunfermline Athletic achieved. While all the commentators and pundits looked forward to a year of consolidation in the First Division, with the avoidance of relegation as the main goal, Jim and Gregor produced a squad which, right from the beginning of the season, took the league by storm and was never out of the top two berths in the table.

Though the team stumbled towards promotion in the final weeks, the real wonder is that they ever managed to get into such a commanding position in the first place. Their failure to win the championship on the last day, a prize which few in Scotland outside Greenock would have grudged them, was certainly a great disappointment. It is a pity that they could not have reproduced the performance that Celtic put in the previous season in pipping Hearts at the finishing post.

This disappointment, however, should be seen in perspective. While a few English clubs (like Ipswich and Spurs) have managed to win league titles in successive seasons, no Scottish club has ever achieved this notable double. If Dunfermline had come from behind, like Raith Rovers did in Division Two, and snatched promotion on the last day of the season by virtue of goal difference, then the team, paradoxically, would probably have won even greater acclaim. Sadly, they became victims of their own high standards set earlier in the season. From August 1986 until May 1987, they became the side that everyone, the relegated clubs especially, wanted to beat. If the league had finished after the customary 39 games, Dunfermline would easily have won the championship. On the other hand, every team goes through a bumpy patch during a long, arduous programme and for Dunfermline's dismal run of only two victories and six goals out of the final eight games to have occurred at the start of the season, then relegation, not promotion, might well have been their fate.

It should also be remembered that Dunfermline have become the first team in Fife, a Kingdom rated highly in the footballing world and a rich supplier of fine players, to reach the Premier League. In the past, Raith Rovers, Cowdenbeath, East Fife and, of course, Dunfermline have all enjoyed their golden years but full credit must be given to the Pars on finally making the quantum leap and securing a place among Scotland's elite.

When the analysis and celebrations have ended and when the fixture lists for the new season are published outlining the return of the Old Firm, Dundee United, Aberdeen, Hearts, Hibs and the others to East End Park, then the full significance of the Pars' achievements will have sunk in — Dunfermline Athletic are back in the big time. Premier Bound. Up the Pars — at last!

Season Analysis

Airdrie	D	0-0	East Fife	L	2-4
	L	0-3		L	1-2
	D	1-1		D	1-1
	L	1-2		D	1-1
Brechin	W	4-1	Forfar	W	1-0
	W	4-0		D	3-3
	W	2-0		W	2-0
	L	0-2		L	1-3
Clyde	W	2-0	Kilmarnock	W	2-1
	L	0-1		W	1-0
	W	2-0		D	2-2
	W	1-0		L	0-1
Dumbarton	W	1-0	Montrose	W	1-0
	L	0-1		W	2-0
	W	2-1		W	2-0
	W	1-0		L	0-1

Morton		
W	1-0	
D	1-1	
D	2-2	
L	1-2	

Partick		
W	2-0	
W	1-0	
W	2-1	
W	2-0	

Queen of South		
D	1-1	
D	2-2	
W	2-1	
W	1-0	

	P	W	D	L	F	A	Pts
Partick	4	4	0	0	7	1	8
Brechin	4	3	0	1	10	3	6
Clyde	4	3	0	1	5	1	6
Montrose	4	3	0	1	5	1	6
Queen of South	4	2	2	0	6	4	6
Dumbarton	4	3	0	1	4	2	6
Forfar	4	2	1	1	7	6	5
Kilmarnock	4	2	1	1	5	4	5
Morton	4	1	2	1	5	5	4
East Fife	4	0	2	2	5	8	2
Airdrie	4	0	2	2	2	6	2
	44	23	10	11	61	41	56

	Appearances				Goals			
	League (44)	Skol (1)	Scottish (1)	Total (46)	League	Skol	Scottish	Total
S. Beedie	6	–	–	6				
J. Bowie	4 (4)	–	–	4 (4)				
I. Campbell	2 (8)	– (1)	–	2 (9)				
G. Connelly	5 (1)	–	–	5 (1)				
J. Donnelly	30	–	1	31	7	–	–	7
E. Ferguson	23 (10)	1	1	25 (10)	6	–	–	6
B. Forrest	40 (1)	1	1	42 (1)	1	–	–	1
R. Hamilton	14 (2)	–	1	15 (2)	2	–	–	2
I. Heddle	10	–	–	10	2	–	–	2
W. Irvine	6 (1)	–	–	6 (1)	2	–	–	2
G. Jenkins	28 (12)	–	1	29 (12)	6	–	–	6
I. McCall	29 (13)	1	– (1)	30 (13)	8	–	–	8
N. McCathie	44	1	1	46	6	–	–	6
B. MacKay	– (6)	–	–	– (6)				
S. Morrison	30 (6)	– (1)	1	31 (7)	5	–	–	5
D. Moyes	5	1	–	6				
G. Reid	16	1	– (1)	17 (1)				
B. Robertson	31	1	1	33				
T. Smith	7 (7)	1	–	8 (7)				
G. Thompson	38 (3)	1	–	39 (3)				
J. Waddell	1 (1)	–	–	1 (1)				
J. Watson	40	1	1	42	13	–	–	13
I. Westwater	42	1	1	44				
H. Whyte	2	–	–	2				
D. Young	31	–	1	32	1	–	–	1
						own goals		2
								61

Season 1986-87

Date	Opponents	F-A	Att.	League Position	Division One
1986					
July 30	Cowdenbeath (H)	5-0	–	–	Fife Cup
Aug 2	East Fife (A)	0-1	–	–	Fife Cup
9	Forfar (H)	1-0	3,294	–	
13	Dumbarton (A)	1-0	1,600	1	
16	Morton (A)	1-0	3,000	1	
20	St Mirren (H)	0-2	6,161	–	Skol Cup, Second Round
23	Clyde (H)	2-0	3,530	1	
30	East Fife (H)	2-4	4,448	2	
Sept 6	Kilmarnock (A)	2-1	2,700	2	
13	Brechin (A)	4-1	1,000	2	
16	Partick (H)	2-0	3,852	1	
20	Queen of South (A)	1-1	4,000	2	
27	Airdrie (H)	0-0	5,877	2	
30	Montrose (H)	1-0	3,498	1	
Oct 4	Forfar (A)	3-3	1,892	1	
8	Dumbarton (H)	0-1	4,161	1	
11	Clyde (A)	0-1	1,665	2	
18	Morton (H)	1-1	3,741	2	
25	Brechin (H)	4-0	3,159	1	
29	Partick (A)	1-0	2,579	1	
Nov 1	Kilmarnock (H)	1-0	4,179	1	
8	East Fife (A)	1-2	3,843	1	
15	Queen of South (H)	2-2	4,013	1	
22	Airdrie (A)	0-3	1,800	2	
29	Montrose (A)	2-0	1,200	1	
Dec 6	Forfar (H)	2-0	3,353	1	
13	Dumbarton (A)	2-1	4,000	1	
27	Morton (A)	2-2	3,200	1	
1987					
Jan 1	East Fife (H)	1-1	4,956	1	
3	Kilmarnock (A)	2-2	4,900	1	
24	Queen of South (A)	2-1	2,900	1	
Jan 31	Hibs (A)	0-2	16,500	–	Scottish Cup, Third Round
Feb 7	Airdrie (H)	1-1	4,272	1	
10	Clyde (H)	2-0	3,489	1	
21	Partick (H)	2-1	3,795	1	
24	Brechin (A)	2-0	1,000	1	
28	Forfar (A)	1-3	2,039	1	
Mar 3	Montrose (H)	2-0	3,539	1	
7	Dumbarton (H)	1-0	4,366	1	
14	Clyde (A)	1-0	1,500	1	
21	Morton (H)	1-2	5,959	1	
28	East Fife (A)	1-1	2,730	1	
April 4	Kilmarnock (H)	0-1	3,704	1	
11	Partick (A)	2-0	2,633	1	
18	Brechin (H)	0-2	4,645	1	
25	Queen of South (H)	1-0	5,482	1	Promotion Won
May 2	Airdrie (A)	1-2	2,759	2	
9	Montrose (A)	0-1	2,500	2	

Off the Field

While it was the events on the field which naturally grabbed the footballing headlines, there was a considerable amount of activity on the touchlines which merits attention, especially in the areas of sponsorship and of preparations to bring back full-time football to the club.

As one of the last full-time players when the club was forced to go part-time in 1976, Jim Leishman knew better than most the necessity of having at least a nucleus of players training at East End during the day. He noted with regret how Aberdeen and Dundee United had remained with a full-time set-up and how they had certainly reaped the benefits. A small, tentative step was taken in that direction on August 18 when eight 16-year-olds signed on as football apprentices under the auspices of the Manpower Services Commission's Youth Training Scheme, administered by Dunfermline District Council. The central theme of their course is football training with the rest of their day profitably spent at college following a wide range of general courses. After Christmas three more joined, enough for almost a full team in a few years.

A more significant step was taken in October when, with the team's prospects on the field so good, it was announced that several of the first team would be offered the chance to go full-time. While clearly this would not appeal to many of the squad who were already carving out successful careers elsewhere, the idea certainly had its attractions for many of the younger players. Connelly, Hamilton, Heddle, Morrison, Donnelly and McCall all expressed an early desire to avail themselves of the opportunity. The arrangement would also be a vital factor in persuading quality players to leave other prosperous clubs to come to East End Park in the future.

Hand in hand with this startling innovation went the news that Jim Leishman himself would go full-time, relinquishing his other job as commercial manager which had undoubtedly distracted him from concentrating fully on team matters. The board rightly saw in Leishman the man who had not just succeeded on the park but, equally, had brought a buzz back to the stadium through his infectious enthusiasm. In mid October he signed a two-year contract, a signal for other marauding club chairmen to look elsewhere.

Jim was also making the headlines in other ways. Following incidents at two games at the end of August — both against East Fife — he was reported to the S.F.A. by the referees for his conduct and he was summoned to Park Gardens. As he had already been fined £50 for a similar offence at Stenhousemuir in 1984, the authorities, as part of their clean-up campaign, took a dim view and banned him from the touchline for the remaining thirty games, with a £200 fine added for good measure.

Consequently, the prominent figure of the manager could now be seen taking his seat in the Directors' Box, a stage removed from the action. "The worst experience of my life" was how Jim summed up his first day of exile on October 18. Soon, he and his coach in the dug-out were linked by two-way radio to enable the stream of instructions, which seem to continually emanate from all management teams, to carry on. The dulcet tones of the manager could usually be heard in any case without resort to artificial aids.

Jim, however, was not totally unloved. Earlier in the month, an admiring fan had caused motorists to look twice as they passed around the unfinished roundabout near East End — "Leishman for Prime Minister" proclaimed a hand-painted board.

As a result of the club advertising for a new commercial manager, a new face appeared at Halbeath Road. She was the 29-year-old Karen Grega from Australia where she had 14 years' involvement with football as a player, referee and administrator. Since she arrived in Scotland six months earlier, she had worked with an Edinburgh public relations company which had involved her with the firm's Skol Cup and Hibernian accounts. "To begin with," she explained, "I'll probably just be trying to make the existing business practices more efficient. I'll definitely be looking at other areas that the club have wanted to go into, but have not had anyone with the time to do it."

Karen found that the club had already made great strides in the realms of sponsorship. For several years the club had relied on the traditional boarding around the ground and had usually managed to persuade a local company to sponsor the team. In a major new initiative at the start of the season, the Pars pulled off a major coup in clinching a six-figure deal with Aluglaze, the national double-glazing company.

Indeed, such a deal was due to have been signed in 1985 had the club gained promotion then. "The club's professionalism," remarked a company spokesman, "makes it hard to believe there is a better team for us to sponsor. We are confident Dunfermline Athletic will become a Premier team within the foreseeable future." In return, the club agreed to put the company's name on the strips and the tracksuits worn by the players as well as displaying adverts in the programme, round the track and in the stadium. With Dunfermline figuring three times on the television while still a First Division club and certain to feature more in the future, Aluglaze must already feel that some of their investment has paid off.

In early September, another significant deal was struck with Robert Nicol, the gents' outfitters in Chalmers Street, to supply the team and management with the latest style in blazers and slacks. Like Stein before him, Leishman understood the importance of having his players dressed smartly for social occasions and the value it had in making players think that the club cared for them. "We consider it important," explained Jim Leishman, "that everything is done to present the best possible image off the field." This was followed up by another generous gesture from Jeltek who agreed to donate outdoor gear to be worn in inclement weather.

At the start of the season, another innovation was introduced. Local firms were encouraged to be match sponsors whereby, for a significant donation to the club, the company would be the special guests of the Board at that particular game. As well as receiving free advertising in the programme, the sponsor and his guests are shown round the stadium, wined and dined in the Board Room and given reserved Stand seats. The highlight of the afternoon is the selection by the sponsor of the Man of the Match whom he presents with a special trophy. The scheme has been a great success and has generated additional finance and interest.

Another sponsorship deal, going back several seasons, between Taggarts and the club gives Jim Leishman the use of a car. In January, when severe weather conditions brought West Fife to a halt, a delighted but apprehensive manager received the keys to his new model, an Austin Montego, decorated with the club's name and badge.

In the same month, the old Fife Cash Lottery was wound up and a new Pars Pounds was launched with the guarantee of a £1000 prize every month. The introduction of selling kiosks in the Kingsgate Centre, Fine Fare and Asda has greatly helped this important fund-raising venture. In April, a new supporters' shop, offering a wide range of club goods, was opened and has proved very successful.

In December, the author and Douglas Scott combined forces to produce a three-hour video of the club's exploits in the 1960s called "Dunfermline Athletic – the Golden Years." The video relies on old archive film supplied by S.T.V. which is broken up by current interviews with some of the main participants. The action starts with Dunfermline's Cup win in 1961, continues through the early European action until the 1968 Final and ends with the last European match against Anderlecht in 1970. The nostalgic trip down memory lane proved to be most appealing to young and old fans alike.

The introductions to each match were expertly performed by Bob Crampsey whose own book, *Mr. Stein,* an affectionate but critical look at the great man, was also launched just before Christmas and sold widely in Dunfermline.

In the week before Christmas, Jim Leishman strengthened his backroom squad by appointing Ian Campbell (33) as player-coach to assist with first-team training and to help out with the reserve and youth squads. Only the previous month, it looked not unlikely that the veteran striker might have made permanent his temporary loan to Montrose.

However, it was not all good news at East End Park. At the end of September, vandals climbed on to the roof of the stadium and removed the League Flag which had been proudly hung there at the start of the season. Fortunately, acting on a tip-off, the police raided a house and recovered the precious item from under the floor boards.

The Board of Directors

When Dunfermline Athletic was converted to a limited company in 1919, its constitution stated that the club would be run by a Board of Directors appointed by the shareholders. It has always been the policy of the club never to pay fees nor dividends, but to plough money back into the club.

The post of director is not as glamorous as it might at first glance **149**

In the boardroom: The officials who took Dunfermline to the Premier League. From left: Jim McConville (Secretary), Roy Woodrow, Jim Leishman (Manager), Bill Braisby (Vice-Chairman), Mel Rennie (Chairman), Blair Morgan, Dr John Yellowley and Jimmy Watters. (Dunfermline Press).

seem from the terracing. A quick perusal of the minutes of any Board meeting would reveal the wide-ranging duties to which the directors must attend: the employment of more than 50 workers; the maintenance of the ground and buildings which, as the Government rightly insists on more stringent safeguards, impose many headaches; the balancing of the books; the establishment of overall club policy; liaison with numerous outside bodies such as the S.F.A., the Scottish Football League, the police, local authorities and the press; and dealing with day-to-day business as it arises. In addition to the weekly board meetings, a director can expect to have several other evenings devoted to club business: attending reserve games, supporters' club functions, fund raising events as well as **150** a number of business meetings with interested parties.

The current Board will be remembered as the one which took Dunfermline into the Premier League for the first time. They have a great deal of experience of the game and Mel Rennie is fortunate to have two ex-chairmen to offer advice. They blend together very well, so much so that a board meeting, once the essential business is over, can extend well into the night as more general matters are discussed. All, bar one, live within a stone's throw of the ground. The past two seasons have been particularly nerve-racking ones and the Board, not wishing to count chickens before they were hatched, could never be sure whether they were planning for a continued existence in the First Division or for participation with the footballing elite. To a man, they are ambitious and totally loyal to the club, and are determined that Dunfermline Athletic will not be the whipping boys of the Premier League.

Chairman: Mel Rennie

There are some chairmen in the sport today who regard running a football club in the same way as a game of Monopoly: a stadium to be bought one year and sold off the next for a handsome profit as a shopping development; they view a turn on the Terry Wogan show as more important than attendance at a supporters' club meeting.

Happily, Mel Rennie belongs to that older-fashioned breed of chairmen who quietly gets on with the job behind the scenes, creating the right conditions under which manager, players, officials and fans can all live in harmony. He prefers to let actions on the field take the place of fine, but empty, phrases. He has always taken his involvement with Dunfermline Athletic very seriously, his last season as chairman especially so. He is a quiet spoken, unflappable, generous and able man who exhibits few of the trappings of the self-made millionaire that he is.

William Melbourne Rennie was born in 1924 in Arbroath, the son of a railway signalman. His father spent some time in Australia, hence his middle name. As a boy he watched his local team, the Red Lichties. On leaving school at 14 with no qualifications, he began an apprenticeship as a joiner, a trade which he has never totally given up. The Second World War destroyed his quiet existence and in 1942, when he was 18, he volunteered at the first opportunity for the R.A.F., serving in Air Sea Rescue. In June 1944, he made the short, but hazardous, trip on H.M.S. *Adventure* as part of the D-Day landings. The end of the war brought about his demobilisation and the end of a great period of camaraderie, something which he was later to find in the world of football. He returned to his trade but this time in Dunfermline, the town to which his family had now moved. As post-war austerity gave way to a growing affluence in the 1950s, Mel decided to branch out on his own, employing an extra man each successive year. With remarkable foresight, he anticipated the housing demand of the 1960s and turned his attention to private building in which he fast built up a considerable reputation. In the 1980s, he now has the largest firm of housebuilders in West Fife, employing more than 40 men and sub-contracting many more. Mel also saw the need to diversify, taking up a directorship with Landmark, the furniture retailing group, and also buying a farm in Oakley.

During this time, he was an avid supporter of the Pars and through his friendship with Leonard Jack, who wisely saw the need for a builder on the board, became a director in 1971. This was not the most auspicious time to join the club as it was now suffering a severe financial crisis and, as hindsight was to show, the end of a glorious decade had just occurred. Throughout his term of office, he has personally seen to the maintenance of the ground and its not inconsiderable fixtures and has taken great pride in the many compliments bestowed on the stadium. Like many chairmen and directors before him, the club would have gone bankrupt if he **151** had charged for all the time, labour and materials which were so freely given. For a number of years he also sponsored the team.

But for the premature retirement of Jimmy Watters, Mel Rennie might never have become chairman. The last season has been an immense challenge to him and he has taken great personal satisfaction from subsequent developments. When asked why the club has done so well, he will quickly praise his manager and his colleagues but will not entertain the idea that he had anything to do with it, simply claiming that the wheel of fortune had now spun Dunfermline's way.

One small incident sums up his standing in the club. On the day the club won their promotion, the players washed the ball in the bath (along with the chairman!) and presented it to him, signed by all the staff. Of all the possessions in his house, this is one that money cannot buy.

In his spare time he enjoys gardening, joinery (he built the magnificent Trophy Cabinet which adorns the Board Room) and the pleasure of Gleneagles Country Club.

Bill Braisby: Vice-Chairman

Bill (54) has been a lifelong supporter of the Pars. Brought up in West Fife as a boy, he can vividly remember watching Jim Logie, Willie Harley and Billy Liddle guest for Dunfermline during the war. On leaving school at the age of 14 with no formal qualifications, he started work in the newspaper depot of John Menzies in St. Margaret's Street. From there, he began a five-year apprenticeship as a

slater, earning the princely sum of 25 shillings a week. Two years of national service then intervened which saw him serve with the Black Watch and the Gordon Highlanders in Germany.

In 1962, with a family of 3 to support, he took the bold step of setting up his own business and after a great deal of worry and hard work, he established it into a prosperous venture, employing more than 100 men at one stage. He and his wife also set up "Lin-Lor," a health and beauty salon in their home village of Cairneyhill.

Bill joined the board in 1981 and became vice-chairman in 1986 when Mel Rennie became chairman. A few years ago, he was instrumental in setting up at East End Park the official Supporters' Club of which he is honorary president. He was also Chairman of the Centenary Club for one and a half years during which he helped establish it as a rich source of income for the club. His son, Billy junior, is also an avid Pars' fan and is now vice-chairman of the Centenary Club.

Director: John C. Yellowley

John Yellowley is the longest serving director on the present board and a past chairman. He was born in Northumberland in 1924 and as his father served in the R.A.F., the family had to travel around England and went as far afield as Egypt. The family finally settled in Dunfermline before the war and John enrolled at Dunfermline High School for the start of his second year. As a youth, he enjoyed both playing and watching football and cricket and indeed, after war service in the navy, caught the attention of Queen's Park. He also played football in the Kirkcaldy Amateur League.

It was medicine, however, which was to be his main goal and he graduated from Edinburgh University in 1952. After working in various hospitals, the young doctor served as a G.P. in Gourock and Burntisland before arriving in Dunfermline to the practice of Dr. A. Morris on April 1, 1958. In the 1960s he also served for a while as police surgeon.

An excellent chance to combine business and pleasure came when he succeeded Dr. Robson as the club doctor in 1965. Two years later he was co-opted on to the Board, just in time to help plan Dunfermline's second Cup win in 1968.

When chairman Leonard Jack died in 1971, John Yellowley was elected chairman, little realising that the golden era the club had recently enjoyed was about to end.

In 1982 after a difficult, often frustrating, twelve years, he resigned after holding office for longer than any of his predecessors. John Yellowley has lost none of his enthusiasm for the game and his long experience is much treasured by his colleagues. Currently, he takes an interest in meeting the scouts and in reviewing the progress they have made.

It is often forgotten that he also serves as the club doctor. It is his duty to check that any player joining the club is fully fit, thus ensuring that a valuable investment would be able to give long service. His enjoyment of the game on a Saturday afternoon is often interrupted as he makes his way out of the Directors' Box to the dressing-room to deal with a serious injury, even if sustained by a visiting player. Keeping a watchful eye on him are his two young apprentices, doctors Hugh Whyte and Bobby Robertson.

In his spare time, he enjoys angling, travel, cricket and golf.

Director: Jimmy Watters

Jimmy was born and brought up in Buckhaven and, at the tender age of 16 in 1944, turned out for Hearts as a

From left: Past Chairman Jimmy Watters (1982-86). Current Chairman Mel Rennie. Present Vice-Chairman Bill Braisby.

goalkeeper. He modestly claims that war-time conditions and the slow demobilisation of the soldiers kept the older players from offering an effective challenge. He played for the Tynecastle side and later with East Fife till 1956 during which time he has many memories of appearances at East End Park.

An architectural draughtsman by profession, he and his wife, Mary, later successfully operated two catering businesses, "La Speranza" in Kirkcaldy and "Giacomo's" in Dunfermline. In 1970 he was persuaded to give up his connection with the East Fife Board and to join that of Dunfermline. Alex Wright was then manager. When John Yellowley became chairman in 1971, Jimmy stepped up to become vice-chairman, a post which he diligently held until 1982 before becoming chairman himself. Tom Forsyth was then manager but he did not last long and under Jimmy's guiding hand, the Board made one of their best appointments for years — that of Jim Leishman. The two men got on extremely well together establishing almost a father-son relationship which did nothing but good for the club. The cruel disappointment at the end of season 1984-85 was a bitter blow to both men.

Jimmy found himself presiding over the club's many Centenary celebrations in 1985, duties which he enjoyed but which were also very tiring. More exhausting was the planning — and the watching — of Dunfermline finally winning promotion in 1986. Jimmy has always taken his duties seriously and beneath his amiable disposition lies a worrying nature. He wisely,

but regrettably, followed his doctor's order to take life more easily and resigned as chairman in the summer of 1986.

He was persuaded to remain on the Board to give them the benefit of his long experience in the game as a player and administrator. One of his duties is to oversee the catering contracts at the club and, at a humbler but equally vital level, to provide nourishment at the long board meetings which are now beginning to rival Parliament's late-night sessions.

When not working, Jimmy enjoys a game of bridge and golf.

Director: Blair Morgan

At 39, Blair is the youngest member of the Board. A solicitor in a thriving legal practice in the town, Blair is the first lawyer to serve on the Board since Leonard Jack in 1971. In the complex world of modern football, his talents are much appreciated. He attends to conveyancing matters, lotteries, sponsorship deals and the intricacies of commercial transactions as well as meeting with many outside agencies.

Born on Christmas Day, 1947, Blair has lived in Dunfermline all his life and can recall following the Pars as a young boy when he met heroes like Harry Melrose, Charlie Dickson and Alex Smith on the team bus in the late fifties. From Dunfermline High School, he went to Edinburgh University where he studied law. On graduating, he remained in the city to complete his two-year apprenticeship with a local firm of solicitors.

As a youth, Blair excelled at many sports, rugby and athletics in particular. He represented the university at both of these sports and acquitted himself well. Coached by Jock Thomson from Townhill, Blair won the British Boys' Club Championship at Crystal Palace in 1964. While playing for Dunfermline Rugby Club, he helped them win promotion to Division One in 1974. While there, he was selected several times to play at district level for North and Midlands, then coached by Adam Robson who later went on to become S.R.U. President in the year of the Grand Slam.

Another great passion in Blair's life is music. In 1964 he won the Scottish Accordion Championship and he is also an accomplished pianist. It is with pleasure that he attends to the legal affairs of a number of pop groups like Nazareth, 7 – West, Heart Industry and Billy Rankin. It was Blair, of course, who arranged the recording of the club's anthem, "East Enders", last season.

Blair still plays many sports and is looking forward to beating Bobby Robertson, the club champion, on the tennis courts during the team's visit to Majorca. Another of his hobbies is cars, whether of the classic or modern variety. He and his family enjoy foreign travel.

Director: Roy Woodrow

Roy, born in June 1941, comes from a long established Dunfermline family. His grandfather, James Woodrow, started the family business in Rolland Street under the name of "Aerated Water Manufacturer". The business had grown so much by the early seventies that new premises had to be occupied in the Pitreavie Industrial Estate and it now has depots in Oban and Fort William to meet ever increasing demand.

Roy, born, bred and educated in Dunfermline, has been a Pars' fan for as long as he can remember and his firm have always helped out by taking advertising space in the programme and around the ground.

At the beginning of January 1986, he and Blair were co-opted on to the Board to inject younger blood into their group. "We've got to encourage the paying public to come," he explained on taking up office. "There are so many different attractions for people on a Saturday. It is so easy for them not to come to a match". From that date, whether coincidentally or not, the club has certainly prospered and Roy looks forward to the challenge of the Premier League. He is a past member of the West Fife Rotary Club and enjoys curling and travel.

Secretary: Jimmy McConville

To anyone who has followed Dunfermline Athletic since the last War, the name of Jimmy McConville needs no introduction. He has just completed 35 years of unbroken service to the club – half a lifetime by Biblical standards, and his appetite for the game and his love of East End Park show no signs of abating. Jimmy, born on March 21 1915, has served under 11 managers.

As a 10-year old boy, brought up next to East End, he can recall visiting the ground regularly to lay sawdust markings on the pitch in preparation for Saturday's games. He was a member of **155** the Supporters' Club, then officially attached to East End Park, and in 1952 he was elected to the then seven-strong board. Jimmy was one of those advocates who successfully pressed for the share issue to be tidied up to prevent too frequent changes to the Board which brought instability. It was by bringing about such major constitutional change that the club was able to prepare itself for the football revolution which later took place on the field.

On leaving school, Jimmy served an apprenticeship as a clerk with a local linen manufacturer and then left to join a haulage contractors' business. During the war he joined the forces (R.A.O.C.) and was eventually posted overseas where he saw service in Iraq, Iran and the Middle East. On his return to Scotland, he eventually took up employment with the Gas Board before becoming a sub-postmaster.

In 1954 "Wee Jimmy" then became Secretary. "We were a part-time club then, the old wooden stand held 600 people and the north enclosure was a Nissan hut". The arrival of Jock Stein transformed the club and for the hard-working secretary it meant a great deal of extra – and pleasurable – work in organising all-ticket games and in making arrangements for European travel. Obviously, the 1960s were a great decade for Jimmy – there is hardly a European country he has not visited with the club; there is not a boardroom in Scotland which he has not entered.

Jimmy always claims to have a bad memory but, given the right prompt, he will launch with glee into a story about which everyone else has forgotten – a trip to Wembley, a dinner in New York,

156

a match in the Second Division, a prank which only footballers could dream up in a foreign hotel. He remembers meeting Archbishop Makarios; an escape through a gauntlet of angry fans in France; a police escort; and a host of fascinating memories, the subject of a book in their own right. He has seen the club promoted no less than six times and he is looking forward to the big time returning to East End.

Jimmy, "the Laird of Kelty," has many other pastimes. He has been a J.P. for many years, a member of Cowdenbeath Rotary Club, a patron of Kelty Musical Association, Secretary to the Fife Football Association and he has been actively involved in Trade Union matters. He has also served on various club committees – the Sportsmen's Club, the D.A.F.C. Improvements Society and the Paragon Club. All these positions have been held in an honorary capacity. He lives with his wife, Grace, in Kelty where he still works as a postmaster. In his spare time he enjoys bowling.

The Manager: Jim Leishman

In 1953 Queen Elizabeth was crowned, Mount Everest was conquered and Winston Churchill was prime minister. On November 15 of that year, Mitchell and Mary Leishman announced the birth of their fourth child, James. Already they had two sons, Mitchell and George, and one daughter, Elizabeth. The arrival of a fourth child stretched the family budget at their home in Lochgelly. Mitchell senior was a coalworker in the local pits

A rare moment of relaxation for Jim, Mary and Kate Leishman

and it was a continuing struggle to make ends meet. Jim grew up in a close-knit, loving family and in a small community largely dependent on coal for its survival.

As a young boy, Jim attended Lochgelly South and West primary schools. He enjoyed his football, like most youngsters, and even then acquired the nickname of "Big Leish." His secondary education took place at Beath H.S. where he was a prefect and where he gained six 'O' grades and two highers. At this time he was involved in the scouting movement and was assistant leader with 33rd Fife (Macainsh Church) Scout Troop. He recalls with pleasure the camping trips, the rambles and the competitions he undertook. He gained further experience helping youngsters by running the U-14 team of Woodmill Boys' Club.

While Jim was still at school, he signed an 'S' Form with Dunfermline Athletic and played with the nursery club, Dunfermline United. Jim arrived at East End when the club was at its peak in the late sixties and the impressionable youth could not but be inspired by the set-up: a fine stadium, the Scottish Cup in the Boardroom, European competitions, famous players on the books. George Farm was the manager, Andy Young coached the youngsters and Joe Nelson also assisted behind the scenes.

Jim's promising career was confirmed when he, along with four others from the club, was chosen to play against the English Schoolboys at Airdrie. Manager Alex Wright gave him his break into the first team against Ayr on September 18, 1971. Although Dunfermline were going through a sticky patch which was to end with the club being relegated in 1972, Jim became a regular player, valiantly shoring up the defence. He was a member of the squad which took Dunfermline back into the First Division in 1973 under the guidance of George Miller, one of Jim's idols.

Disaster struck for Jim in a League Cup match against Hearts on August 21 1974 when he suffered a badly broken leg in a tackle with Jim Jeffries. Although the leg eventually healed, Jim was never to be the same player again. Even today, his leg can still give him a few twinges. His career was effectively over, despite making a brave comeback later.

Under Harry Melrose, Jim made only one appearance, as a substitute, and was transferred to Cowdenbeath in a player-swap with Bobby Morrison. He had played 81 full games for Dunfermline over five seasons, scoring six goals in the process, one of which was a real beauty against Rangers in 1972. The move to Central Park did not work out — he made only 11 appearances during which he suffered the indignity of being sent off against his old club, for only the second time in his career. After a short spell with Glenrothes and Oakley, he gave up football completely on doctor's orders. This was a cruel blow for someone who was only 23 years old with a full career ahead. When he sees Sandy Jardine and Kenny Dalglish playing today in their late thirties, he can only feel but saddened by his premature retiral.

For a brief spell, Jim managed Kelty Hearts and then he returned to Central Park to assist Andy Rolland. Jim's big chance to return to East End came when Pat Stanton, who had seen him at Cowdenbeath, invited him to take control of the youth team. Tom Forsyth

Jim Leishman proudly holding the Second Division Championship Cup. (Dundee Courier).

then appointed him as a coach in charge of the reserve team. Outside of football, Jim worked in a job centre at Cowdenbeath.

When Forsyth resigned in 1983, Jim was appointed caretaker manager and so impressed the Board that, in a bold gamble, they made his position permanent, but part-time. On starting his new career, Jim promised: "The club can expect honesty, enthusiasm, 100% effort and loyalty from me." They got that, and a great deal more.

Jim made an excellent choice in securing the services of Gregor Abel as his coach. The two worked together extremely well, neither afraid to speak his mind to the other. Gregor trains the players and works out the set-pieces;

The pressures on the Manager can at times be overwhelming. (Dundee Courier).

Jim, who bears overall responsibility for the team, takes the general policy decisions. What followed is now part of Dunfermline's long history.

It is premature at this stage to compare Jim Leishman with his more famous predecessors but certain points should be made. On his appointment in October 1983, he was Dunfermline's youngest manager at 29 years and indeed the youngest in Scotland. When Jock Stein came to the club he was 37 years old and a year older when he won the Cup. While Jim's colleagues of yester years were winning medals, Leish was thrown in at the deep end with a club desperately trying to get back on the rails. In a relatively short time, he has achieved what few thought was possible: he has produced a winning team, he has taken Dunfermline into the Premier League for the first time, a feat which eluded his four immediate predecessors, and he has helped the club financially to get on its feet to enable it to contemplate full-time football once again. At local schools, pupils who used to wear the scarves of fashionable English clubs, now sport once again the colours of Dunfermline Athletic. Above all, perhaps, he has given the club and its supporters new hope and confidence for the future.

Coaching Staff
Gregor Abel, Team Coach

Partnerships in football management have blossomed in recent years. Brian Clough and Peter Taylor hit the headlines with their work at Derby and Nottingham Forrest; more recently Graeme Souness and Walter Smith have brought the Premier League title to Ibrox. At East End Park there is another successful duo to add to that list — Jim Leishman and Gregor Abel. While Jim is obviously the more extrovert, the one who can displace politicians and celebrities from the front page of the local *Press,* Gregor is much quieter, solidly and conscientiously going about his business in the background.

Gregor himself is no stranger to football or indeed to football management. Born on April 9 1949 as one of three children, Gregor went to Falkirk H.S. where his talent for sport generally, and for football in particular, quickly shone through. His cousin, Ian Cowan, played for Dunfermline and Partick Thistle. While deciding to train as a physical education teacher at

Gregor — as a formidable, uncompromising player with Clydebank.

159

Jordanhill College, Gregor pursued his footballing career with vigour. He was first farmed out to Bo'ness United to "toughen him up".

He spent six good years at Brockville from 1966 to 1972, making 82 appearances and playing full back alongside Alex Ferguson and Andy Roxburgh. Under the guidance of Willie Cunningham, the former Dunfermline manager, they won the Second Division Championship in season 1969-70. In 1972 he went to Clydebank, not the most glamorous of postings perhaps, but while at Kilbowie he helped the Bankies to win promotion in successive seasons from 1975 to 1977, a feat which he has just repeated with Dunfermline. He made 283 appearances and scored the only three goals of his senior career.

As the twilight of his playing career approached, he moved to Alloa at Christmas 1979 and six months later he took the significant step of also becoming a coach. In all, as a professional player, he had made 400 first-team appearances before giving up the playing side in October 1980. With Alex Totten as manager, Gregor's golden touch again worked miracles and Alloa were promoted to the First Division in 1982. His excellent working relationship with the ex-Dunfermline player continued in Christmas 1982 when he followed him to Brockville to be his deputy there.

It can only be a matter of conjecture what the pair might have done for this ailing club had not the summons to assist Jock Wallace at Ibrox proved irresistible to Alex Totten. Unable to resist a challenge, Gregor accepted the vacant manager's job. It was a promotion which he very quickly regretted. While furthering his football and coaching careers on the field, Gregor had worked away steadily and faithfully in his job as a P.E. teacher at Falkirk and Inverkeithing High Schools before finally becoming Head of Department at Alva Academy, a full-time, demanding job. The extra strain which the Falkirk job imposed almost ruined his love for the game and it was not surprising that he resigned after only 3 months. It was, he noted on reflection, a part-time job with full-time commitments.

The football grapevine was at work, however, and Jim Leishman moved in quickly to make possibly his best ever signing in persuading Gregor to join the staff at East End at the end of February 1984. The acquisition of Gregor was to prove invaluable to the club. As a fully qualified S.F.A. coach — in fact, he coaches the coaches — Gregor knew the business inside-out and his good working practices were soon to shine through at the stadium, relieving a hard pressed manager to concentrate on other urgent matters.

Gregor gets to know players, to work out their strengths and weaknesses and how to get the best out of them. He devotes a lot of time to devising varied training schedules to keep the players sharp and interested; he meticulously keeps a record of everything he does with his players. A lot of time in training is spent in rehearsing moves and the fans have noticed a big improvement in the taking of free kicks. The high level of fitness of the squad has been a telling factor as a gruelling game neared its conclusion and the team could draw on that little extra they had in reserve. His knowledge of the game is so complete that his authority over the players is unobtrusive, yet total. He is quietly spoken, yet commanding. It has given him a tremendous thrill to see Dunfermline twice promoted; it surely cannot be a coincidence that every club he has been associated with, has also been promoted.

Joe Nelson, Assistant Trainer

Football clubs could not survive without the like of Joe Nelson in the background. Although officially designated one of the backroom staff, Joe's influence is to be seen everywhere. He attends to the players' every need on training nights and on match days, taking particular care that all their kit is clean and ready. At the end, he is responsible for seeing that everything is properly put away. During matches he takes his place in the dug-out, ready to deal with any unlikely emergency which might arise. Jim Leishman knows a job entrusted to Joe will always be done efficiently and well. Joe was a miner who took early retirement and he enjoys helping out at the club.

John Jobson, Reserve Coach

The past season was also a very successful one for the reserves. They thought they had won the Scottish Reserve League (East) before Christmas, only to discover that the goal-posts had been shifted. The competition continued after the New Year and the lads went on to finally emerge as winners, despite losing to Raith Rovers in the last game on May 4.

The official who looks after the reserves is John Jobson, born in Tayport on February 20 1957. From 1974 to 1984 he played for no less than five clubs, beginning with Raith Rovers whom he helped to promotion in 1976. From there, he moved to Central Park in 1977 to Berwick with whom he scored a hat-trick in just six minutes, then on to Meadowbank with whom he made 137 appearances and scored 59 goals. He played with Falkirk for one season 1982-83, then went to Recreation Park along with Gary Thompson. While there, a complicated fracture after only 11 appearances ended his career. After a brief coaching spell with a juvenile team in Kelty, he was invited to help out at East End Park, being appointed reserve coach when Andy Young left in 1985.

Philip Yeates

Philip (26), the team's physiotherapist, is the man whose job it is to get the players fit in time for matches. His treatment room at East End is one of the busiest places in the stadium at the height of the season as he desperately tries to massage a back or strengthen a limb to ensure that a player is ready for the line-up on Saturday. On a match day, he also carries the magic sponge, or spray as it is more likely to be, to revive a concussed player or to quickly patch up a gaping wound. His services have also been recognised by his selection as physio to the Scottish 'B' team in May 1987.

Pip, who is married to Joe Nelson's daughter, lives in Edinburgh and enjoys golf and a game of football with the lads. **161**

The Players

To be privileged to interview and photograph the players during training sessions at East End Park at the end of a memorable season, gave one a rare insight into the individuals who make up the team. Although the results had not always gone as planned on the field, the atmosphere was still that of one big, happy family. There were no recriminations, no harsh words, no slaggings; just honest enthusiasm, a good esprit de corps, a healthy respect for each other and desire to do better to please a fanatical, yet demanding, support. On one half of the field, hoses had been set out to water the fiery pitch; on the other half, Jim, Gregor and Ian were putting the players through their paces. A guided tour of supporters, organised by the Centenary Club, watched admiringly from the touchline.

On a lovely evening, when everyone was amazingly relaxed before the fixture that was to clinch promotion, it was not difficult to see why footballers take up the game: not necessarily for money or indeed glory, but simply for the opportunity to enjoy one another's company, to keep fit and kick that magic ball about.

All the players, without any encouragement, spoke highly of their boss and coach. They enjoyed the liberal, yet firm, discipline and the varied

The players who took the Pars into the Premier League for the first time ever: *Back:* Gordon Connelly, Trevor Smith, Stevie Morrison, Hugh Whyte, Ian Westwater, Grant Reid, Bobby Robertson, Davie Young. *Middle:* Joe Nelson, Philip Yeates, Willie Irvine, Rowan Hamilton, Ian McCall, Grant Jenkins, Norrie McCathie, Gary Thompson, John Donnelly, John Jobson, Ian Campbell. *Seated:* John Watson, Stuart Beedie, Gregor Abel, Jim Leishman, Bobby Forrest, Eric Ferguson.

training courses which had been established. They all singled Jim out as a great motivator, stressing how he could lift players before a game. They all commented on his pre-match talks which dealt with a wide variety of topics, not always directly related to tactics, but which nonetheless seemed to have the desired effect.

Jim is very much a players' manager. On the eve of what turned out to be the promotion-winning Saturday, he contacted the chairman and suggested a continental holiday for the players if they made the Premier League. Mel Rennie immediately contacted his fellow directors and within hours a trip to Magaluf in Majorca had been arranged. Alas, this book will have gone to print before the stories and the photographs will have filtered back from the Mediterranean.

The gesture, however, will perhaps take on a greater significance. Although this trip was purely for relaxation, it will be heartening to see a Dunfermline Athletic party climb on to an aeroplane at Turnhouse on their way to Europe. In 1959 the Dunfermline team received a similar treat (at a cost of £29 per person) and they, though they never even dreamed of the possibility, were on the verge of an historic era. It would be pleasant to hope that this Dunfermline squad might be on the threshold of another golden decade. They certainly deserve it.

Stuart Beedie

Stuart is a relative newcomer to East End Park but is already making his

Stuart Beedie

mark. Born on August 16 1960 in Aberdeen, Stuart attended Hilton Academy where John Hewitt, Neil Cooper and Ian Wilson were also pupils. He started his footballing career with Montrose in 1978 and later joined St. Johnstone for £15,000. While at Muirton Park he helped take the club into the Premier League, a level at which he has ample experience. He became their captain aged only 22 due to his ability to motivate others. Pars' fans will remember, with regret, how he played such a prominent role in helping to relegate their team on the last day of season 1982-83 at Perth where Dunfermline lost 1-0.

From Perth, he made the short trip to Dundee United where his finest, but saddest, moments occurred in 1984-85. The Taysiders made it to the final of the Skol Cup where they lost to Rangers. In the same season, Stuart returned to Hampden for the final of the Scottish **163**

Cup on May 18. In front of 60,000 fans, he scored United's single goal which looked like winning the cup until two late goals from Celtic took the trophy to Parkhead.

He then moved to Hibs for a substantial fee in 1986 and scored on his debut. A serious knee injury, however, kept him out of action for much of the season. At the end of March, Leishman stepped in with a £35,000 cheque to bring Stuart to Dunfermline. He is looking forward to regular first-team football again and his skilful midfield play and his experience of Premier League football should work to Dunfermline's advantage.

He now lives in Edinburgh where he enjoys golf and cricket. He is full-time with Dunfermline.

Jim Bowie

The departure of "Ziggy" at the end of March 1987 to St. Johnstone was a sad day for manager Jim Leishman and the fans at East End who highly valued this dedicated servant to the club. Jim had increasingly found it difficult to secure a first team place – his game on October 18 1986 against Morton as a substitute was his last outing – and the chance of full-time football at the tender age of 30 still appealed to him, though he left with great reluctance.

Jim was one of that small band of players who had been brought to East End about a decade earlier by Harry Melrose. He was born on February 2 1957 in Edinburgh. He played junior football with Pumpherston and joined the staff at East End on September 22 1976 when Dunfermline were struggling

after failing to enter the Premier League. He made his debut that day in a match against Clyde.

Over the years he has delighted the crowds with his delicate skill and application. Injury and problems at work have not always made him an automatic choice for the team, though he seldom complained at being left out. Initially, he started as a midfielder but was converted by Stanton to a winger, a role which he did not always relish but one which he accomplished with verve. High scoring forwards like John Watson depend on his excellent crosses to build up their goal tally. A fine example of this was displayed on September 30 1986 in the match against Montrose when a perfectly flighted cross was met head on by a diving Watson to score a glorious winner.

His contribution in Dunfermline's promotion-winning season of 1985-86 will never be forgotten. He made 30 league appearances, nine as substitute, and though he scored only two goals, he made more and undoubtedly helped the club to achieve its goal. During his stay at Dunfermline, his only senior club, "Ziggy" made the line-up in 187 games plus 40 as substitute and scored 13 goals.

Ian M. Campbell

Born in Dunfermline on November 22nd 1953, Ian is easily the eldest of the squad. He is one of seven children and is a twin to Richie whom older fans will remember at East End. Two of Ian's uncles played senior football – Alex and Willie Menzies.

Ian did well as a pupil at Beath H.S., excelling in particular at all forms of

Ian Campbell

Welfare he scored 25 goals in one season and then joined the Dunfermline team which had regained First Division status in 1973. He played with the club for two seasons making over 50 appearances and scoring 13 goals. When Ian refused to accept a part-time contract after the club failed to reach the Premier League in 1975, he was given a free transfer and found himself at Arbroath where an unhappy season saw him make only one full appearance. His sojourn with Cowdenbeath for a single season brought little more satisfaction though he did make 25 full appearances and scored three goals.

A move to Brechin City, by contrast, gave him seven and a half happy seasons, the highlight of which was winning the Second Division Championship in 1983 under Ian Stewart. Moving from the midfield to the forward line, Ian scored no less 137 goals in over 300 appearances.

He was persuaded to return to East End in March 1985 to help his old club in the final push for promotion in their Centenary year. In his first match at Stranraer, he showed the fans that he had lost none of his old magic by scoring a goal. Last season he played a major part in the Pars' successful push for promotion and although he did not play the full 90 minutes in many games, he managed to become the club's second top goal scorer on 18 goals. Ian tries to slow the pace down in a game and build up the play, a feature which does not always endear him to some sections of the crowd.

sport, and it was no surprise when he went to Jordanhill College where he trained to be a P.E. teacher and graduated with a B.Ed. (Hons.). He taught at Kirkcaldy H.S. for six years but was reluctantly persuaded to join a local double-glazing company as their staff development manager.

Football has always been the love of Ian's life and he can recall playing either against or with Jim Leishman at almost every level. At primary school he played against a Lochgelly team which had a young Leishman in goal. He recalls that Jim lost so many goals to him that he gave up as a 'keeper and turned his talents to the outfield. He and Jim went on to play together at under-14, under-16 and under-18 level. With Lochore

Increased competition and an annoying knee injury have kept him out of the first team for much of the past **165** season and he was sent out on loan for a month to Montrose. Happily for Dunfermline, the arrangement did not work out and "Pink" returned to East End at Christmas to be appointed a coach, assisting Gregor Abel. He is often referred to as a good, model professional and his qualities of honesty, loyalty and integrity are sure to be appreciated by the younger players. He reckons he has only been booked twice in his long career.

It would be a rash person who would write off Ian's playing career at this stage. He is keen on all sports, especially athletics, and keeps himself in excellent trim. He has threatened to continue playing to the age of 40 – don't be surprised if he does.

He and his wife, Rona, have two children, Allan and Alistair, with another one expected in June.

Gordon Connelly

Born on September 20 1967, Gordon (19) is one of the club's youngest players. When he left St. Modan's H.S. in his native Stirling at the age of 16, he went straight into professional football with Burnley. When that once proud English club was later relegated to the Fourth Division, the management had a great clear-out and Gordon was one of the victims. He returned north and was signed by Leishman in 1985.

A slightly built player – 5'5" tall and weighing only 9 stones 7 pounds, Gordon operates in the midfield and forward departments. Last season he played well in the reserves but only managed to break into the first team on one occasion. That was on the night of Wednesday March 12 when his team

Gordon Connelly

struggled in their promotion bid at Ochilview. Gordon, in fact, was substituted. This season saw him have an extended run of five games before Christmas during which the team only lost one game. Injury and the increasing tempo of the struggle for promotion have kept him on the sidelines. He has undoubted skills and could be challenging for a permanent berth in the not too distant future.

Gordon is one of the players who jumped for full-time training during the season at East End Park, having previously lost his job as a painter. He has put his coaching to good use by running an under-15 team in Stirling, Carse Thistle, which won the Scottish Cup in 1986. Unmarried, Gordon enjoys all sports, especially golf, tennis and snooker.

John Donnelly

The signing of midfielder John Donnelly last September was a real sign that Dunfermline was serious in attracting

John Donnelly

top class players to the club. John, born and bred in Glasgow, is a true professional and was quick to sign full-time papers with the club during the winter. As a schoolboy at St. Mungo's in Glasgow, John was keen on athletics, coming third in the Scottish Schools Championship in the cross-country, a pursuit which still interests him. It was football of course which was his main interest and, on leaving school, he immediately went to Notts County as a young apprentice. He was, like so many others, homesick and he returned for one season to Motherwell, then in the Premier League. With them, he gained a Scottish Youth Cap. From there, he moved to Dumbarton where he spent three successful years which saw him move down south once again for £30,000 to Leeds United. Under Eddie Gray's management he made 50 first team appearances, scoring eight times, and he savoured the big-time atmosphere of full-time training facilities.

After one and a half years, he was transferred to Partick Thistle, Dunfermline then failing to catch his signature.

The acquisition of John for £5,000 was a shrewd piece of business on Jim Leishman's part. John rightly felt that Dunfermline, with its fine stadium and good crowds, was the place to be and his ability to slow the game down in midfield has paid dividends. Another notable factor in his play has been his talent to strike the ball cleanly and fiercely, whether from set-pieces or during the play. Such skills have already brought him seven goals, the most spectacular being his last one against his old club at Firhill in April which tied up two valuable promotion points.

His brother Tom played with Hamilton until forced out through injury. John travels with the others from Glasgow – Grant Reid, Stevie Morrison and Gary Thompson. In his spare time, John enjoys horse racing and athletics.

Eric Ferguson

Eric is one of the new players who joined Dunfermline at the start of the season. In July, he got off to a cracking start by knocking in two goals against Cowdenbeath in the Fife Cup but has only managed six league goals since then. Unfortunately, illness and niggling injuries plus a healthy competition for places in the forward line have kept him from establishing himself regularly in the first team. Fans have probably yet to see the best of the young striker who has just turned 22.

Eric, one of four brothers, was brought up in Kincardine and attended Dunfermline High School where the **167**

Eric Ferguson

a dozen appearances over three seasons with no goals to show for it. Once again he was loaned out, this time to Southampton on a monthly basis. New manager Souness did offer Fergie a one-year contract but Eric, impressed by the set-up at East End, decided to come to his native Fife and was signed by Jim Leishman on May 22 1986.

Though sorry about giving up full-time football, Eric has found a job as a sales rep with a chemical company and is enjoying his spell at Dunfermline. Eric lives in Dalgety Bay and enjoys golf, driving and snooker.

Bobby Forrest

Though born in Hamilton on August 9 1960, Bobby lives in the East of Scotland and works as a gardener at Loanhead in Midlothian. He is married to

author remembers him as a mild-mannered, quiet boy, eager to assist in any way. While at school he played juvenile with Gairdoch, occasionally playing at centre half but normally operating up front. His ability attracted both Dundee and Rangers but it was the latter club which secured his signature on an S-form. He went straight to Ibrox on leaving school but inevitably found himself a small cog in a very big wheel. In season 1983-84 he was loaned out to Clydebank to gain experience and while there scored eight goals in 18 appearances.

He returned to Rangers and managed to play for them in Australia when he was flown out to replace the injured Bobby Williamson. With so much talent at Ibrox, he still found it difficult to make **168** it to the first team, managing only about

Bobby Forrest

Ruth and they have one child, Nicola. Like most of his mates, Bobby likes to relax over a game of golf or snooker.

Bobby was one of the last signings that Harry Melrose made in November 1980 before he resigned the following month. His form as a winger with junior club, Penicuik Athletic, had impressed the scouts and new manager, Pat Stanton, called him up in the following spring along with Grant Jenkins to inject new life into an ailing team. Though Bobby made a promising debut against Aberdeen in a friendly match in July 1981, during which he scored a goal, he found it difficult to break into the first team as there were plenty of wingers on the staff and in his first season he made only 12 full appearances, scoring two goals in the process. Pat Stanton played him once as a full back in a reserve game, a fact which was remembered when Leishman decided to play him in that position in the now famous Cup-tie at Ibrox in January 1984. From then on, Bobby has made the left back position his own and has carried out his duties remarkably well for someone with little experience of defending. There is still something, however, of the winger in him and he continues to delight the crowd and occasionally shames his younger forwards, by charging down the left wing at full pelt and delivering an accurate cross. Nor has he forgotten how to score good goals, as those at Rugby Park last September will remember when he scored a remarkable winner.

Bobby has never been with another senior club and his loyalty and dedication to Dunfermline Athletic have made him a favourite with the crowd. He has already chalked up more than 200 appearances for the club, scoring 17 goals, with the prospect of many more to come.

Rowan Hamilton

Rowan was born on December 29 1964 in Ballingry and attended the local High School there. While still at school, he played in a Sunday League for Hill of Beath Swifts. Despite attracting a lot of attention from local clubs, Rowan went straight from school to play full-time for Dundee in 1981.

Unfortunately, the Dens Park side seemed to spend most of its time avoiding relegation and Rowan failed to break into the first team. However, under the guiding hand of reserve coach, Jockie Scott, Rowan and his mates won the Reserve Scottish Cup. After three and a half years at Dundee and apparently getting nowhere, Rowan was happy to sign for Dunfermline in 1984, especially as he continued to live in his native Fife. He made his debut against Stranraer on August 11 and went on to

Rowan Hamilton

make another 31 appearances that season though he failed to score any goals. He played a major part the following season in helping the Pars to win the Second Division title. He made no less than 32 League appearances and scored five goals, one of the most important being at Broomfield when he notched the one that confirmed Dunfermline as winners against Albion Rovers.

During the past season he has failed to confirm the promise he showed earlier. As with others in the squad, he has found that the new arrivals to the ground have made competition for a place all the harder. He made three appearances as full back and 12 in the midfield, scoring two goals in the process.

Rowan (22) is unmarried and works as a storeman with Taggarts Garage, next door to East End Park. He is still friendly with Ian Heddle and both of them coach youngsters at Dunfermline Centre. Rowan is 5'9" and weighs 12 stones.

Ian Heddle

Although Ian was transferred to St. Johnstone at Christmas 1986, he will be remembered at the club for several reasons and his contribution to Dunfermline's double promotion was not inconsiderable. Ian was Jim Leishman's first signing as manager in October 1983 and on August 7 1985, his left-foot volley against Aberdeen won the Pars the Centenary Challenge Cup.

Ian was born in Dunfermline on March 21 1963 and has spent all his life in the town, the only player so to do. He

Ian Heddle

has supported the Pars since he was a boy of ten. Ian attended Woodmill High School and always showed promise there as a footballer. Perhaps that was not surprising as his grandfather, Jimmy Birrell, had played for Celtic in the late 1930s. As a youth, Ian played for Hill of Beath at under-16 level and Inverkeithing at under-18. He then went on to play juvenile with Dunfermline Railway Club and so impressed the scouts that he was quickly brought to East End as a midfielder.

Ian made his debut against Forfar on January 9 1984 in the Scottish Cup, one of just two first-team appearances that season. The following season saw him make only slightly more – three outings – which brought him his first goal, against Queen of the South in the league. Season 1985-86 was his best with the club. He made 30 appearances, scored five goals and seemed to be establishing himself as a first team regular.

He is a naturally left-sided player and can unleash a powerful shot. He has, however, suffered from inconsistency and a less than tolerant crowd did not always give him an easy time, especially when he was playing out of position at full back. Though he made several first team appearances in the past season, his future was put in doubt when John Donnelly, another left-footed player, was bought from Partick. Ian returned to the reserves once again and indeed so impressed the Perth mananger in a match that he decided to buy him. The prospect of regular first team football appealed to Ian and he volunteered to go to Muirton Park. It was no surprise that he scored the winning goal against Berwick on his debut.

Ian, single, continues to live in Dunfermline and works as a welder. He enjoys all sports, especially golf. He and Rowan coach youngsters at Dunfermline Centre and enjoy the experience.

Willie Irvine

Willie Irvine

Willie is another of the newcomers to East End this season, having signed along with Stuart Beedie from Hibs at the end of March 1987. He was born in Stirling on December 28 1963 and attended Woodlands H.S. in Falkirk. He played juvenile football with Dunipace and then joined Stirling Albion in 1982 for whom he was a regular goal-scorer. In season 1984-85 he notched up 21 goals in 35 league matches, form which saw him snatched up by Hibs for £35,000. He never settled at Easter Road, making only two full league appearances for them in 1986-87, so a move to Dunfermline for £15,000 suited all concerned.

Willie, who is married to Lynn, currently lives in Linlithgow and works as a sheet metal worker at Bonnybridge. Like most of his new team-mates, he enjoys golf and snooker in his spare time.

He made a dramatic entry to the team on March 28 at Bayview when he stepped straight into the side and coolly stroked home a penalty equaliser to give Dunfermline a much needed promotion point. He will be remembered even more for the historic goal he scored against Queen of the South on April 25 to send his new side into the Premier League for the first time. He has already shown some fine touches and could be a good buy for the Pars in their bid to consolidate their position in the Premier League.

Grant Jenkins

In many ways, it is quite remarkable that Grant Jenkins is with Dunfermline Athletic in the season of their promotion to the Premier League. At the age of 22 years, by which time most budding professionals have tucked away a few honours, Grant was still playing junior football in Perthshire, near his home in Crieff. When he was 16 he played with Crieff Earngrove and stayed with them for six years before moving on to Jeanfield Swifts. It was then that scout Ned McGeachie noted his goal-scoring feats and on his recommendation, he played in a trial match at East End and manager Pat Stanton signed him in February 1981. Within a fortnight he was playing in the first team – against Hibs – and by the end of the following month he had scored his first league goal, against Motherwell. For the next five seasons he has never been able to command a steady place in the team

172   Grant Jenkins

but he has generally managed to play in more than half of the games over the season. In the past season, he has found the competition for places greater with the arrival of new strikers, Eric Ferguson and Ian McCall, but the bearded forward has always persevered and generally is never far from making at least the substitute's bench. During his stay at East End, he has made over 200 appearances and scored more than 50 goals, some of them real beauties like the one against Montrose in March.

Travelling difficulties and personal problems have also taken their toll of him and once or twice a move to another, more suitable club like St. Johnstone seemed imminent. Just when it seemed he might be departing, the deal was called off, he was recalled to the first team and another scintillating display reassured him that this future lay at East End Park.

During the week Grant works as a scrap metal merchant in Perthshire. He is married to Jane and they have one boy, Adam. Grant enjoys a game of golf and tennis to help him relax. His elder brother played for St Johnstone.

Ian H. McCall

Ian, no relation to his famous namesake of earlier years, has in his single season at East End proved to be a very entertaining player to watch. Not unlike Maradona, in stature if nothing else, he can set matches alight with his excellent control, his fast pace and his quicksilver turns. His jinking runs down either wing and his ability to take on a defence single-handedly are talents which delight the crowd. Ian was born in Dumfries on September 30, 1964, one of three children, and attended the local Academy where he picked up three highers and six 'O' grades. On leaving school he went straight to Motherwell and signed on as a professional under the ebullient Jock Wallace. He had just been made player of the Tournament in an S.F.A. youth competition and, though the future looked bright, Ian dropped out of the game at the end of the season, reverting to a minor grade with Bellevue A.F.C.

After a few months, he decided to return to senior football and secured a place with Queen's Park in 1984. Although he only made a couple of appearances in his first season, the next two seasons saw him make over 60 appearances and score nine goals.

Jim Leishman was impressed by his form against the Pars and secured his services in May 1986. Ian jokes that he was glad now to be playing alongside and not against, Norrie McCathie whom he found to be a formidable player. Ian has asthma but, as young sufferers reading this will be pleased to learn, the illness has not handicapped his career in any way. Before each game he uses an inhaler to help his breathing.

Ian made 11 successive appearances in the opening games of the season when the team got off to a flying start. Much of the rest of the season has seen him come on from the substitute's bench, often with remarkable effect. One recalls his goal against Partick in February which secured two precious points for the Pars. The end of the season has seen him restored to the side and he too is relishing the prospect of Premier League football at East End Park.

Ian is unmarried and enjoys playing all sports, golf and rugby in particular.

Norrie McCathie

Norrie, 26, has picked up Man of the Match awards and Supporters' Club trophies with the same regularity that Frank Sinatra has picked up gold discs – and it is not hard to see why. Week in, week out, he turns out immaculate performances with well timed tackles and skilful midfield moves. He is strong in the air, reads the game well and is equally at home defending at the back or pushing forward to grab a vital goal.

His talents have been recognised much further afield than Dunfermline, causing a string of scouts and managers to send back rave reports to their boardrooms. Thankfully the Dunfermline board have resisted all such moves and Norrie has been kept at East End Park, a firm favourite of the crowd. Further recognition came his way last October when he was invited to play alongside Craig Levein, Sandy Jardine and John Blackley in a select team to honour Cowdenbeath goalkeeper, Ray Allan.

A greater honour came when he was selected by Craig Brown for the Scotland Semi-professional team to take part in a tournament in Fife in May against other nations. Norrie also deputises as team captain in the absence of skipper Bobby Robertson. He has never missed a game this season, having turned out in all 46 major games.

Yet, it was almost chance which first brought him to East End in August 1981. On leaving Forrester H.S. in Edinburgh, Norrie started his playing career with Edina Hibs as a centre forward and in his last season there **173** scored 36 goals, sparkling form which took him to Central Park. When Stanton moved from there to East End, he remembered the young star and in an astute piece of business, swapped Craig McFarlane for him. After taking a season to find his feet, Norrie quickly settled into a regular place in the team, missing only a handful of games in the last four seasons. He has now made over 200 appearances for the Pars during which he has scored a remarkable 36 goals, not bad going for a defender. One has only to remember some of his strikes against Morton and Dumbarton the past season to realise how important a player he has been to the Pars. The Premier League will give him an excellent platform on which to further display his undoubted talent.

During the week, Norrie works as a whisky blender in Leith and shares a flat with Ian McCall in Edinburgh. He enjoys all kinds of sport, squash and tennis in particular.

Ian McCall and Stevie Morrison

Stevie Morrison

One player who has taken to full-time training at East End like a duck to water is midfielder, Stevie Morrison, who has just completed probably his best season at the club. Over the years he has found difficulty getting employment and the travelling from his home in Glasgow had also taken its toll. It was unfortunate that circumstances toward the end of last season took him to Australia while the club was celebrating promotion to Division One. While in Australia, he met up with Paul Donnelly who is adapting well to his new life down-under.

Standing 6' high and weighing in at 12 stones, Stevie is not easily moved off the ball. At free kicks, he is a tremendous hitter of the ball and his rasping shots have brought the club many superb goals. It is little wonder that he regards Platini as his favourite player. In 1984, when Dunfermline lost their Cup-tie at Ibrox, Stevie had the satisfaction of receiving the "Mr. Super Fit" Award from the sponsors. In over 200 appearances for the club he has scored 45 goals, the most recent at Firhill in April being one to particularly savour.

Stevie was born in St. Andrews on August 15 1961, though he later moved to Glasgow, his current address. He began his career as an amateur with St. Mirren Boys' club and then moved to Love Street under Alex Ferguson. He followed his manager to Pittodrie where he went full-time. He never broke into what was a very fine Aberdeen team and was pleased to accept the invitation of Stanton, the former depute manager there, to return to the central belt with Dunfermline. He signed in May 1981 as a forward for £7,000 and made his debut in August. At the end of the season he played in the Scottish Semi-Professional squad which won the Four Nations' Tournament at Pittodrie.

Although signed as a striker, Stevie was converted to a midfielder and it is in that position that he has excelled. He has been a regular player for the Pars over the seasons and has become a firm favourite with the crowds. He is looking forward with great anticipation to the larger stage of the Premier League.

His brother, Stewart, also played for Dunfermline and St. Johnstone but never made the grade. Stevie enjoys a game of golf or tennis in his spare time.

Davie Moyes

Although Davie has not been seen much by the fans during the past season, he is not the sort of player who is easy to forget. From the minute that he made his debut for the Pars on March 19 1985 against East Stirling, he has become a favourite with the crowd. He is acclaimed, not for his delicate touches or his breathtaking passes, but for his determination, his commitment and single-mindedness which cause him to lose few tackles, even if it causes apoplexy with the referees.

Davie was born in Haddington on October 14 1955 which makes him, at thirty-one, one of the older members of the squad. He began his playing career with Royston Juveniles in Edinburgh and then stepped up a grade to play with Preston Juniors. He was signed by Berwick in 1976 and spent eight seasons at Shielfield Park during which time he moved from the role of sweeper to that of full back. He was a member of that famous Berwick team which won

Davie Moyes

the Second Division Championship in 1978-79, giving Dunfermline a good run for their money that season. He was particularly fortunate to play under Dave Smith, a player for whom he had tremendous admiration for the way in which he could effortlessly stroll through a game and yet make a telling contribution to it.

After making 248 appearances with 13 goals for the English club, Davie moved to Meadowbank on a free transfer with whom he made around 50 appearances. His move to Dunfermline two years ago came out of the blue, Davie arriving at East End in his working clothes to make his debut. It is a move which he has not regretted.

Unfortunately, the last season has been a trying one for him. As a bricklayer he has found it difficult to **175** combine football training with the tight schedules which housebuilders demand and his games have been limited to six successive appearances at the start of the season when the club got off to a flying start.

Davie, married with two children, hopes to continue playing an important part at East End for some time.

Grant Reid

Grant has only been with the club for one season during which he has enjoyed mixed fortune. After making his debut on July 30 at the start of the season against Cowdenbeath in the Fife Cup, it seemed as though he had ousted Davie Young and secured the centre-half spot for himself. He then played in 14 successive league and cup matches during which Dunfermline lost only three games. A long-throw expert, Grant is a formidable opponent, aggressive and quick off his mark, a good tackler and always prepared to go forward in search of goal.

Grant Reid

However, he did not realise he had broken his nose at Forfar and when the injury was finally diagnosed, complications developed in the re-setting. He lost his place to Young who never looked back. Although Grant has played the occasional game at full back, not his natural position, he has never managed to re-establish himself into the team and has sat patiently in the wings awaiting his recall which will undoubtedly come.

While still at school in his native Glasgow, Grant played as an amateur with Possil Park Y.M.C.A. He also played alongside Eric Ferguson for Rangers in the Croix Tournament but when he received no encouragement from the Ibrox club, he signed for Norwich City in 1981. His spell there was unsuccessful and when the East Anglian club was relegated, Grant returned to Scotland, signing for Morton. They too were relegated and Grant found himself on his way to Stenhousemuir where he at last enjoyed regular first-team football. In his three seasons at Ochilview, he made over 90 appearances and managed to score four goals.

He was delighted to sign for Dunfermline in July 1986 for £10,000, impressed by the set-up and the electric atmosphere which larger crowds generate. Although the past season has not worked out as happily as it might have for him, he is looking forward keenly to playing in the Premier League for the first time.

During the week Grant works as a tax officer and lives with his wife and son in Dennistoun. Grant enjoys most sports, golf and swimming in particular.

Bobby Robertson

There are few players at East End Park as proud of Dunfermline's promotion as Bobby Robertson. As captain of the team, he has achieved an ambition which has escaped a dozen of his predecessors – to take the club into the Premier League. When Bobby joined the club in 1976, morale was undoubtedly low. He recalls there was a great preoccupation with "the good old days" which had just slipped away and he and his generation had to live under this foreboding shadow, aggravated by the publication of club histories extolling that golden age, for a whole decade.

Born in Leslie on St. Valentine's Day 1959, Bobby spent six years at Auchmuty H.S. collecting the necessary highers to gain entry to Edinburgh's prestigious Medical School. From school football he graduated to playing with Kirkcaldy Y.M.C.A. during which time he attracted the attention of Manchester City and Hearts. It was with Dunfermline Athletic, however, that his destiny lay and he signed for them on an S-form, later being called up by Harry Melrose. Bobby started as a midfield player but was later converted to full back and he also played at centre half, such is his versatility. Indeed, he claims to have worn eight different jerseys in his career at East End. From September 1978 to February 1982 he played in 154 successive League and Cup games. As a player, Bobby will be remembered for being an eager competitor, a man who gives 90 minutes to a game. He latches on to attacking forwards and snaps away at them like a terrier, harassing them and forcing them to hurriedly give the ball away.

Bobby Robertson

From his debut in the Fife Cup in 1977, he has played in more than 400 games for the Pars, scoring eight goals, a figure which would have been higher but for his medical studies which increasingly bit into his time. The five year medical course, which gave him his M.B., Ch.B., was relatively easy, but four gruelling years of post-graduate work in hospitals often made him unavailable for selection. At one stage, while studying for a diploma in gynaecology, he was putting in a 78-hour week in 1985 at Dunfermline Maternity Hospital. Under these circumstances, training, not to mention playing, especially away from home, was difficult.

Now that he is fully qualified and working in General Practice in Glenrothes, he finds that by working a rota system with one of his partners he **177** can get Saturday afternoon off relatively easily. When his medical colleague, Hugh Whyte, relinquished the captaincy, the mantle fell to a very proud Bobby Robertson whose inspiration on and off the field has in no small way contributed to Dunfermline's success these past two seasons.

Bobby and his wife, Susan, who is a dentist, live in Freuchie and he enjoys all sports, especially golf and tennis, in what little spare time he can find.

Trevor Smith

For someone as young – he is only 22 – it is incredible that Trevor is now the seventh longest serving player in the squad, although disappointingly he has only played in just over 40 games. He was born on May 6 1965 in Whitburn where his father, George, was a teacher. His father will be well remembered by older fans as a successful winger in the 1960s with Partick and later as player/manager at Ballymena in N. Ireland.

As a promising youngster, he played in Scottish Schoolboy Teams against England and Wales and met up then with Ian McCall. While at school, Alva Academy, he played for Sauchie Juveniles and from there signed for Dunfermline. His first appearance for the club was as a substitute against Berwick in November 1983. Over the years, he has shown he can run at defences and, given more luck and freedom from injuries, he might well have added to the nine goals he has so far scored. He has good ball control, a fierce shot and has always hinted at having more potential than he sometimes exhibits. Everyone will remember the two penalties he expertly fired home against Berwick in

Trevor Smith

the final game of season 1984-85 which seemed to have put Dunfermline into Division One.

Formerly a bank official, Trevor is presently studying sociology and history at Stirling University but he would also like to go full-time at football. At his home in Menstrie, he enjoys collecting a wide range of records and playing most sports, especially golf. It has to be stated that all the players in the squad who play golf grudgingly admitted that Trevor is probably the best, a fact which is not surprising as he played at Dunbar a few years ago in the Scottish Schoolboys' Championship. Among his dislikes is pre-season training. Trevor, unmarried, is 5'9" tall and weighs in at 12 stones.

Gary Thompson

It would be fair to say that Gary has made a considerable impact on the team since arriving from Alloa for £5,000 in April 1986. He is a tenacious, hard-tackling midfielder who, even when not playing well, does not like to lose a game. His close marking of opponents and his gritty determination have often seen him fall foul of referees, which has caused him to be suspended several times.

Gary was born on June 11 1956 in Glasgow and grew up in the shadow of four sisters. His father once played football for Derby and Queen's Park and encouraged his son to pursue his footballing interest. He began his career as a striker with the junior team, Benburb, and signed in 1977 for Morton for whom he made only one appearance as a substitute. He moved on to Falkirk where he spent five successful seasons during which the club won the Second Division Championship in season 1979-80. Never a regular in the team, he made 81 full appearances and scored 19 goals.

A player-exchange took him to Alloa in 1983 and at Recreation Park he was pulled back to play at full back. He was a member of their successful team of 1984-85 which just pipped Dunfermline for promotion. In three seasons there, he scored nine goals in 98 appearances.

At the age of 29, he was quite surprised, but nonetheless delighted, to join the Pars in 1986 and his extra bite undoubtedly helped the club in their final push for promotion. He has been a regular member of the side over the past 12 months and looks forward to playing

Gary Thompson

in the Premier League.

Gary works as a roofer in Glasgow and currently lives in Dennistoun with his wife and three children. In his time off, Gary enjoys coaching a boys' team in Glasgow. At 5'6" Gary is one of the smaller members of the squad, but certainly not the lightest either, at 11½ stones.

John Watson

If John Watson had not taken a chance and signed for the Pars in 1983 after Jim Leishman took over, it is highly unlikely that his name would ever have hit the back pages of daily newspapers. There was little to suggest in John's early background that he had a promising career ahead of him. Born in Edinburgh on February 13 1959, John was brought up along with his two sisters in the capital and went to Liberton H.S. There were to be no schoolboy caps for him and during his formative, teenage years he was simply a

John Watson and Norrie McCathie

spectator at Easter Road where his uncle, Tony D'Arcy, had occasionally deputised for Lawrie Reilly.

When he finally did take up playing football seriously, it was as an amateur in the seventh division of the Edinburgh Amateur League and for one season he played in goal – Ian Westwater beware! While continuing to earn his living as a plumber, John was signed up by Willie McFarlane in 1980 to deputise at Meadowbank for John Jobson, now of course on the coaching staff at East End. John stayed there for two, undistinguished seasons making only 23 appearances and scoring, believe it or not, no goals.

When McFarlane left Meadowbank, John drifted back into the amateur ranks and would have remained there had not a recommendation by his former manager taken him out to Hong Kong Rangers. He did not settle there and on his return was given a trial at East End Park. Since then, he has not looked back and he has certainly engraved his name into the history books. His first season, 1983-84, saw him score only three goals in 18 full appearances. The following season, however, saw him get fully into

his stride and in August 1984 he was nominated Player of the Month by Scottish Brewers, a rare honour for the club. It will be season 1985-86 for which he is best remembered. He scored his 50th goal for the club and then went on in April to become the first striker in Scottish football to score 30 goals in the season for which he received an award from the *Daily Record*. Indeed, by going on to record 31 strikes, he proved to be the most prolific scorer since the days of Alex Ferguson.

In the past season, his goalscoring prowess has tailed off somewhat, partly because of the tighter defences in the First Division which have got to know him very well over the four games and partly because of several niggling injuries which he has not always shaken off. With 13 goals, however, he was still the club's top scorer. National recognition finally came his way when he too was selected for the Scottish Semi-Professional team to play in the Four Nations' Tournament in Fife in May involving England, Italy and Holland.

As a centre forward, John is almost as fearless as his namesake on the racing track. His ability to reach a high ball is spectacular and it is often a great pity that there are not more forwards running beside him to benefit from his head flicks. He particularly impressed T.V. commentator Archie McPherson when the cameras visited Easter Road for the Cup-tie in January 1987. His unselfishness extends to him retreating into defence when the opposition is taking a corner kick and his red head can often be seen clearing a dangerous ball out of his own box. On the ground, he has shown he can score goals equally well with either foot. With over 150 league appearances to his credit, the fans can be assured that this late developer is still good for more goals yet.

John, who vies with one or two of his mates for the title of the club's most eligible bachelor, is a good all-rounder at many sports. He particularly enjoys a game of snooker, potting the ivory ones with the same regularity as he does the leather ones. Though occasionally out of work, he has turned down lucrative contracts in Hong Kong and in the North Sea to allow him to enthrall his fans each week.

Ian Westwater

Few fans would doubt that Ian has been one of the best acquisitions at East End in recent years. His transfer fee of £4,000 from Hearts was a real bargain. On countless occasions, the columns of sports pages are full of how Westy has come to the aid of his mates. So far in his career he has enjoyed 45 shut-outs, 19 in the past season. At 6'2" and weighing in at over 13 stones, he is clearly the biggest on the staff and yet few would guess that as he acrobatically leaps around his goalmouth. He is not a 'keeper to keep quiet when disarray breaks out around him, a tip he picked up from one of his heroes, Peter Bonetti.

Though born in Loughborough on November 8 1963, Ian was brought up in Scotland and attended Currie H.S. and later Telford College where he took a diploma in business studies. He is currently a sales rep for an industrial company and lives with his newly-wed wife, Debbie, in Linlithgow. He enjoys a game of golf in his spare time.

Ian Westwater

A big influence on Ian's career was his father who played in goal for Queen of the South and Arbroath before retiring through injury. Ian has always played in goal, though to see him waltz around in midfield in a training session, he might well have found a niche further up the field.

Ian began his career with Salvesen Boys' Club, playing alongside the likes of Dave Bowman and Gary Mackay, and was selected to play as a Scottish Schoolboy for the under-15, under-16 and under-18 teams in the company of Paul McStay and Eric Black. He was soon snapped up by Hearts with whom he gained honours in the Scottish Professional squad. One of the highlights of his early career was playing against St. Mirren on November 1 1980, an appearance which made him, just a week short of his 17th birthday, the youngest goalie to appear in the Premier League. He had shut-outs in both his **181** debut and the match that followed, but was then rested by manager Bobby Moncur. While subsequently playing for the Scottish team against Brazil, he was injured and a quick recall to the Hearts' first team was ruled out. By the time he had recovered, he found that new goalkeeper Henry Smith had firmly established himself. In a bid to secure first team football, Westy jumped at the chance to join Dunfermline in March 1985. His debut for the club one week later against Stranraer quickly confirmed him as an excellent buy. Recently, Gordon Marshall of East Fife was transferred to Falkirk for £65,000. One can only guess at the value on Ian's head.

He is looking forward immensely to playing again in the Premier League and hopes to be able to record many more shut-outs against the best Scotland can throw at him.

Hugh Whyte

At the age of 31, Hugh Whyte has a great deal of goalkeeping experience behind him. As a youngster, Hugh attended Kilmarnock Academy and while he excelled in his academic studies, he found he enjoyed playing in goal at football. Since his school favoured rugby, he had to sign for Ayr Boswell, a boys' club, to satisfy his craving. At the age of 16 he signed for the junior club, Hurlford United, and after a few games was recommended to Hibs. This suited Hugh fine as he was soon to embark on a long, demanding six year course in medicine at Edinburgh University from 1973-79.

He impressed manager Eddie

Hugh Whyte

Turnbull and his big chance came at the start of season 1975-76 when regular 'keeper, Jim McArthur, was sidelined with a broken hand. Hugh deputised well, holding Dundee United to a goalless draw in the first game. His dream was shattered when chairman Tom Hart, realising his full potential, invited him to go full-time. Not unnaturally, Hugh did not wish to give up his other great love, medicine, especially as he was half way through his studies and he politely refused the offer for which others would have given their eye teeth. The Hibs management promptly relegated him to the stand and Hugh's days at Easter Road were effectively finished.

Ironically, this was excellent news for East End Park because Hugh was duly snapped up by Harry Melrose on a free transfer in 1976. At that time the Pars had a goalkeeping problem following the departure of Norwegian internationalist, Geir Karlsen, in 1975. Graham Barclay had come on loan from Celtic and then Jim Herriot had made a brief reappearance to tide the club over.

Arriving in the summer of 1976, along with Bowie, Robertson and Donnelly, Hugh made the goalkeeping position his own for the next nine years. Up until 1981, he clocked up 227 appearances, with only one absence – and all that while continuing with an arduous course and tiring hospital work. In his time, Hugh has seen off two challenges to his position – Jim Moffat and George Young – and has delighted the crowd with many breathtaking saves. His record of 362 appearances with 116 shut-outs is one of which he can be proud, especially when one looks at the struggle the team then had. Latterly, he served the club as captain, a rare honour for a goalkeeper.

When Ian Westwater arrived on the scene, Hugh was already established as a general practitioner, in the same surgery as director John Yellowley, and he and his wife had seen the first of their children, Graham, arrive. He was thus quite content to see Ian do so well but was nonetheless pleased to deputise for him against Montrose and Forfar in the past season to allow Westy's groin strain time to heal.

Hugh is still a regular attender at training sessions and is only too keen to help the club out whenever he can. In the last home game of the season, for instance, he donned his strip to be the goalkeeper in the William Rennie penalty kick competition for the Junior Supporters' Club, Hugh enjoys all sports, especially golf and squash. He and his wife, Helen, also enjoy dining out together 'whenever we get the chance'.

Davie Young

It is remarkable that Davie ever took up senior football. His secondary school, Forrester H.S. in Edinburgh, concentrated on rugby and he had to join North Merchiston Boys' Club to pursue his interest in soccer. John Clark, on the backroom staff at Celtic Park, secured the signature of the tall 16-year old and brought him to Parkhead where he never really settled. He decided to move on to Arbroath where there was the chance of regular, first team football. While at Gayfield from 1980-84 he turned in 141 performances and grabbed six goals. There was a disagreement with new manager George Fleming over training – he wanted all the players to come to Arbroath instead

Davie Young

of Stirling – and Davie was freed. At that point Jim Leishman was looking for a solid centre half and he brought Davie to East End. In his first season he did not miss a single game and in the season of the Second Division Championship, he missed only one game. His height – he is over 6' – and his long legs have greatly helped to steady the Dunfermline defence. There are few attackers, if any, who can outjump him in the air.

Yet the past season did not start too well for Davie. New signing Grant Reid, also a centre half, was given the opportunity to win his spurs, a chance which he accepted with great alacrity, keeping Davie out for 14 games. His subsequent injury, however, allowed the patient reserve, who had been doing extra training and exercises, back into the team and he has proved difficult to dislodge. His strength, determination and cool head have been significant factors in Dunfermline's push to the Premier League, a level at which he is desperate to play. At the age of 25, he feels he has a lot to contribute at East End.

A great influence on his career has been his father who seldom misses a game. He is married to Caroline and is employed as a buyer for an electrical contractor. He enjoys most sport, especially golf.

Seven other players also turned out for Dunfermline during the past two seasons. JOHN WADDELL (21), signed on a free transfer from Dundee during the close season in 1986, made a promising debut in the Fife Cup at the end of July. However, the tall defender blotted his copy book in his first league match by being sent off at Kilmarnock in September and, although he made an appearance as substitute, he never really fitted in and was freed before Christmas.

BILLY MACKAY (26), the ex-Rangers forward, was signed on loan for a month from Hearts in January 1987. Although he was never listed in the team from the start, he did suggest promise in the six appearances he made as substitute. He certainly gave the impression of having fully recovered from the serious knee injury which almost destroyed his career. Billy, a publican in Coupar Angus, was recalled to Hearts in February to aid an injury-stricken side.

HAMISH McALPINE made one surprise appearance in goal at Meadowbank in April 1986 but this was essentially a one-off affair and there was never any intention that the partnership would be renewed. Indeed, he went to neighbours Raith Rovers to assist them in gaining promotion to the First Division.

DAVIE HOUSTON, born in Glasgow on December 4 1956, played for the amateur side, Glasgow United, and for Clydebank before moving to Alloa. He signed for Dunfermline in 1985 on a free transfer and made only seven full appearances for the Pars in the league plus as many again as substitute. He was a skilful midfield player but was never able to command a regular place and was freed at the end of his first season.

IAN GORDON, born in Broxburn on October 30 1960, joined Dunfermline from Airdrie in 1984 when a broken leg seemed to have put him out of the game. Ian never had a regular run in the first team. In season 1984-85 he made eight league appearances and though he made 15 appearances the following season, he was transferred at the end of it to Raith Rovers for £3,000.

IAN PRYDE and GORDON WILSON each made two appearances for the club during season 1985-86. Ian was born in Dunfermline in July 31 1965 and signed for East Fife in 1981 from Hill of Beath. He joined Dunfermline early in 1986 but only made two appearances as substitute and was released at the end of the season. Gordon, signed from Meadowbank, made two full appearances, deputising for Norrie McCathie when the team suffered two ignoble defeats in April 1986. He, too, left East End one month later.

The Centenary Club

Chairman   Jim Harrison
Vice-Chairman   Bill Braisby, junior
Secretary   Jessie Arnott
Treasurer   Bill Rolland

The Centenary Club has gone from strength to strength since it was launched two short years ago. Jim Leishman first heard of a similar scheme at a meeting for commercial managers and he and Bill Braisby journeyed to Bolton to learn at first hand how that club had successfully launched and run a lucrative fund-raising scheme. The weekly draw of £500 and the quarterly prize of £2,500, plus other generous prizes such as a colour T.V., have all helped to swell membership to almost the thousand mark. The football club now receives more than £25,000 as a result, the largest single donation to club funds.

There are also other incentives for members. During the Easter and Christmas holidays, special coaching sessions are arranged for members' children and vast numbers of budding Peles turn up to benefit from the advice of the club's backroom staff. At Christmas the committee booked the Carnegie Hall for one night and treated members and their families to a special production of the pantomime, "Dick Whittington." Jim and a few of the players made a guest appearance, making it an extremely popular evening. On May 6 1987 the hall was again booked, this time for "Guys and Dolls" in which Jim's wife, Mary, starred as Adelaide. Once again, a most pleasant evening was enjoyed by an appreciative audience.

Members can also take advantage of a vast number of discounts which local suppliers and businesses offer, as well as receiving a limited number of free stand tickets; discounts are also given on season tickets for members. For those sportingly minded, special evenings of darts, dominoes and snooker have been arranged in the Paragon Club. Recently, a golf competition at Muckart was thoroughly enjoyed by those who took part, Keith Moffat winning the tournament.

Also proving extremely popular have been the cabaret nights in the Glen Pavilion. In the autumn, Tony Christie was the guest star while in the spring, a packed hall was entertained by Django and Mr. Abie. On that particular evening, a draw was made for a Mini car, supplied by Taggarts, which was won by a delighted Robert Easton from Dunfermline.

Designed by Ken Forbes, the Jock Stein lounge commemorates the man whose reputation was first established at East End Park. The lounge is used to entertain the club's ever-growing number of sponsors.

Future Prospects

Jim Leishman would be the first to admit that, with promotion to the Premier League secure, his problems have just begun. Life amongst the elite of Scottish football will be a totally different proposition from doing battle in the lower divisions. The prospect of seeing half the Scottish International squad, and indeed some of the English team, such as Butcher and Woods, grace the turf at East End Park will certainly whet the appetite not just of the Dunfermline faithful but also of the vast untapped seam of football fans in Fife's hinterland who have been denied Premier League football. "At least," quipped Jim Leishman, "we will be able to beat Rangers and England on the same afternoon".

Visiting fans to East End Park in the past few seasons have been noticeable by their absence, the east end of the ground holding very few supporters. By contrast, loyal, dedicated contingents of Dunfermline supporters often found themselves in a majority when their team played in numerous away fixtures.

That cosy and peaceful picture will now dramatically change, perhaps not always for the best. As a quick look at the map of Scotland will demonstrate, Dunfermline is ideally placed for visits to and from Premier League clubs; all the grounds, apart from Pittodrie, will be within about an hour's drive. While Dunfermline in the past season found the First Division to be dominated by clubs from the West of Scotland, the new Premier League has, unusually, over half the clubs placed in the East of Scotland. Large crowds can once again be expected at East End and while the turnstiles will whirl merrily with paying customers, problems will inevitably arise over crowd control, policing and parking. On home match days, the town centre will have a vitality and expectancy about it, not seen for more than a decade.

The close season will no doubt be marked by the arrival of new players, though quality players at the right price are always difficult to find. George Cowie has already been signed from Hearts for £15,000. With three clubs to be relegated at the end of 1987-88, only Dunfermline's best and most consistent form will ensure their survival. The example of St. Johnstone, who plummeted from the Premier League to the Second Division in successive seasons, and the sad demise of Hamilton last season, are there for all to draw lessons from.

Though East End Park has always been an attractive stadium, too good for the Second Division, the Board have long been conscious of the need to upgrade it and entry to the Premier League has been the necessary catalyst that they required. During the summer, they will be among the busiest men in Dunfermline, supervising the planned improvements.

Ground safety is a major priority and the stadium will undergo rigorous fire safety and crowd control inspections. During the past season, the club experimented with a "hoolivan" which surveyed the crowd during the game against Montrose from T.V. cameras in a parked van. However, the plan is now to install a permanent close-circuit T.V. system, monitored by the police from a specially erected building beside the

'Radio Pars' box. They will be able to view in detail any part of the ground which will allow them to deal with any trouble as soon as it arises. A new perimeter fence is also to be erected.

Existing crush barriers have been declared unsafe and will have to be dug up and replaced during the summer. It is hoped that these improvements will allow the ground to have a capacity in excess of 22,000 which will make it one of the largest in Scotland, bigger than Easter Road or Pittodrie. Improved facilities for the disabled will also be looked into.

With the comfort of the fans in mind, the centre of the stand is to be renovated. Seats for up to 742 season ticket holders will be reserved in the centre of the stand around an enlarged Directors' Box. The old seats in the centre – all 1,015 of them – which are now rather tatty and uncomfortable, will be ripped out and replaced by red folding chairs. Eventually the seats of both wing stands will also be replaced by new ones, black on one side, white on the other. A family area will be created as well.

Two familiar landmarks to the Pars' faithful will disappear shortly. New, modern, efficient floodlights are to be installed under the roof of the stand and on the enclosure opposite, at a cost of £65,000. The old pylons, erected in the summer of 1958 for the sum of £12,000, and inaugurated in a special match against Sheffield United on October 26, will eventually be dismantled. As metallic structures, their lifespan is finite and they had always been awkward to maintain. The new lights will cope well with colour T.V. and

the broadcasting companies will be welcome at East End Park once again on a regular basis.

The old turnstiles at the west end of the stadium are also to go, to be reconstructed in black and white brick. The new gate mechanisms will be easier to operate and keep a more detailed check on entry. The exit doors have also to be enlarged to allow easier departure at the end of a game.

There is also a proposal, subject to planning permission, to purchase the considerable area behind the enclosure and convert it into a large bus and car park for the expected crowds on a big match day. Negotiations are at present being conducted with British Rail who own the land. If this initiative materialises, match traffic will filter along Leys Park Road, park behind the stadium and then make their way out through the present car park. The most ambitious plan of all, however, is the erection of a large sports complex to the east of the ground on a one and a half acre site. According to the architects' drawings, it would include a bowling alley, a new social club and a large sports arena to cater for a number of sporting and cultural activities. An attractive feature would be the installation of executive-style boxes which would allow special guests to have an excellent view of the match from luxurious surroundings. As yet, this is still a pipe dream, but it does give an indication of the kind of forward planning that the Board is making.

As soon as the Four Nations' Tournament is finished, the groundsmen will move in to treat the pitch. The sand-slitting and the re-sowing of the playing surface should boost the turf for the start of the new season. Improved training facilities are also being considered.

The improvements earmarked for the summer will cost around a quarter of a million pounds. This sum will be met through increased borrowing, from donations from the Paragon Club and the Centenary Club, from sponsorship and lotteries, from grants from the football development trust and from large increases in projected gate money as crowds in excess of 20,000 might be expected for top-class matches. It is hoped that the population of Fife and indeed Central Scotland will find East End Park an attractive and safe ground to visit.

Last season, 181 season tickets were sold. For next season, a big increase is expected by Karen Grega, the club's commercial consultant. "We intend to market these tickets aggressively so they are likely to go quickly". Open days at the club at the end of the season certainly resulted in hundreds of tickets being snatched up. Karen also plans to increase yet further the advertising space in the ground, in the programme (which is to be restyled) and in more sponsorship of matches. She is also pleased at the success at the newly opened Supporters' Shop beneath the east stand. The shop carries a wide range of Athletic souvenirs, photographs, keyrings, glass tankards, pennants, pens and other items. The enterprising Karen would also like to start a crêche at East End where very young children could be left while their parents and older members of the family enjoy the game upstairs. Another idea she has might be more difficult to implement – she would like to take an aerial picture of the field, covered by supporters marking out the initials D.A.F.C. If anybody can achieve this, Karen can.

Everyone at East End Park is ready for the Premier League. It will not be through lack of preparation or support if Dunfermline fails to make the grade. Given the break of the ball, which every team needs, the Pars could be on the verge of another great era.